CW01034372

The UTS Law Review No. 1

The Courts
and the Media

HALSTEAD PRESS

First published in 1999 by
Halstead Press
19a Boundary Street
Rushcutters Bay, New South Wales, 2011

© Copyright: Faculty of Law, University of Technology, Sydney, 1999

This book is copyright. Apart from any fair dealing for the purposes of private study, research, criticism, or review, as permitted under the Copyright Act, no part may be reproduced by any process without written permission. Inquiries should be addressed to the publisher.

National Library of Australia Cataloguing-in-Publication entry
    The courts and the media.
    ISBN 1 875684 28 X
        1. Mass media – Law and legislation – Australia. 2. Free press and fair trial
        – Australia. 3. Crime and the press – Australia. 4. Mass media and criminal
        justice – Australia. I. Keyzer, Patrick, 1966– . (Series: UTS law review no. 1).
        343.94099

ISSN 1442-4959

Typeset by Brevier Design, Kensington, NSW
Printed in Sydney by Alken Press

ERRATA

Mr Albert Yuen is Associate Editor of the UTS Law Review.
Professor Michael Chesterman's name should have appeared on the cover
of the Review.
The Editor
This publication may be cited as (1999) 1 *UTSLR*. For further information about
the UTS Law Review please contact utslawreview@law.uts.edu.au

CONTENTS

Contents *Continued*

FOREWORD

It gives me great pleasure to introduce the first volume of the *UTS Law Review*: a special issue entitled *The Courts and the Media*. The papers in this volume are drawn from a conference convened at our Law School in November 1998 that brought together senior members of the judiciary, executive government, leading scholars, and practitioners in the field of media law. The relationship between the courts and the media is a significant topic and this volume will do much to enhance and further debate.

The publication of the first volume of the *UTS Law Review* marks a coming of age for the Faculty of Law. The University of Technology, Sydney is the home of the leading journalism school in the country and the Faculty of Law now has a developing profile as a centre for research and scholarship in communications law. The next volume of the *Review* will comprise papers drawn from the upcoming Second Conference of the Australasian Legal Information Institute, the leading research centre of law and information technology in Australia.

Professor David Barker
Dean
Faculty of Law
University of Technology, Sydney

INTRODUCTION

This book, the first volume of the *UTS Law Review*, comprises the papers presented at the Courts and the Media Forum convened at UTS Law School in November 1998. It brings together contributions from senior members of the judiciary, government, scholars, reporters and practitioners engaged in the debate. I hope *The Courts and the Media* will prove to be a useful resource for everyone interested in the relationship between the "third branch" and the "Fourth Estate".

I would like to thank the busy judges, scholars, practitioners and reporters who participated as speakers, panel chairs and panel members: Richard Ackland, Professor David Anderson, Kimberley Ashbee, Professor Wendy Bacon, Chief Justice Michael Black, Jenny Brockie, Rod Campbell, Professor Michael Chesterman, Chief Justice John Doyle, Julie Eisenberg, Justice Tony Fitzgerald, Professor David Flint, Liz Jackson, Andrew Kenyon, Margo Kingston, Bernard Lane, Susannah Lobez, the Hon. Robert McLelland, Chris Merritt, Professor Chris Nash, Professor Denis Pearce, Alan Rose, Justice Bernard Teague, Professor Rod Tiffen, Professor Sally Walker, the Hon. Daryl Williams, and George Williams.

I would also like to thank: Francesca Wraith, Juilee Pryor, Yasmon and the students who assisted with the staging of the Forum and editorial tasks—Kon Asimacopoulos, Rhys Bollen, Julia Colagiuri, David Dimouski, Julian Hammond, Lyndall Foldvary and Michelle Shek; Professor David Barker, Andrew Mowbray and George Marsh for their unstinting support for the event and for the *Review*; the Faculty of Law for the opportunity to be the *Review*'s inaugural editor; Halstead Press for its efficiency and diligence in the preparation of the final product; and Gilbert and Tobin for their financial support of the *Review*.

Patrick Keyzer
Editor

OPENING ADDRESS

The Honourable Justice Michael Black

Chief Justice of the Federal Court of Australia

It gives me great pleasure to open this forum on the courts and the media and I do so with enthusiasm. There are several reasons for this.

First, the topic to be addressed by this forum is critically important. Nearly all the papers that will be presented acknowledge that and explain why it is so. Fundamentally, we are concerned with public understanding of, and hence confidence in, Australia's system of justice. This involves access to the courts, which not only means access by being present in person as is the right of every citizen, but access to the workings of the courts by the reports of journalists. There are few topics more important than public access to the courts and public confidence in them; independent courts in which the public has confidence underpin our democratic system of government.

Secondly, the topic is one in which the public interest can clearly be advanced by the writings of those who, by scholarship, profession or both, are best qualified to offer insights into the topic and the issues it raises. It is also a topic that can be illuminated by informed discussion and by an understanding of different viewpoints—something that today's program is calculated to achieve.

This leads me to the third reason for my enthusiasm. Patrick Keyzer has assembled what, if I may say so, is an outstanding group of presenters, panel chairs and panel members from the universities, the law and the media. Quite a few of the speakers are qualified in at least two of these fields. I am not aware of any comparable forum on the subject where there has been such a high level of expertise and such a breadth of expertise.

As well as having enthusiasm for today's forum, I approach it with a fair degree of optimism. Whilst I hasten to agree with Mr Roderick Campbell's comments that the relationship between the courts and the media is hardly likely to be a marriage made in heaven, nevertheless I think that recent history—in which many of us here have been personally involved—gives cause for optimism. Of course, it must be recognized that tensions are inevitable and indeed they are to a large extent healthy, but I believe that there have been great changes in the attitudes and practices of many courts in Australia over the past five or six years, and I would like to open this forum with a brief first hand overview of the changes that have occurred during the 1990s which I think justify a certain optimism. Perhaps what I want to convey was better expressed in the heading of today's leader in *The Australian*: "Cause for hope, not celebration".

For the first two years of the present decade, the attitude of the courts towards the media was, in general, much as it had always been. The importance of the media was recognized but the approach was essentially passive. The courts would provide a press box and perhaps even a press room. They did their work and the press reported it as best it could. The prospect that the electronic media might be allowed into the courtroom for any purpose was viewed with apprehension, even though the Alice Springs Coroner had shown in 1981 that the world did not come to an end when a judgment was delivered in front of a television camera. There had been one judgment summary—in the *Tasmanian Dam Case*[1] in 1983— but that experiment had not been repeated.

The only media liaison officer was in the Family Court; none of the Supreme Courts had one and nor did the Federal Court. The media was generally not supplied with any visual information about the courts, with the consequence that the most common visual image of the courts was of red-robed long-wigged judges, some with buckled shoes, proceeding into church at the opening of the legal year. The Chief Justices never, or hardly ever, gave press interviews about their courts, and the idea that they might appear on talkback radio was the stuff of an extreme judicial nightmare.

And so 1993 arrived, a year in which the courts seemed to receive nothing but adverse press. Even the inappropriate comments of judges in England were reported here and were seen to reflect a universally out of touch judiciary. Then two things happened which marked, it seems to me, the beginning of a new era. The first was the appointment of Jan Nelson as a media officer at the Supreme Court of New South Wales. I came to know Jan and her work and I greatly respected her. It seems to me to have been both fitting and significant that her obituary in Tuesday's edition of *The Australian* was written by the Chief Justice of Australia.

The other important event of that year was a statement made by the former Chief Justice of Australia, Sir Anthony Mason, in his "State of the Australian Judicature" address in Hobart in September 1993. In that address, Sir Anthony suggested that it would from time to time be appropriate for judges to explain publicly their work and the issues they faced. In effect, he said, judges should take advantage of the marked upsurge in the public interest in the courts, and should not be afraid of telling the public what they were doing and why.

Let me now give a brief summary of what are, in my view, the most important developments since then.

The appointment of Jan Nelson was soon followed by the appointment of media liaison officers to the Supreme Court of Victoria, the Federal

---

[1] *Commonwealth v Tasmania* (1983) 158 CLR 1.

Court of Australia, the Supreme Court of Western Australia and the Courts Authority of South Australia. From the time of their appointments these media officers, with the strong support of their Chief Justices, have played what I see as a very important part in facilitating media access to courts and improving understanding between the media and the courts.

Whereas there were no judgment summaries in 1993, in the Federal Court such summaries are now routine. Recently the Court decided, as a matter of general policy, to prepare them wherever possible in cases of public interest. I understand that the same view is taken by the Supreme Court of South Australia.

In many courts, journalists are now allowed to use tape recordings to facilitate their reporting of cases and in some instances the recording of whole cases for the purposes of a later broadcast has been allowed. The recording and subsequent broadcast of the entire reasons for sentence of Chief Justice Cox in the case of Martin Bryant in 1996 provides a notable example of a broadcast of taped court proceedings. Earlier, in May 1995, Justice Teague had allowed the televising of his reasons for sentence in a murder case. The next day *The Australian* carried the headline: "Murder sentence broadcast divides the nation". It may be that Justice Teague was ahead of his time, but I for one would not criticize him for that and, to me, the goal of explaining to the public the true reasons for sentence— one of the most difficult tasks that a judge has to undertake and one that he or she undertakes in public and in the interests of the whole community—is a goal worth striving for.

In my own court we have adopted an incremental, if cautious, approach to the electronic coverage of our cases, but it is nevertheless the fact that we have now allowed cameras into our courtrooms on no fewer than 25 occasions, including a number of cases in which judgment summaries were recorded for later televising. Almost half of the judges whose primary work is with the Federal Court have now had first hand experience of television in their courts. Many judges of the Federal Court, and judges of other courts also, have permitted cameras to record file footage of themselves in court or in chambers for use in news and current affairs reports. We were, I think, the first superior court in this country to permit the recording and subsequent broadcast of a judgment, to allow a whole trial to be recorded on video tape for potential broadcast (the *Yorta Yorta Case*[2]) and to facilitate the live telecast of the delivery of one of its judgments.

In what seemed a radical step at the time, the taking of the oath of office of a judge of the Federal Court at her swearing-in ceremony was recorded for television by the ABC in 1993. This now occurs routinely when a new judge is appointed to the High Court of Australia. In South

---

[2] *Members of the Yorta Yorta Aboriginal Community v The State of Victoria & Ors*, Olney J, 18 December 1998, unreported.

Australia an entire trial has now been the subject of a radio broadcast, and in both South Australia and Western Australia judges now take part in talkback radio programmes. I should also mention the increasing willingness of the country's Chief Justices to respond to invitations by the media to explain the work of their courts and, if necessary, to defend them (although opinions continue to differ about the appropriateness of that role being left to Chief Justices). Some Chief Justices, myself included, have also written articles explaining the law and the work of their courts and thus have developed some understanding of the constraints within which journalists work.

This summary is not exhaustive, but it is intended to convey something of what I believe is a great change in the way our courts see the world and their place in it. In the Federal Court we now aim to take the next step which, subject to getting the necessary funding, is the appointment of a Public Education Officer to develop and co-ordinate a program of court-based education about the work of the court. Some valuable work in this area has already been done in other courts. The appointment of a Public Education Officer will be in addition to that of the Media Liaison Officer, who now forms an indispensable part of the court's staff.

What I have said so far bears more perhaps upon the need for continuing reform, which is to be discussed at session 1, than upon the topic of session 2, "The Law and Freedom of the Media", or upon session 3, "Access to the Courts and its Implications". But the reforms outlined so far are by no means irrelevant to these other topics. Here too, court media liaison officers have played an important part in increasing the level of understanding between the courts and the media. In some jurisdictions work has also been done to assist journalists to avoid the unintentional publication of material that has been the subject of a suppression order.

Overall, we find that in the space of a very few years there has been a rapid and substantial change in the way that many courts see the media and the extent to which the courts have a role in explaining their work to the public.

Of course, all change involves risks, and where courts are involved there is a need for special care to avoid conflict with the fundamental values of the administration of justice. The requirement of impartial justice according to law must remain paramount. But the existence of risk, even when fundamental values are involved, should not be allowed to stand in the way of desirable change. Those who seek to change need to be well informed and to move forward with appropriate care. Recent history shows that if this can be done, what appear to be problems turn out not to be problems, and what are in fact problems can often be overcome. That is another reason why an informed discussion such as this is so valuable. I will say something about judgment summaries to illustrate the point that I am seeking to make.

I was the presiding judge when we first used these in the Federal Court as recently as 1995.[3] While I believe that judgment summaries should be encouraged, one objection to them has been that they could be used to put a "spin" on a case. The answer to this, as borne out I think by experience, is that the judgment summary is released simultaneously with the judgment that it summarizes and the two stand immediately for public comparison. The world of the spin doctor, by contrast, is the world in which the spun message is the primary source. Moreover, the development in recent years (and here some Australian courts, including the High Court and the Federal Court, were again the leaders) of virtually instantaneous internet access to judgments has, as a practical matter, dramatically increased access to both judgments and judgment summaries.

Then it is said that judgment summaries may divert attention from the real judgment. Experience does not bear this out and, in any event, in the real world of the radio or television journalist there is likely to be a very tight deadline with an extremely narrow window of time available for presentation of their material. The relevant moment is now, and it is no use a court saying otherwise. If the moment is now there will be no time to digest 40 or 50 pages of close legal analysis. This, of course, in the ideal world, should be done—but it can be done later.

Also, I do not think that judgment summaries are really very hard to do. I would be very interested in the views of journalists here today, but it seems to me that if, for example, the point in issue in an application for judicial review is whether a minister followed the procedures required by law in making a decision that resulted in the demolition of, let us say, a historic building, what the general public has an immediate interest in knowing is why the court set aside the minister's decision. If the judgment summary says no more than that the minister's decision was set aside because the court found that her department had not advertised the proposal as the law required and had not given an interested party a right to be heard, that conveys to the public the essence of the decision. The legal reasoning is available to anyone who wishes to read it on the internet. In most cases of judicial review the essential point, and with it an understanding of the different roles of the court and the executive government, can be conveyed very simply. Our experience with the *Hinchinbrook Case*[4] shows that the essence of judicial review can even be conveyed in a short television bite.

In some cases this has an added advantage. If we believe, as we surely must, that it is possible to facilitate informed debate and that society is better for it, then a clear and understandable statement of what a court has actually done, and why, is a powerful antidote to unfounded political comment about court decisions. A climate of readily understandable truth

---

[3] *Norvill v Chapman & Ors* (1995) 57 FCR 451.
[4] *Friends of Hinchinbrook Society Inc v Minister for Environment* (1997) 77 FCR 153.

is not a climate in which that type of behaviour—one that undermines public confidence in all three branches of government—can readily thrive.

Likewise with television in court: this is one of the most controversial topics in this area, but in our court we have taken the view that the dangers and difficulties likely to be encountered should not stop us from proceeding incrementally, if cautiously. By doing so we have, I think, had success in explaining our work to the public. At least the public now knows what it looks like inside the Federal Court. Some of the apprehended problems have not materialized simply because the technology has improved and in other respects because the court's Media Liaison Officer and television broadcasters have worked in co-operation with each other.

An interesting result of this incremental approach was that when, in the *MUA Case*[5], the court's requirement to complete its reasons for judgment and media deadlines came into collision, the three appeal judges felt able to permit their judgment—and not the judgment summary as intended—to go live to air. This was the first time that this had happened in Australia. Although there was some comment that the technical legal analysis in the judgment was not in itself riveting television, this was balanced by others who said that the insight into the reality of the legal process, on national television, was itself something of great interest and significance. Even in the admittedly controversial area of television in courts, where the demands of justice and the demands the media makes may come into conflict, there is a strong case for incremental movement so as to give the public greater access to the courts.

In stressing some of the positive elements, I do not wish to minimize the difficulties. These are particularly acute in the areas to be discussed in the second and third sessions. There is also the overriding question of the unswerving independence that is required of both the courts and the media. But the answer in today's world is surely not the complete isolation of the past.

There is one additional reason why today's topics are so important. It seems to me that they are elements of an even larger and more fundamental matter, which is the broader need for a well informed society. That would be a society better able to make decisions about itself, based upon an understanding of all its institutions of government. This is a matter of profound importance.

I also see the process of change that I have described as part of a larger movement of change as today's courts assume an ever greater responsibility for their own management and for adapting the system in which they play a pivotal role to meet the changing needs of modern society.

---

[5] *Patrick Stevedores Operations No 2 Pty Ltd v Maritime Union of Australia & Ors* (1998) 77 FCR 478.

THE COURTS AND THE MEDIA: WHAT REFORMS ARE NEEDED AND WHY?

The Honourable Daryl Williams

*Attorney-General for the Commonwealth of Australia**

This forum would not have taken place 20 years ago. It is evidence of remarkable changes that have taken place in attitudes in recent times. All our institutions have been opened up to critical scrutiny. The community demands accountability of those in public office.

There have been similar panels held, not only in Australia, notably at the recent conference of the Australian Institute of Judicial Administration,[1] but also overseas.[2] We are seeing in Australia not an isolated phenomenon, but a world-wide increase in demand for information about, and accountability of, democratic institutions. The judiciary is one of those institutions being carefully scrutinized by its public. As the Chief Justice of the High Court of Australia, the Honourable Murray Gleeson AC, said recently: "We live in an age of accountability. What is required of judges is changing. That is a good thing, but it does not make life easier for judges."[3]

I propose first to focus on the relationship between the courts and the media. Secondly, I will distinguish the different types of information that the media conveys about the courts, such as:
- information about the judicial process generally; and
- information (and criticism) about specific judicial decisions.

My argument will be that courts the and the media must adopt different approaches, depending on the information they are conveying to the public.

Relationship Between the Media and the Courts

It is a fact of life that the courts and the media do have a relationship. A similar panel discussion in the United States was entitled "Shall We Dance?". One of the participating judges observed that it was

---

* I have been greatly assisted by Ms Kerry O'Kane of the Attorney-General's Department, Canberra, in the preparation of this article.
[1] Held in Melbourne, 4–6 September 1998.
[2] See "Shall We Dance? The Courts, the Community, and the News Media", (1996) 80 *Judicature* 1 at 30.
[3] Gleeson, A.M., "Performing the Role of the Judge", (1998) 10 (8) *Judicial Officers' Bulletin* at 59. The article was based on an address entitled "The Role of the Judge and Becoming a Judge" delivered at the National Judicial Orientation Programme on 16 August 1998, Sydney.

too late to ask such a question. Justice Femia remarked that: "These are the 1990s, and we're dancing whether we like it or not."[4]

It is no secret that the relationship is an uneasy one. I suggest that this is because the roles of the judiciary and the media are very different. Not only are these roles different, I do not think each understands the other's job. Ultimately, they should both be acting in the public interest, serving the community. Their responsibilities are owed to the community, not to each other. Further, the obligations the courts and the media owe to the public are quite different.

The role of the courts is to uphold the law fairly and independently. Judges maintain the rule of law, uphold the Constitution, and administer civil and criminal justice according to the law.[5] The judiciary is granted unique conditions of service to achieve this aim. It is guaranteed tenure and salary. It is not dependent on any group or body in society, least of all the executive which appoints it. It stands between the citizen and the state and maintain the lawful balance of power between the executive, the legislature and the citizen.

The term "judicial independence" is used frequently, and sometimes inappropriately, when describing the role of judges. It is helpful to remember the explanation of judicial independence proffered by the former Chief Justice of the High Court, the Honourable Sir Anthony Mason AC KBE. He said that:

> ...judicial independence is not a privilege enjoyed by judges, although judges sometimes mistakenly encourage that notion by invoking the privilege as if it were their own. Judicial independence is a privilege of, and a protection for, the people. It is a fundamental element in our democracy, all the more so now that the citizen's rights against the state are of greater value than his or her rights against other citizens.[6]

However, as I have stated elsewhere,[7] the principle of judicial independence is consistent with the requirement of judicial accountability. Both are aspects of the duties owed by the judiciary to the community.

There are significant restraints on the judiciary.[8] It does not set the judicial agenda. It does not choose which cases or subjects will come before it for decision. Even in the limited circumstances of the High Court's decisions on granting special leave to appeal, the subject matter before the court is

---

[4] *Ibid.*, n. 2 at 33.

[5] *Ibid.*, n. 3 at 57.

[6] Mason, A., "The Independence of the Bench; the Independence of the Bar and the Bar's Role in the Judicial System", keynote address to the 1992 Conference of English, Scottish and Australian Bar Associations (London), 4 July 1992 at 3.

[7] Williams, D., "Judicial Independence, the Courts and the Community", address to the South Australian Chapter of the Australian Institute of Judicial Administration Incorporated, 7 February 1997. See also The Hon. Anthony Murray Gleeson AC, *op.cit.*, n. 3 at 58.

[8] Kirby, M., "Judicial Activism". Bar Association of India Lecture, 6 January 1997.

controlled by litigants. The information on which decisions are based is dictated by the requirements of the adversarial system and the rules of evidence governing proceedings.

The media, on the other hand, has a very different job. It has obligations of accuracy, fairness and objectivity. It must also entertain and produce profits for its owners. It has a responsibility to understand the legal processes only to the extent necessary to fulfil these obligations. There are also significant restraints on the media in its ability to grasp the complexity of court proceedings.[9] The media works within extremely tight time frames. Not all papers can have full time court reporters. While we are well served by some specialist reporters, many reporters are not legally trained and legal reporting is only one aspect of their portfolio. There may not be continuity in the allocation of court reporting within a newspaper and young reporters, with insufficient knowledge of the legal system, may be appointed.[10] The articles, even on lengthy, complex cases, must be absurdly brief. They must mould a decision into a newsworthy item. It is not hard to see how accuracy and completeness may be casualties.[11]

The media is interested in newsworthiness. It will rarely publish the success stories.[12] It usually reports when the judicial process is either not functioning well or when it appears to clash with other branches of government—notably the legislature.

What should the courts do for the media? The courts should help the media understand their processes. This is not because they owe the media anything. On the contrary, the judges, by the oaths they take on assuming judicial office, must perform their duties without fear or favour to any person or group. The courts should provide information because they are the most competent body to do so and because the public is entitled to the most accurate information.

What should the media do for the courts? The media should simply fulfil its duties to the public of fair and accurate reporting. It is not qualified to be a spokesperson for the judiciary, and nor should it be. The courts themselves have to maintain and enhance public confidence in the judiciary by the quality of their work.

The accountability of the courts and the media differs enormously. The courts are accountable to the community by the requirement that their duties be performed in public and are publicly reported, and by the

---

[9] Cunningham "Courts and media can't avoid some tensions", *Australian Financial Review*, 1st edn., 5 June 1998, at 20.

[10] Nicholson, R D., "The Courts, the Media and the Community", (1995) 5, *Journal of Judicial Administration*, 1 at 18.

[11] Dawson, D., "Judges and the Media", (1987) 10, *University of New South Wales Law Journal* ,17 at 23. This article is based on an address given to the Queensland Bar Practice Centre, Brisbane, on 13 November 1986.

[12] For an exception, see Ackland, R., "A case of justice seen to be done", *Sydney Morning Herald*, 30 October 1998, at 17.

appeal process. In the case of courts which have separate financial administrations, such as the High Court, the Federal Court and the Family Court, they are responsible for, and must account publicly in annual reports for, the proper expenditure of significant amounts of public moneys.

As for the media, why should it be held accountable? I quote the rationale provided in the report of the Ethics Review Committee, Media Entertainment and Arts Alliance (MEAA) Australian Journalists' Association Section:

> In a democratic society no power is legitimate unless it is accountable. Journalists have a special obligation to be accountable, because it is they who claim to be one of the main methods for holding to account, on behalf of the public, others who wield power.
>
> If the public becomes convinced that journalism will not accept accountability, and is hypocritical as well, then gradually the media will be perceived as illegitimate, as lacking in credibility, as being unworthy of trust. When people don't trust you, they can't rely on you. Journalists cannot fulfil their responsibilities to the Australian community unless it relies on them. Without that reliance, democracy suffers, and eventually freedom wanes.
>
> We are not saying that doom is nigh. We are saying the stakes are high.[13]

How is the media held accountable? Short of the sanctions of defamation and contempt laws, accountability is governed by and large by self regulation. In his foreword to that report, Father Frank Brennan SJ AO, Chair of the MEAA Ethics Review Committee, highlighted some of the accountability problems. They were:

- journalism is a self regulating profession in which most practitioners are not self employed;
- the stock in trade is free speech practised in a world of revolutionary technological change; and
- half the journalists are not members of the union that formulates the code of ethics.[14]

The report makes recommendations[15] to improve accountability, such as the inclusion of non-journalist members on the committees which hear complaints, an escalating scale of penalties for breaches of the (recommended revised) code of ethics and publication of decisions on such breaches.

The report also notes that there are many media self regulation systems other than that used by the MEAA, such as the Press Council, in-house

---

[13] Ethics Review Committee, Ethics in Journalism, Media Entertainment and Arts Alliance, *Australian Journalists' Association Section Report*, Melbourne University Press (1997), at 20. That report recommends the adoption of a revised MEAA *Code of Ethics*.

[14] *Ibid*. at (vi).

[15] *Ibid*., summarized at 104–106.

systems and the commercial broadcasters' codes of practice. While the report did not review the effectiveness of these other systems, it said that:

> ...we have highlighted the importance of a combined effort by MEAA members and employers to improve media accountability. Several practical initiatives will work effectively only if they co-operate.
>
> We see no reason in principle why the commercial, national and community broadcasters could not also establish better liaison among themselves and with publishers and the MEAA. Consistency of standards, decisions and shared expertise would improve media accountability, in particular in an industry characterized by a highly mobile workforce.[16]

This is not the occasion for elaboration, but the adequacy of media accountability mechanisms is open to question.

Information about the Courts

THE JUDICIAL PROCESS

It is appropriate to distinguish two different types of information the media conveys about the courts. Firstly, there is information about the judicial process. This is general, educative material about the judiciary. Secondly, there is reporting of particular decisions. Different considerations apply to these different categories. My argument is that the courts and the media should take different approaches to these different situations.

We would all agree that the judicial process will not headline the evening news. It does not have the immediacy required for short term news stories. It is also a very complicated story. It involves explaining the separation of powers, the interlocking relationship between the legislature, the executive and the judicial arms of government. It includes the constitutional basis for judicial powers, including issues of tenure and terms of appointment. There is the added complication that we have separate Commonwealth, State and Territory courts and tribunals. This is hardly the stuff of the 30 second grab.

Nevertheless, the community has a right to this information. Who is best placed to deliver it? I would say the courts themselves. It is not the role of the media. The courts are already pro-actively performing this precise community education role. Judges have for many years considered it appropriate to address conferences and other educational forums. The courts have their own annual reports and home pages on the internet. Many have appointed media liaison officers and have conducted user forums. Some judicial officers have agreed to interviews with the media. Professor Parker has summarized these initiatives in his report, "Courts and the Public"[17] Dr Wood, in the publication "Judicial Ethics", stated:

---

[16] *Ibid.* at 99.

[17] Parker, *Courts and the Public*, Australian Institute of Judicial Administration Incorporated (1998), at 86–92 and 174.

Judicial officers are valuable contributors to public education and debate on legal matters. Although some hold that judicial officers should generally remain silent, others believe that they should be encouraged to speak and write informatively about matters concerning the law, the legal system, and the administration of justice. Groups addressed might include meetings of community service clubs, press club luncheons, and university students.

This may be seen more as an extension of the judicial role—or even an integral part of it—rather than a departure from it.[18]

As Professor Parker acknowledges in his report, the courts have initiated many of these developments themselves, with enthusiasm. Many courts and tribunals have produced helpful materials for the public to explain their jurisdictions. This is an ongoing process. For example, I understand that the "Guidelines for the Media" published by the Western Australian Courts in 1996 is being revised. I understand that the South Australian Supreme Court is also producing a media handbook. Such reforms are a matter for the courts themselves. However, if the courts develop a good working relationship with the media, this information can be provided to the public even more effectively.

The topic for this particular session invites the question — who or what should be reformed? It would be inappropriate for politicians, academics or the media itself to try and impose reforms on the courts concerning their relationship with the media. It is important to remember that the independence of courts is a crucial feature of their credibility and the vitality of the democratic process generally. Having said that, the presence of so many senior members of the judiciary at this forum reinforces my earlier observation that the judiciary is not only aware of its duties to the public in providing information, but embraces them enthusiastically.

The reforms I have referred to above have been initiated on a court by court basis, and there is a place for them in specialist jurisdictions. However, I have many times expressed the view that the Australian judiciary, and the community, would benefit enormously by hearing a representative voice for all the judiciary.[19]

JUDICIAL CONFERENCE
I would like to see the Judicial Conference of Australia emerge as this representative voice for the judiciary on broader questions that arise in relation to the judiciary as an institution.[20] The Conference could relieve

---

[18] Wood, *Judicial Ethics*, Australian Institute of Judicial Administration Incorporated (1996), at 29.

[19] Williams, D., "Who Speaks for the Judges?", Australian Judicial Conference, 3 November 1996; and Williams, D., "Judicial Independence, the Courts and the Community", address to the South Australian Chapter of the Australian Institute of Judicial Administration, 7 February 1997.

[20] Williams, D., "Judicial Independence: Australian Initiatives", (1998) 24 (2), *International Legal Practitioner* at 108.

the strain of the responsibility increasingly placed on individual courts or members of the judiciary to present more general judicial views to the public and to the media. Such a representative body could also be a focus of support from, and liaison with, other key players such as the legal profession.

One of my initiatives in the previous Government was the grant of $60,000 to the Judicial Conference to establish a secretariat so that it will be able to perform these functions.[21] Another initiative was a grant to the Judicial Conference of a further $40,000 to conduct a research project on "Judicial Independence in Australia Today". This is a practical research project on the concept of judicial independence and its meaning to the community in a modern democratic society.

The project will provide materials for use by members of the Judicial Conference on judicial independence and the rights and responsibilities it entails for the judiciary. It will also produce briefing materials for the community, parliamentarians and the media to explain judicial independence.

COMMONWEALTH STUDY ON JUDICIAL INDEPENDENCE

Another practical initiative I have taken has been to initiate a Commonwealth Law Ministers' project on Judicial Independence. My Department drafted a comprehensive survey on behalf of the London-based Commonwealth Secretariat. Twenty-eight Commonwealth member countries responded. All Australian courts also provided data which has been included in the results.

The result is a comprehensive database on the judiciary which is located on the internet.[22] The project will not only benefit developing countries and their judiciaries, but add to the easily accessible data on Australian courts.

AIJA STUDY ON COURTS AND THE PUBLIC

Many of you will be aware of the important, recent publication of the Australian Institute of Judicial Administration (AIJA)[23] entitled "The Courts and the Public" written by Professor Stephen Parker, to which I referred to earlier in this paper. It was launched at the AIJA conference in Melbourne in September 1998.

I am pleased to say that the report was made possible by a grant of $50,000 by my Department. It represents a significant addition to

---

[21] The address of the Judicial Conference of Australia is care of Professor Stephen Parker, Faculty of Law, Griffith University, Nathan, Queensland 4111, Australia. Professor Parker's e-mail address is S.Parker@law.gu.edu.au. The Conference's internet home page address is http://uniserve.edu.au/law/pub/law_reform/jca/

[22] The internet address for the Commonwealth database on the Independence of the Judiciary project is http://jis.ag.gov.au

[23] The address of the Australian Institute of Judicial Administration is 103–105 Barry Street, Carlton South, Victoria 3053, Australia.

Australian research on its courts. In particular, the study is about how we can improve relationships between Australian courts and their public.[24]

Media Coverage of Judicial Decisions

I have discussed appropriate ways the courts themselves can contribute directly to the community's education about judicial process. The more problematic area is media reporting of particular decisions and court proceedings. Undoubtedly, this is where tensions emerge between the courts and the media.

I want to highlight three different situations and suggest appropriate responses. These are:

• firstly, where factual inaccuracies occur in press reports, either about the facts of a case or about a courts's processes;
• secondly, where a criticism of a judicial decision becomes a personal attack on a judge or a number of judges; and
• thirdly, where the criticism becomes an attck on a court, such as the accusation that a court is making policy, not law.

(There are, of course, other situations where the nature of appropriate responses may differ.)

FACTUAL INACCURACIES

Firstly, where criticism is based on a misunderstanding of the law or on inaccurate reporting of a case, it is entirely appropriate, in my view, for a court to correct public misunderstanding by dealing with the media directly, either through its Chief Justice, media liaison officer or chief executive officer. Such occasions can be a valuable opportunity to raise community awareness about legal issues and the functioning of the court system. For example, judges could use the occasion to explain the rationale for judicial reticence in commenting on judicial decisions generally. The public interest in judges generally refraining from commenting on decisions will not be supported by the public if it does not understand the rationale behind it.[25]

Criticism of a court's administrative processes, at least under the federal system of judicial self administration, seems to be a clear example of a situation in which the courts can and should respond in their own defence. However, the courts must remember that they do not have the final say. Correct information supplied to the media may not necessarily be printed. Courts need to take care in seeking to prolong an issue and must be conscious they do not control the forum.

---

[24] *Op.cit.*, n. 17 at v.
[25] Cunningham, "The Role of the Judiciary in a Modern Democracy", Judicial Conference of Australia Symposium, 8–9 November 1997.

PERSONAL ATTACKS

Secondly, and most seriously, what should courts do when the media attacks judges on a personal level? Unfortunately, this has become more prevalent, not just in Australia, but in many countries.[26]

Personal attacks against individual judges are likely to undermine public confidence in the judiciary and thereby damage the legitimacy necessary to its effective functioning as the third arm of government. The former Chief Justice of the High Court, the Honourable Sir Gerard Brennan AC KBE has said that the judiciary has public confidence as its necessary, but sufficient, power base.[27]

In this situation, it is appropriate for not only a court itself, but also the Judicial Conference and the leaders of the legal profession, to respond to such criticisms. In some situations it may be appropriate for the Attorney-General to respond, such as where the report is of an attack on the judiciary conducted under parliamentary privilege, a venue which the judiciary has no other means of addressing.

We must bear in mind that there is a great deal at stake for our community if public confidence in the judiciary is unnecessarily eroded by sensational, personalized attacks. Our remarkably stable democracy can be attributed in no small part to the community's acceptance of the legitimacy of our courts to maintain the balance between the executive, the legislature and the community.

THE NATURE OF DECISION MAKING

The third situation I wish to address is where courts are criticized because they are perceived by the media, or by others who are reported in the media, as making, not applying, the law. This has applied particularly to the High Court.

Mabo,[28] *Wik*[29] and the so-called implied rights decisions of the High Court[30] are examples of cases that have attracted significant public criticism. I do not believe this is solely because of disagreement with the substance of the decisions themselves. Rather, criticism has been directed at a perceived intrusion of the court into areas of law making rather than adjudication.[31]

I do not subscribe to the view that judicial decision making is a task

---

[26] Kirby, M., "Attacks on Judges: A Universal Phenomenon" (1998) 81 *Judicature* (6).

[27] Brennan, G., *The Australian*, 8 November 1996.

[28] *Mabo v The State of Queensland [No 2]* (1992) 175 CLR 1.

[29] *The Wik Peoples v The State of Queensland* (1996) 187 CLR 1.

[30] *Australian Capital Television Pty Ltd v Commonwealth* (1992) 177 CLR 106; *Nationwide News Pty Ltd v Wills* (1992)177 CLR 1; *Theophanous v Herald and Weekly Times Ltd* (1994) 182 CLR 104; *Stephens v Western Australia Newspapers Ltd* (1994) 182 CLR 211.

[31] Thompson, "Two reactions to the speech on the role of the High Court given at Cambridge University by Chief Justice Sir Anthony Mason" , *AM*, 14 July 1993.

free of interpretive activity.[32] The common law is not a static entity but is clearly a dynamic living thing that develops as new problems are put before it, and as new standards develop in our legal and social worlds.[33] Many judges have explained this and I think it is appropriate for them to do so. However I do not believe it is universally understood. This is also an appropriate task for the Judicial Conference and the leaders of the legal profession. The media also has a responsibility to convey this reality to the community.

This role of the High Court has been emphasized since the reforms in the 1980s, when the appeal processes were changed. Now, generally, civil appeals can only go to the High Court by special leave, not as of right. The Chief Justice of the High Court has explained one consequence of this reform as follows:

> ...the result has been that most civil appeals before the court are cases in which at least one party intends to argue that established common law principles should be modified or changed, or that existing precedents should not be followed. A court whose business consists largely of dealing with cases of that character is more likely to take on the appearance of being radical, not necessarily by reason of the disposition of the members of the court, but by reason of the nature of its business.[34]

The more significant a judicial decision, the more important it is that the community, including the media, understands that decision. The media has a role to play in reporting not just the decision, but the reasoning behind it.

Even allowing for the significant restraints on the media I have referred to above, this is not a role it is performing well. For example, Dr Robert Austin (now Justice Austin of the Supreme Court of New South Wales) observed that the press summarised 217 pages of legal reasoning in the *Wik* decision "by and large, in a sentence".[35] He also said that: "Readers could not possibly have gained an impression that the judgments of the justices were supported by extensive and careful legal reasoning."[36]

As I have already indicated, the media is unlikely to summarize complex decisions accurately. Therefore, the courts have a responsibility to make their decisions as understandable as possible. Several suggestions have been made. For example, I agree with the views of Chief Justice Gleeson that the style of judgments and the necessity for reserved written

---

[32] Williams, D., "Who Speaks for the Judges?", Paper delivered to the Australian Judicial Conference, 3 November 1996.

[33] *Ibid*.

[34] Gleeson, A.M., "The Role of the Judiciary in a Modern Democracy", Judicial Conference of Australia Symposium, 8–9 November 1997. See also Kitto, F., "Why Write Judgments?", (1992) 66 *Australian Law Journal* 787.

[35] Austin, University of Sydney Graduation Ceremony (Postgraduate Law), 2 May 1998. This address will be published by the Judicial Commission of NSW.

[36] *Ibid*.

judgments should be reconsidered.[37] Secondly, I agree with calls that have been made for the provision by the courts, where considered necessary, of summaries of judgments.[38]

Thirdly, I have expressed the view previously,[39] and will do so again, that the members of courts, particularly the High Court, should consider, wherever possible, publishing joint reasons for decision. It is difficult enough for learned constitutional lawyers to analyze seven separate decisions in an important case, let alone a journalist on a tight deadline, or a member of the community.

Roles of the Judiciary, Executive and Legislature

I have attempted to defend decisions of the High Court, which have been mistakenly branded as judicial legislation, as legitimate exercises of judicial power. As I have stated above, it is appropriate also for a court to defend its decisions if they have been erroneously reported, trivialised by personal references or if the media has misrepresented the nature of the judicial role.

However, we must be clear about the parameters of the judicial role. It is another matter entirely for a judge to use the media to convey views on policy which is rightly the domain of the legislature and the executive. In the public's eye, there is no such thing as a judge's personal view on a matter of policy. Judges should always refrain from expressing such views publicly. Just as politicians should refrain from personal attacks on our judges, which undermine public confidence in the judiciary, so should judges respect the territory of the executive and the legislature.

It is readily apparent that such mutual restraint is necessary for the healthy balance between the three branches of government. Ultimately, all three are serving the public interest. That public interest demands a mutual appreciation of the limits of each other's roles.

Conclusion

The relationship between the media and courts is an uneasy one. This is partly because of misunderstandings about each other's roles. Also, it is partly because both the courts and the media should be serving the public interest, but they do this in different ways. Their responsibilities are owed to the community, not to each other.

Courts are attuned to the need for changes. They should assume, and have assumed, responsibility for explaining their processes and role.

---

[37] Gleeson, A.M., "The Role of the Judiciary in a Modern Democracy", Judicial Conference of Australia Symposium, 8–9 November 1997 and Gleeson, A.M., "Performing the Role of the Judge", (1998) 10 *Judicial Officers' Bulletin* (8), at 59.

[38] Samuels, G., "Public Relations For the Courts?", paper delivered at the Annual Conference of the Supreme Court of New South Wales, 10–11 April 1992 at 11.

[39] Williams, D., "Welcome to the Chief Justice, the Hon. Anthony Murray Gleeson, on the occasion of a special sitting of the High Court of Australia", 22 May 1998. This speech was reported in (1998) 50 *Administrative Review* 45.

Reforms are taking place in the courts' attitudes to the media. These are consistent with courts maintaining their necessary independence.

There is also room for improvement within the media. It could refrain from personalizing criticism of judgments, explain reasoning behind judgments and resist the temptation to simplify and sensationalize. It could improve its methods of implementing accountability.

It is appropriate for courts to respond to inaccurate factual reporting, personalizing of criticism and misreporting of their function. Different situations call for different approaches and the media retains ultimate control over the messages the judiciary seeks to convey through the media.

The judiciary should also be aware of the appropriate parameters within which it should use the media. Politicians and the media should not attack the judiciary on a personal level and judges should avoid venturing into the domains of the executive and legislature.

An expanding dialogue with the media through such forums as this is very constructive. This forum is not about finger pointing. Rather, I see it as a mutual commitment to providing the public with a better quality of information about its institutions. We will be on the right path if we bear in mind that both the third branch and the fourth estate are required to serve the public interest.

THE COURTS AND THE MEDIA: WHAT REFORMS ARE NEEDED AND WHY?

The Honourable Justice John Doyle

Chief Justice of South Australia

I am sure that the question of whether changes are needed to the relationship between the courts and the media will attract a variety of answers. Before I give my answer, I think that it is helpful to consider, if only briefly, the nature of that relationship. I believe that an understanding of the nature of the relationship is relevant to the answer to the question posed.

I propose to focus on the role of the print, radio and television media as a means by which Australians are informed about the work of the courts and about the administration of justice. That is, on the relationship between the courts and the media as a source of public information about the work of the courts. I will deal only with the news media. I leave to one side the entertainment media and the internet, although the latter is of considerable importance.

I consider this role of the news media, this relationship between the courts and the news media, to be of fundamental importance. The courts are an institution of government. Highly simplified, our system of government has three arms or elements—the legislature, the executive and the judiciary.

The significance of the judiciary, as the third arm of government, is self evident. The judiciary is significant because the administration of justice is important. We must have a state-backed system for the resolution of disputes between Australians, between Australians and their governments, and for the trial of criminal charges. That system of justice must be one in which the law is applied impartially and fairly, and must be administered by judges who are truly independent.

The judicial arm of government has a relationship to the Australian people that differs from that of the other two arms of government. It must administer laws enacted by Parliament, whether it agrees with those laws or not. It does not set its own agenda or formulate and implement policies in the manner of the executive government. The judicial arm of government depends upon the legislature and upon the executive government for funding. It cannot raise its own resources. The enforcement of its decisions depends, ultimately, upon the executive government providing the necessary backing. This is just another way of expressing Alexander Hamilton's famous proposition that the courts, lacking the power of the sword and the power of the purse, are the least dangerous of the three branches of government. The judicial arm of government does not have the democratic legitimacy that comes from popular election. The judicial arm of government does not deal with and draw support from interest groups in society in the way which the executive and legislature do. It stands apart from the community in many ways, although it acts for the community.

The point I make is that the legitimacy and effectiveness of the courts, and indeed of the system of justice, rest upon public confidence and support. That in turn must be derived from the public's perception of the manner in which we discharge our function. While our system of justice is underpinned by the power of the state, I believe that public confidence in the courts and public support for an independent judiciary is essential for the proper functioning of our system of justice. The courts have to earn that public confidence, or to be more precise, have to maintain the public confidence which I believe they presently have.

That is my starting point. Public confidence in the courts is vital and the courts must earn that public confidence by the manner in which they discharge their function.

My other basic premise is that because the courts are an arm of government, and because our concept of justice is one of justice done in public, public access to the courts is a basic right. The right of access seems to me to rest upon our concept or theory of government and upon our concept or theory of justice. These two fundamentals are linked because, I believe, the confidence of the public in the courts depends upon the public having access to the courts, in the sense of being able to observe and to understand what the courts are doing.

The courts have long accepted the right of public access to the courts as an incident of the administration of justice. It is accepted as fundamental to the administration of justice. The courts have not paid the same attention to the idea that public access to the courts has a democratic or governmental aspect. I do not mean that the courts would deny this point of view, although whether my analysis is correct might be debated. What I mean is that the right of public access has rested on the notion of justice administered in public, which means that the doors of the court must be open to the public. That in turn means those who choose to resort to the courtroom, which is usually relatively few people.

My approach is somewhat different. My approach is that the courts try to reach those who choose not to exercise the right of access in person and to inform them of what the courts are doing and why they do it. The courts must do this because Australians have a democratic right to be told what the courts are doing. As an arm of government we should do what we can to inform Australians about our work and not simply take the view that those who choose to come to court to observe the administration of justice are free to do so. As well, because I believe that public confidence in the courts rests upon public understanding, it is our duty as officers of justice to maintain public confidence in the courts, and therefore to do what we can, once again, to give Australians information about what the courts are doing.

It is this latter approach which I think the courts have been slower to accept. That is, the notion that the courts, as an institution, have an obligation to inform Australians about their work. This is much more than an obligation to permit access to those who seek it. I realize that many judges would differ in view from me and I recognize that I may not be right. Many judges would take the view that our only task is to administer justice in court and that we are not suited or equipped to undertake an active role in the process of communication with the public.

I recognize the force of that point of view. In response to the point about our competence, I wish to make it clear that I am not suggesting that every judge has to be closely involved in the process. Nor am I suggesting that what is done is to be done entirely by the judges. My view is that the relevant responsibility rests upon the courts as a body or institution, to be discharged by such persons as are appropriate. This will, of course, include professionals with relevant qualifications. There is a part for the judges to play and it is important that they co-operate with the work of informing the public. However, the task is not necessarily one to be discharged by the judges. The responsibility is not ours alone. It also rests upon the executive government. But the courts have a part to play as well, and at present, the executive governments of Australia do not, as far as I know, do much in this area.

My argument has a theoretical underpinning but there is a practical aspect to it. If the courts are going to leave it to others, the media in particular, to determine how much and what sort of information the public gets about their workings, then the courts are saying that they are content to leave it to others to shape the public understanding and perception of the courts. That, to me, is not acceptable. I believe that the courts are well placed to explain their function. I consider that experience shows that leaving that task to others is, in the long term, unsatisfactory. I do believe that the courts retain the confidence of the public but I believe that the uninvolved approach of the courts, to date, puts that at risk and certainly makes it much harder to maintain than it otherwise would be.

This leads me to the conclusion that the courts should co-operate with the media in this area. I say that because the media is the means by which Australians get much, probably most, of their information about the courts. That being so, and because Australians have a right to that information, we have a responsibility to assist the media. As I have explained, I believe that public confidence will be enhanced if we assist the media to communicate accurate information to the public. In other words, we should see the media as the means by which Australians exercise their democratic right of access and a means by which we can maintain public confidence in the courts.

We are not working with the media to protect ourselves or to cultivate a desired image. We are doing it because Australians have a right to know and this is a way of recognizing that right. Also, public confidence and the independence of the judiciary depend upon public understanding.

Of course, the media is not the only means by which the courts can communicate with the public. But it is a very important means. Treating the media as an important means by which the public exercises its right of access has a number of ramifications. It means that the courts should do what they can to facilitate that form of public access. The courts should do what they can to make their processes comprehensible to the media and, through the media, to Australians generally. Assistance given by the courts to the media is not an act of generosity on our part. It is done on the basis that the media is exercising a right on behalf of the public and on the basis that we wish to communicate to Australians through the media.

This is simply said, but it is a demanding charter. It will take a long time to implement. I do not imply by this that the courts should give uncritical assistance to the media, just as I do not imply that the courts would then expect to escape criticism. We are entitled, indeed obliged, to point out deficiencies in the manner in which the media informs Australians about the courts. On the other hand, I accept that we have to move with the times and we have to understand, even if we do not agree with, the nature of contemporary journalism.

It is important that the media recognizes the constraints on the courts in doing this. When sitting in court we are engaged in the administration of justice. That is a serious business. It is demanding work and usually requires all of one's energy and attention to be done properly. The parties before us have a right to be treated properly and justly. We cannot allow court proceedings to become, as it were, a media event. We must find ways to maximize public access without damaging the process of justice. Television cameras in court are an obvious example of the difficulties that can arise. In theory, enabling the public to watch court proceedings as they happen, or more or less as they happen, on their television screens at home is an ideal way of informing the public of how the courts work. However, bringing television cameras into court brings with it many problems for the fair administration of justice. We have to balance the interests of the administration of justice and the rights of Australians to know what happens in court. It is not simply a matter of making arrangements that best suit the media.

There are real limitations upon what the courts can do. But having said that, I believe that there is plenty that the courts can do. We can be accessible for interviews, participate in talkback radio, talk to community groups, produce informative videos and so on. All of these activities depend upon the courts having the human and financial resources that arc needed and we do not always have these. We need to persuade the executive government of the need for appropriate funding. However, we should be willing to do what we can.

The course that I suggest is not risk free. The judiciary has a lot to learn about working with the media. If we aim to make use of the media as a means of communication with Australians, we must learn how to make proper use of the media. If we do not, mistakes will be made.

It is also appropriate to recall that in this area the media has responsibilities. As I understand it, the function of the news media is to report the facts. A lot of the reporting of the work of criminal courts is quite superficial. Reporting of sentencing decisions is often relatively poor because there is rarely an attempt to capture the reasons for the decision. The emphasis tends to be upon the bare facts of the crime, the sentence, and the reaction of the victim. I believe that accurate reporting requires an attempt be made to report the reasons the judge(s) gave. I believe that the media can, and should, do better than it does when reporting the work of the courts, even allowing for the restraints under which it works. I also believe that the media should, and could, give more attention in current affairs programmes to aspects of the administration of justice but I accept that this requires the co-operation of the courts. I am not suggesting that the news media in particular is there to argue the case for the courts. I accept that it is there to report facts. However, I do believe that its reporting of the facts at times is incomplete and superficial.

In short, I believe that the courts must change their attitude to the media and to making use of the media as a means of informing Australians. I believe that there is a sound democratic argument for doing so and that to do so is in the interests of the administration of justice in the broadest sense. As for the media, I hope that it will listen to our views and consider the part that it plays in informing Australians about the system of justice. I hope that the media will accept a responsibility to provide Australians with sound information and not just with "news". I hope that the media will take a close interest in the subject matter of justice and will try to establish a reputation for accurate reporting.

Changes are occurring in the relationship. I hope that the courts and the media can work together to achieve a better informed public.

THE COURTS AND THE MEDIA: WHAT REFORMS ARE NEEDED AND WHY?

Professor David Flint

AO; Chairman, Australian Broadcasting Authority and Professor of Law, University of Technology, Sydney

In a modern democracy, the courts and the media must have two essential characteristics. First, they must be independent. Second, they must be separate, not only from the executive and the legislature, but also from each other. The best we can hope for in the relations between them is that each will have a degree of respect for the other, but certainly not deference.

It is inevitable of course that there will be friction between them. And certainly criticism. In 1819, one of the first justices of the Supreme Court of New South Wales, Barron Field, published a small book of poetry. This was *First Fruits of Australian Poetry*. Soon after this, a critique appeared which was also in verse:

> Thy poems, Barron Field, I've read
> And thus ajudge their meed
> So poor a crop proclaims thy head
> A barren field indeed!

Lord Jacobson once issued this admonition about another state institution and the press:

> My Lords, relations between Government and the press have deteriorated, they are deteriorating, and they may deteriorate even more. And on no account, on no account must they be allowed to improve.

It may well be desirable that government and media relations be adversarial and based on mutual suspicion. Nevertheless, a more respectful *modus vivendi* has traditionally prevailed in relations between the judicial branch and the media. Yet these relations have certainly deteriorated in Australia in recent years.

Can relations be improved? Should they be improved? My answer to both questions is a definite "yes".

How then can they be improved? They can be improved, I believe, by reference to two sound principles. The first principle is based on international law and in the application of the freedom of political communication found in our Constitution. The second arises from the Constitution and is fundamental to the common law. It is the principle of judicial restraint. That is, that the courts should restrict themselves to the judicial role which is implicit in the separation of powers and the very independence the judiciary must have.

1. Restrictions on the Media

I come to the first principle. This principle operates in the context of the High Court decision in *Lange v Australian Broadcasting Corporation*[1] which has now settled the meaning of the constitutional freedom of political communication. This acts as a restraint on the making of legislation. And the common law must be consistent with it. Legal restrictions on freedom of political communication must only be those for an object which is necessary in a democratic society. And the restriction must be proportional to the achievement of that objective. This principle calls not only for a reconsideration of existing restrictions, it also means that every proposed restriction, however well intended, should be subject to the same test.

DEFAMATION

In *Lange*[2] the Court gave a signal to trial courts in defamation cases involving the media to give new life to qualified privilege. This should, over time, have the desirable result that the media will be freer to examine matters of genuine public interest. Although the constitutional defence created by *Theophanous v Herald & Weekly Times Ltd*[3] and *Stephens v West Australian Newspapers Ltd*[4] was no longer available after *Lange*, the practical effect would be much the same. The media would be free but this would, and should, only be available in the airing of matters of genuine public interest. The publication of mere rumours about the private lives of public figures, à la Kitty Kelly—remains totally unjustifiable. It is appalling that once great publishing houses can today bring themselves to publish such material. The law must continue to provide a remedy against this.

There are two aspects of substantive law related to the application of this principle which I believe do need reconsideration. First, the assumption that a jury, properly instructed, remains more susceptible than judges or lawyers to media reporting. This is unjustified today—if it ever was. However, it is not suggested we introduce "trial by media", just a reform of the law of contempt.

Second, the provision of information to journalists, on the basis that the source not be named, is fundamental to the free flow of information

---

[1] (1997) 189 CLR 520.
[2] *Ibid*.
[3] (1994) 182 CLR 104.
[4] (1994) 182 CLR 211.

in a democratic society. This should be protected by shield laws which ensure a court's procedures are not compromised. Processes which should be protected are those of the courts, not of administrative inquiries or bodies such as Royal Commissions or anti-corruption agencies for instance.

CONTEMPT LAW

When the cream of the world's lawyers met in Melbourne a few years ago at the International Bar Association Conference, the Australian and English lawyers were at pains to demonstrate how the law of contempt ensured juries remained unexposed to media reports. After hearing this in a bemused silence, a Dutch lawyer said that it could have been a story "from the other side of the moon".

And yet we persist in trying to quarantine our juries. In a major fraud case in England, the judge decided that, while the jurors were locked up to arrive at a verdict, they ought to be able to relax by watching television. So the judge banned any report of the trial on the electronic media! Admittedly an extreme example, but one which illustrates the requirement that the jury should come to the trial completely fresh.

Yet juries were originally expected to report on what they knew. Even by the 18th century, when the United States Constitution expressly prescribed impartial juries, the great Chief Justice of the United States, John Marshall, refused to stand down jurors merely because they had been exposed to media reports. He would only do this if a juror had already made up his mind. John Marshall was right. Insisting on an unexposed jury is wrong. What is needed is an unbiased jury.

Even today in America, the courts actively seek those who have not been so exposed. As Mark Twain wrote, no matter how intelligent or how willing to put aside any prior exposure, it is assumed that "ignoramuses alone could mete out unsullied justice".

The contempt law of this nation equally assumes the ordinary Australian is affected or indeed infected by whatever he or she reads, sees or hears. (This is tempered by the assumption that he or she also has an extremely poor memory!) When Neville Wran was fined for affirming his belief in Lionel Murphy's innocence, it was because of the potential impact on the jury. Yet any reasonable person would have accepted this as Mr Wran's genuine personal belief. Evidence of his affection and loyalty, certainly, but hardly proof of Mr Justice Murphy's innocence. When a Minister of the Crown not so long ago in this State spoke in the most general terms about the Government's campaign against paedophilia, Australians would not have thought that he had said anything which would affect a jury, which just happened to be about to hear a charge of paedophilia. Yet the judge aborted the trial.

The assumption that jurors are putty in the hands of the media has been demonstrated to be untrue. The fact is juries can be singularly impervious to the media. This has been shown in a series of cases which have attracted maximum media exposure. For example, Jeremy Thorpe and the Kray Twins in the United Kingdom, and O.J. Simpson in America.

If the purpose of contempt law is to quarantine the jury from information and debate, it doesn't work. The *sub-judice* rule normally doesn't apply until arrest. All the photographs, all the stories beforehand, cannot be withdrawn. So it is assumed jurors have poor memories. Where there is media saturation, any attempted quarantine is pointless. Had Martin Bryant pleaded not guilty, would there have been even one potential juror in Tasmania not well informed on the Port Arthur massacre? And no juror can be completely isolated from the gossip and rumour that surrounds a notorious crime, made worse by the absence of counter-information by the media restrained by contempt law.

Sometimes it will even be official policy not only to relax the quarantine, but to egg the media on. If an accused escapes from custody, and is thought dangerous, the media is encouraged to publish photographs and warnings. In London in July 1998, people were arrested carrying bombs ready to go off. The media reported the police speculations— who they were, what they planned to do—well beyond the constraints of contempt law. Perhaps the public's legitimate rights to know and hear police advice outweighed the need to have a virginal jury?

There is a lesser inclination to apply contempt law where no jury is involved. Nevertheless, *The Sunday Times* was found to be in contempt when it dared to suggest the makers of thalidomide should offer more by way of damages to settle several cases before the English Court. As a Law Lord once said (Lord Salmon), "no judge would be influenced in his judgment by what may be said by the media. If he were, he would not be fit to be a judge."

And if judges, and presumably lawyers, cannot be tainted, we just witnessed the extraordinary case of a judge who actually chose to be tried by the media. When Justice Vince Bruce was called before the New South Wales Legislative Council to defend himself, he campaigned vigorously and robustly. In Parliament and in the media, even appearing on the "60 Minutes" television programme. Had this been the trial of an ordinary citizen, he and any journalist who interviewed him or commented on the case would have been charged. Presumably, Members of Parliament are as impervious as judges to media speculation. Unlike all other Australians.

I must stress that I am not calling for trial by media. The media should act with special restraint when identity is likely to be in issue. Not to protect the jury, but the witness. But I repeat, identity should be likely to be in issue as it never really was with Martin Bryant. And much of what is trial by media in the United States results more from the misbehaviour of the lawyers, including those who depend on popular election.

CONFIDENTIAL SOURCES

Confidential sources are fundamental to the very concept of journalism. Without the guarantee of protection, "fear of exposure will cause dissidents to communicate less to trusted reporters. And fear of accountability will cause editors and critics to write with more restrained pens."[5]

Not long ago, journalists in Australia knew that, on rare occasions, a court might require them to expose their source, and by refusing they risked a fine or gaol. This did not happen often.

We have had a rash of cases: in 1990, Tony Barrass—gaoled and fined; in 1992, Joe Budd—gaoled; in 1993, Chris Nicholls—gaoled; David Hellaby—fined; John Synott—threatened with contempt proceedings and Deborah Cornwall—found guilty of contempt. There have been raids on newspaper offices and those of the ABC around the country.

In 1995, *The Courier-Mail* ran a story that the Federal Police had gone soft on an investigation into allegations that a former federal Minister had been provided with services of prostitutes in return for government favours.

No doubt, wanting to find out who leaked the story, there were raids late last year on the journalist's home and on offices of *The Courier-Mail.* They were unsuccessful. The raid at *The Courier-Mail* was forestalled by television cameras arriving to film the event.

What is the reason for this acceleration? Are these isolated instances or is there a sinister campaign against journalists? Is it acceptable in our Australian democracy that when incompetence, bad administration and even worse have been exposed, that it is journalists who suffer?

Journalists in Australia have always known of the risk they run. Apart from the broad undefined power of Parliament to find contempt, journalists, in the past at least, thought that they would not have to reveal sources except at a trial and then only when this was relevant to the proceedings. Not any more.

There have been two pernicious developments which have come about—without our noticing.

The first is the use of pre-trial discovery to punish journalists. Pre-trial discovery seemed a good idea at the time. Before you start an action, the court helps the citizen to find out more about a case he or she may wish to bring. It is meant to stop clever lawyers winning by surprise—trial by ambush. It is now a superb weapon which has been added to the armoury of the rich and powerful. It has the potential of stopping a journalist (and setting an example to others). It is also very satisfying. You won't find out who gave the information—but you certainly can make the journalist suffer.

The second development is the creation of statutory bodies which have wide investigative powers. Not only bodies like the New South

---

[5]*Branzburg v Hayes* (1972) 408 U.S. 665 at 721 per Douglas J.

Wales Independent Commission Against Corruption (ICAC). Others are given ancillary powers to require the production of documents or compel the answering of questions. ICAC conducts its own investigations and determines its own terms of reference. So one of the few protections for witnesses—relevance to the proceedings—has gone out the window. Deborah Cornwall could not have been asked the question put to her by ICAC in a court unless it had been relevant to a specific charge against the accused. When eventually her recalcitrance was referred to the Supreme Court, her lawyers pointed out that convicted criminal, "Neddy" Smith, too, had refused to answer questions. But no action was taken about his recalcitrance.

Did we ever intend to give powers to bodies like ICAC greater than those of the Supreme Court, to use against journalists and the media—the very institution that has done more in the initial exposure of defects in public life than any other?

As Justice Douglas of the United States Supreme Court said:

> A reporter is not better than his source of information ... Unless he has a privilege to withhold the identity of his source, he will be the victim of governmental intrigue or aggression ... [He warned that the] reporter's main function ... then will be to pass on to the public the press releases which the various departments of government issue.[6]

Many jurisdictions recognize, to a greater or lesser degree, that journalists should be able to protect their confidential sources.[7] The Australian Press Council, many years ago, initiated a call for the introduction of shield laws in Australia. A shield law needs more than a direction to the court to balance the competing interests of the litigants with the desirability of protecting the various degrees of confidentiality which may prevail in our society.

The Council proposed that New South Wales legislation should include reference to the proposition that:
- protection of journalists' sources is one of the basic conditions of press freedom;
- without such protection, sources may be deterred from assisting the press in informing the public on matters of public interest with a consequent chilling effect on the free flow of information; and
- the protection of sources is of particular and high importance for press freedom in a democratic society and is consistent with Australia's international obligations particularly under Article 19 of the *Universal Declaration of Human Rights* and the *International Covenant on Civil and Political Rights*.

The Council proposed that a New South Wales shield law be based on the American approach and include the following ingredients:[8]
- that the plaintiff be required to show that there is a probable cause to believe that the newspaper has information that is clearly relevant to a

specific violation of the criminal law, with the exception of "official secrets" offence (not as in England "necessary for the prevention of crime" generally);

• that the plaintiff be required to demonstrate that the information sought cannot be obtained by alternative means less destructive to freedom of speech and of the press. This would involve a demonstration that alternative avenues in seeking sources had been attempted;

• that the plaintiff be required to demonstrate a compelling and overriding interest in the information.

II. Judicial Restraint

At the beginning of my paper I argued for judicial restraint, that, as a matter of principle, courts should restrain themselves to the judicial role. In fact most do. But it is the exceptions that have put the courts under such serious attack in recent years. This principle of judicial restraint flows from the very independence the judiciary must have. It is implicit in the constitutional separation of powers. Obviously then the courts are not to intrude into, for example, what is the preserve of the legislature. Nor should trial judges stray beyond the judicial role.

I hasten to add that I am only speaking of the role of judges in court. I make no criticism whatsoever of judges who make thoughtful and considered comments on matters of public interest outside the courts. Indeed, many of these have been significant contributions to the intellectual debate the country must have.

Now judicial expansionism, as I define it, has nothing to do with the development of the common law by some of the world's greatest judges. Judicial expansionism is the active intrusion into the preserve of other bodies, usually for the best of intentions.

It is generally assumed the phenomenon of judicial expansionism has the origins in the United States. Let me give you an example. The Supreme Court of the United States has read into the *penumbrae*, the shadows of the Constitution, a right to privacy. This arises by implication from the express provisions of the Bill of Rights. I make no criticism of this. The drawing of necessary implications is unavoidable, indeed desirable, in the proper interpretation of legal documents. But then the judges decided to peer even further into those *penumbrae*, which for others, including the Founding Fathers, must have been an impenetrable fog. And lo and behold, from the implied right to privacy comes a right, a constitutional right, to abortion!

---

[6] *Supra* n. 5 at 722.

[7] Wilhelm, *Protection of Sources*, Norwegian Institute of Journalism, Fredrickstard, (1988).

[8] Australian Press Council Submission of 15 August 1996 to the Hon. Jeff Shaw, Attorney-General for New South Wales, in protecting *Confidential Communications from Disclosure in Court Proceedings, Discussion Paper*, (1996).

Now at this point let me stress, let me underline, that I am not entering into debate on the legality or morality of abortion. What I am saying is that to anyone but the most extreme judicial expansionist, it is obvious that the Constitution of the United States intends that this matter be one for the legislators to determine.

The absurdity of the Supreme Court's position became even more apparent when it had to determine the point during a pregnancy at which the *soi disant* constitutional right disappeared. As I understand, this is at the end of the second trimester. Judges rushing in where legislatures fear to tread, as one Law Lord put it. And no doubt the legislators were delighted to be let off the hook and not to have to determine a truly difficult question.

The results of siezing the legislative role in this, and other matters, should have been obvious. The Supreme Court attracted the same opprobrium as the political branches. In brief, it had become politicised. The confirmation hearings of nominations to the Court have since come, sometimes, to resemble tabloid soap operas. It is hard to imagine a more undignified way of selecting a judge, one which is sure to put off many a good candidate.

Our own High Court resisted this forbidden fruit for almost two decades. Then on 2 August 1988, the Court made a puzzling announcement. It would abandon, it said, the wig, the robe, as well as the more recently introduced jabot. Now there are those, including editors, who think that judges who cling to traditional dress are out of touch, even ridiculous.[9] Juliet Greco, in the film *The Roots of Heaven*, plays a comfort woman in the Second World War and muses: "Men are not at their worse when they take their uniforms off. Its when they put their uniforms on." Perhaps judges are not at their worse when they put their wigs on. The problem may be when they take them off.

For the High Court was about to enter its most controversial years. And *Mabo v Queensland [No 2]* (the *Mabo Case*) is among the most controversial of its decisions of this period. The case related to Eddie Mabo's claim to own land on the Murray Islands. The Islands are occupied by the Meriam people who are Melanesians, not Aborigines. The people are agriculturists, not nomads. And unlike Aborigines, they recognize individual rights to identifiable parcels of land.

The Court could merely have decided that their title to land survived the annexation of the Islands by the Governor of Queensland in 1879. This would have been a just decision. Moreover, it could have been justified by precedent and on principle. Rather, the Court decided, in effect, to legislate. That is, to legislate with respect to the native title of the Aboriginal people, who were not represented. To legislate with respect to the title of people who were nomadic, not agriculturists. To legislate

---

[9] Editorial, *The Weekend Australian*, 5–6 September 1998, at 18.

with respect to land title across the whole of mainland Australia and Tasmania—matters not before the Court. And in doing all this, the Court did what a common law court should not do. It is elementary that findings of fact in controversial areas can only be adduced from evidence. Yet the judges actually refer to research they have themselves undertaken to make their significant findings! The decision was expressly based on evidence not put before the Court, on arguments not heard in the Court, and affected persons not represented in the Court.

I have no doubt that the judges in *Mabo*[10] acted with the best of intentions. They wanted not only to do justice to Eddie Mabo, but they also wanted to redress what they saw as the injustice rendered to the Aboriginal people. However, this was not their function. Nor were they well equipped to do this.

This question was one which the Australian people had already determined in 1967. The people decided, overwhelmingly, that they would grant the Federal Parliament the power to deal with Aboriginal issues. This was not to be exclusive. It was to be concurrent with the States.

Let me repeat. The people gave the power to legislate on Aboriginal issues to the Parliament. They did not give the power to the High Court.

No doubt the judges were impatient with the legislators. But this was no reason for them to rush in where legislators feared to tread.

The decision, and its aftermath, did little to improve reconciliation. The French academician, Emmanual Todd, measures this by the degree of female exogamy, marrying out, of the minority concerned. Comparisons with, say, American blacks, demonstrates that reconciliation in Australia has been working well. Indeed very well, in this regard. And Australians had shown a regret for the wrongs of the past and a strong commitment expressed in money terms and in laws and policies to ensuring the equality of all our people.

The judges, having legislated a broad proposition, decided that detailed supporting parliamentary legislation was necessary. A poorly drafted and inadequate solution, the *Native Title Act*, was put through Parliament. (The Canberra press gallery, in an extraordinary abdication of its role, stood and applauded when the Bill finally passed the Senate!)

In the following period, especially after *The Wik Peoples v The State of Queensland* (the *Wik Case*),[11] reports of land claims, including claims from groups unknown to surprised land holders, were given limited coverage. Worse, there was a danger that the process of reconciliation would be derailed. Relations between the races in some parts of the country were becoming embittered. Fortunately, the serious defects in the *Native Title Act* apparently have now been cured, at least to a significant degree. And notwithstanding the rhetoric, it is unlikely any future parliament will seek to restore the repealed provisions.

---

[10] (1992) 175 CLR 1.
[11] (1996) 187 CLR 1.

However, *Mabo* was not the high point of this aberration. That surely must have been the case of *Minister for Immigration and Ethnic Affairs v A Hin Teoh* (the *Teoh Case*)[12] where the High Court told us something which a neophyte student of public international law knows is wrong. Students are well aware of the fundamental principle that a treaty has no legal effect without legislation. By then, both Government and Opposition had had enough and moved to overrule the Court.

The result of these intrusions was that the Court was engulfed in a storm of criticism. Yet the judges seemed surprised and bewildered. They still expected to be treated as judges. After all, the High Court had previously handed down decisions in the most controversial of matters, including the case of *Bank of New South Wales v The Commonwealth* (the *Bank Nationalisation Case*)[13] and the case of *Australian Communist Party v The Commonwealth* (the *Communist Party Case*).[14] Nevertheless, in both of these cases, the government of the day sought to reverse the decision by legal means. It is only in recent times that it is suggested that High Court decisions are sacrosanct. But after those two cases, there was no wave of criticism directed to the Court. Why? Because in those two cases, the Court acted judicially. In *Mabo*, the Court strayed from its role and as a result the Court was now politicised.

New appointments to the Court would come under the closest political scrutiny. As in the United States, appointees were assessed as to where they were thought to belong politically and ideologically. There were calls for an inquiry into the advice one judge gave as counsel where the allegations, if true, could not have amounted to grounds for removal. Fortunately, the High Court has now reverted to its traditional role. I expect that it will regain the position it once enjoyed.

The phenomenon of judges straying from their role is fortunately not common. However, it is not limited to the High Court. It can also apply, fortunately rarely, to trial judges and magistrates.

If a judge were, for example, to adopt the common excuse that unemployment is a principle cause for the increase in crime in our society and to accept this as, if not as a justification for, a significant reason to mitigate a sentence, there would be an outcry. (The fact is, of course, the judge would be wrong. There is not even any statistical correlation between unemployment and the level of crime.) For, in substituting some general malaise for the concept of individual responsibility, the judge is also striking a fundamental tenet of our civilization. That is, each individual is responsible for his or her own actions. So when a Sydney magistrate praised environmentalists who invaded the Prime Minister's home, there was a similar outcry.

---

[12] (1995) 183 CLR 273.
[13] (1948) 76 CLR 1.
[14] (1951) 83 CLR 1.

Let me refer now to an editorial in *The West Australian*.[15] This did not escape the notice of Mr Ackland's ABC programme, "Media Watch". And "Media Watch" itself did not escape the scrutiny of Mr Evan Whitton in *The Australian*.[16] It was about an incident far too common today—a violent robbery of an elderly person by a young man. Kenneth Robert Maley, aged 28 years, had threatened the elderly man with a knife. When he did not get any money, he knocked him down. He cut him twice with the knife. (The judge was satisfied that the cutting was not intended.) The old man hit his head on the pavement, which stunned him. While the old man was on the ground, Maley tore his trousers and took his wallet, stealing $465. A witness chased Maley, and the police later arrested him.

When Maley subsequently pleaded guilty, his solicitor told the judge that Maley was having trouble supporting his young partner and children and was motivated by a desperate need for food and money. Drugs, the solicitor said, were certainly not the problem.

The judge, Mr Justice Wallworth, said,

> Yes, there is very little being said generally in the media about the terrible problems a lot of these people are facing. It is just a cry for extreme punishment, one after the other, and until the community takes some responsibility for its citizens we are going to have this type of crime being committed.[17]

Needless to say this was controversial. Mr Evan Whitton wrote in *The Australian*[18] "The community erupted; some felt the judge was accusing them of being responsible for the mugging of an old man."

In any event *The West Australian* thought it would be reasonable to find out whether Maley was in receipt of welfare payments. So *The West Australian* indulged in a little investigative journalism. Maley's former partner came forward and said he received almost $700 a fortnight and spent most of it on drugs. At the subsequent sentencing, the Department of Public Prosecution suggested the judge's comments had been taken out of context and misinterpreted by the media. He said the editor had a conflict of interest which he should have declared. This was because he had once been criticized by the judge! But *The West Australian* has since reported many of the judge's decisions without any criticism. In any event, you can see the general principle, that the community will obviously be concerned if, in sentencing a criminal, any judge were to act more as a sociologist than a judge. And you can see the impact this will have on the respect and confidence that the community has in its judges.

---

[15] "Mugger—What the judge said", *The West Australian*, 21 September 1998, at 6.
[16] Whitton, "They shoot the messengers, don't they?", *The Australian*, 21 September 1998, at 13.
[17] *Ibid.*
[18]*Ibid.*

Maley, incidentally, was sent to gaol for six years and was declared eligible for parole. Would it have been different had not *The West Australian* intervened?

We have inherited sound institutions and superb constitutional arrangements. They represent the very best the world has to offer. If we change them, we should do so with great care. Not inadvertently. Not just because it seems like a good idea at the time.

The judges will command respect, if not deference, if they act as judges. As most of them do. Of course, this does not mean that they cannot develop the law. There is room for the Dennings, the Holmeses and the Mansfields. We are fortunate in Australia in having a judiciary selected by merit. To perform their tasks independently, they must be secure. They should only be removed on conviction for a high crime. Calls for a representative judiciary, if realized, would undermine this institution. We do not have, and no one would suggest we should have, a representative college of surgeons, representative teams of athletes, representative ballet dancers and representative opera singers. Any other method of choice would be thought ridiculous and rightly so. I was almost about to say no one would suggest we should have a representative professoriate ... but that is another story.

Conclusion

In conclusion, let me make these points. First, that we need to review those laws restricting speech and the media to ensure they are for an objective necessary in a democratic society. And that they are proportionate to that objective. Similarly, we need to test any new proposal, however well intended, to restrict that freedom. I have specified the areas of contempt law and the protection of journalist's sources as areas for reform, and defamation law for monitoring.

My other point is that if the judiciary, at all levels, is to maintain public confidence and respect and to ensure the level of criticism remains within reasonable bounds, it must act with judicial restraint. It should not act as a legislator or as a sociologist. To its credit, the great bulk of judges and magistrates do act with judicial restraint.

Of course, it is equally true that media practitioners too should not stray beyond their role. As Mr John Alexander warned in the 1988 Andrew Olle Lecture, they should not seek to be players on the political stage. But that, again, is another story.

THE COURTS AND THE MEDIA: WHAT REFORMS ARE NEEDED AND WHY?

Chris Merritt

Law Correspondent, *The Australian Financial Review*

Firstly, I want to start with a warning: what follows is likely to be very depressing. So let's get the worst part out of the way: it is becoming increasingly clear that the judiciary has an image problem.

Some would go so far as to call it a public relations disaster. This is not a criticism of the very effective information officers who now operate in many superior courts. They do a terrific job.

But an unfortunate collection of issues has arisen in the last year that is doing the image of the judiciary no good at all.

If the public were to be called upon right now to express an opinion about the judiciary based on nothing more than what they have read, seen or heard in the news media, I feel sure that most judges would be pretty disappointed with the outcome.

Now before the judges get too annoyed, let me make it clear that at least some of the causes of this problem are beyond the control of information officers and the judges themselves. Later in this paper it should become fairly obvious which issues I believe are harming the standing of the judiciary. I also propose to put forward a few suggestions on what can be done to fix the problem.

But before getting into that I want to dispose of a distraction from the main argument.

There are those in the legal profession generally and even in the judiciary who may think that the blame for the erosion in the public standing of the judiciary can be sheeted home to biased journalists. This point of view has a superficial logic, starting with the cultural gulf that exists between the courts and the media. It is more than a cultural gulf, it is a cultural Grand Canyon.

Chauvinists in both callings—and there is no shortage of them—make a virtue of their refusal to see the other side's point of view. The law reports are packed with the views of judges who see the media as something akin to oxen who need to be firmly controlled. And sometimes it does appear that some journalists put on blinkers whenever they deal with lawyers generally and judges in particular. Whole careers have been built on lawyer bashing.

So why is it that journalists write such nasty things about judges and the legal system?

To lawyers, the explanation might appear to lie in the way generations of judges have built a legal framework for the Australian media that is increasingly out of step with the countries with which we like to compare ourselves.

On issues that are of fundamental importance to the media, the performance of the judiciary makes it very difficult for journalists to ever be truly fond of the courts.

This should come as no surprise to those who are familiar with the way judges deal with issues such as the right to free speech and the protection of journalists' confidential sources. Under the Mason High Court, it looked for a while as though things might be changing. But that was a false dawn.

While all this makes for a pretty awful starting point for a relationship—and should of course be addressed by the courts—I don't think this is the reason for the judiciary's bad press. On the whole, I think most journalists actually try to give people a fair hearing. If they don't, there is always the risk that their bias will be exposed by an accurate report by one of their competitors. Consequently, I think there are far more substantive reasons for the bad press and the public's poor opinion of the judiciary and the legal system. It is in this area that the need for reform is urgent.

At this point, I think it is important to keep in mind that this gloomy assessment is merely the opinion of a journalist—and we all know what the public thinks about journalists. However in both callings, public opinion does count.

A long term erosion of public respect and credibility should make it impossible for individual practitioners to continue. For the judiciary, there is an added danger. In our system of government, the judiciary is in a perpetual state of dynamic tension with the executive and sometimes with the Parliament. If the courts lose public respect and credibility, there is a risk that the other arms of government will be tempted to expand their constitutional territory—or more accurately, their unconstitutional territory.

And if that happens, the public, not just the judiciary, will eventually feel the adverse impact.

I can think of no better example than the way the New South Wales Government keeps trying to pass laws to keep people in gaol when their sentence has expired. While this sort of behaviour is constitutionally obnoxious, the politicians clearly think they can not only get away with it, but they will be cheered on by the public.

Such an assessment by politicians suggests that they believe the public will see nothing wrong in Parliament attempting to encroach on the judicial function. If this assessment of the public's understanding of the judicial function is accurate, the question arises as to what the judiciary plans to do about it.

Traditionalists would probably argue that the best response is to do nothing. Eventually, so this argument goes, the High Court will strike down such constitutional effrontery and everyone will be happy. The politicians will still be able to ingratiate themselves with the redneck constituency by blaming judicial activism for preventing them doing what should be done. The judiciary will be happy because the threat will be removed.

I don't think that's good enough. On issues such as the separation of powers, the role of the judiciary and the operation of the courts, the voice of the judiciary should regularly be heard. The traditional response is, of course, that judges say all that needs to be said in their judgments. Well, if that were ever correct, I don't think it is these days. Individual judgments are, by definition, a perfectly adequate explanation for the way an individual court behaves in an individual case. But the judiciary is an arm of government and it owes the public a better explanation about the way it operates.

So who should speak for the judiciary on issues that go beyond individual disputes?

Some Chief Justices have begun to reject the taboo about speaking to the press. This is a step in the right direction. Chief Justices Black, Nicholson and Spigelman spring to mind. However, there are limits on what sitting judges can say before they might need to disqualify themselves from some future case.

Federally, the Attorney-General has imposed limits on the circumstances in which he will defend the judiciary. He has nominated the Judicial Conference as the preferred defender of the judiciary.

The Judicial Conference is a fine organization and has provided forums for judges to speak publicly and have arranged sessions with politicians to improve their understanding of the judiciary. But through no fault of its own, the Judicial Conference is poorly equipped to become the spokesperson for the judiciary. As currently structured, it generally refers issues back to the judges, which limits its ability to participate in fast moving public debates.

What about the Law Council? This organization has frequently defended the judiciary. But as the peak national body representing the legal profession, I question whether it is the right body to speak on behalf of an arm of government. Logically, the media is fully justified in seeing any statement issued by the Law Council as being motivated by what is good for the legal profession. This gives rise to a potential problem. For example, when the Law Council talks about legal aid cuts and the importance of a fair trial, there are those in the press who are cynical enough as to construe this as merely a plot in which lawyers are trying to get their hands on more public money. The Law Council's argument might be perfectly valid, but it would be better coming from someone else.

The other way in which the judiciary can sometimes get its point across is through what is fondly known in the media by a number of terms such as the "inspired leak", the "quiet little chat" or the "background briefing". While I would encourage all judges to avail themselves of this technique, I would be less than honest if I failed to point out some of the drawbacks.

While an "off the record" chat is a terrific way of influencing public debate, it usually means that the journalists concerned are unable to reveal the source of the material they publish. That diminishes its authority and means that it can more readily be dismissed as the mere ramblings of a journalist. As a result, on most big issues that have a direct impact on the judiciary, the point of view of the judiciary is either missing, late or it appears obliquely, through the voices of others whose interests are not always exactly in alignment with those of the judges. If this continues, the judiciary will effectively be vacating the field and leaving it to others to set the parameters of debate on these matters.

Public debate will continue, with or without judicial input. But the consequences of such lopsided debates can be alarming. This is best illustrated by a hypothetical example. Let's make a big assumption. Let's assume that a trainee reporter emerges from the now mandatory lectures in media law with his respect for the judiciary intact. This reporter has just been taught some of the basics of defamation law such as how it compares to the United States, how much money Australian judges regularly hand politicians in defamation cases and how the High Court changed its mind on the constitutional importance of free speech.

While such an introduction to a new career might have had an impact on new recruits in the past, our trainee still harbours a deep reservoir of goodwill for the courts dating from what he was taught at the University of Technology, Sydney about the constitutional necessity for a strong and independent judiciary.

Now, let's put this recruit to work.

His first assignment is to review the latest book by Mr Evan Whitton, a winner of multiple Walkley awards and a former editor. Our reporter is instructed to place his review in the context of what has been happening of late in the Australian legal system. He does a library search on his computer and is rattled by what he finds.

In New South Wales he finds that one Supreme Court judge survived an attempted dismissal over late judgments; a retired Supreme Court judge committed suicide when it appeared that his sexual misbehaviour over a lifetime was about to be made public; and a sitting District Court judge had been charged with sexual offences.

Federally, he discovers that the Law Council of Australia wants a Parliamentary inquiry into the behaviour of a High Court judge while he was still at the Bar; and that this same judge—who was close to the National Party—was appointed after the Deputy Prime Minister called for a "capital C conservative on the High Court."

Our reporter also finds that the Allen Consulting Group has produced a report for twelve of the nation's biggest companies warning of an American-style litigation explosion. That report, he notes, covers much the same ground as a series of papers from the Australian Law Reform Commission on the adversarial system of justice.

Armed with this context, our new reporter then reads Mr Whitton's book which attributes much of the ills of the legal system to a conspiracy by lawyers to defeat the search for truth by using nine magic tricks. Being legally educated, our reporter is initially inclined to produce a review that is, shall we say, unfavourable. Some would see this as evidence of the effectiveness of the legal cartel that is referred to in the title of Mr Whitton's book. But our law graduate is now a journalist and has been instructed to follow normal journalistic practice by placing things in context. He asks himself whether Mr Whitton's jaundiced view of lawyers and the legal system really is that unusual. Under the influence of the weight of published material our new recruit tones down his review so that Mr Whitton's book is treated as one more serious contribution to the debate about the future of the legal system.

So who is responsible for this chain of events? Is it the reporter who lacked the fortitude to break away from the orthodoxy, or is it the judiciary whose comparative silence and muted public statements has enabled that orthodoxy to become so orthodox in the first place?

The task confronting the judiciary is to improve its effectiveness in the market for ideas. While the legal profession is well attuned to even the slightest change in judicial nuance, the market for ideas extends far beyond the profession. Occasional speeches by judges and the appointment of information officers are admirable developments. But much more is needed. As an arm of government, I see nothing fundamentally objectionable in creating an institution that would, among other things, put the point of view of the judiciary.

What I have in mind is the creation at a Commonwealth level of an institution based loosely on the New South Wales Judicial Commission, but with the additional responsibility of informing the public about issues affecting the judiciary. If such an institution reported to the Chief Justices of the federal judiciary and were chaired by someone like Sir Anthony Mason, it could become an extremely effective advocate for the judiciary. But it could also do much to neutralize one of the substantive issues that is currently undermining public confidence in the judiciary.

Like its New South Wales equivalent, a federal judicial commission could be given responsibility for assembling conduct divisions made up of other judges to investigate complaints against federal judicial officers. If such a system operated in private, it would be possible to investigate judicial conduct without harming the standing of judges who were ultimately found to be without fault. It would also take at least this part of the process out of the political arena. Parliament would, of course, retain the final say on whether any adverse factual findings against a judge fell within the constitutional grounds for dismissal.

If such a system had been in place a few months ago, the Law Council would never have needed to have sought a Parliamentary inquiry into the conduct of Justice Ian Callinan. The fact gathering and initial assessment could all have been handled in private using the procedures that were recently used in New South Wales concerning Justice Vince Bruce.

Without such a system, the decision on whether to even investigate the facts surrounding this affair fell to the Attorney-General. It would be in the interests not just of the judges, but also the Attorney-General, for such a decision to be removed from the political arena.

In the wake of the fuss over Justice Callinan, a few calls have also begun to be made for a new way of vetting and selecting potential candidates for federal judicial office. While nobody who has seen the full disaster of an American Senate confirmation hearing would ever advocate adopting that system in this country, there is a good case for injecting a great deal more rigour into the process of assessing the background of potential federal judges.

Again, this is a fact-gathering role that could be done in private and would sit comfortably within the scope of a federal judicial commission. But it could just as easily be given to officers of the Attorney-General's Department—so long as somebody did it. The effect of these changes would not be immediate. But over time, they would change the nature of the debate over the judiciary and that, eventually, would have an impact on public opinion.

PANEL DISCUSSION

Susannah Lobez[1], Professor Denis Pearce[2], Alan Rose AO[3], Margo Kingston[4] and Bernard Lane[5]

PROFESSOR PEARCE:

Back in the 1920s an English judge called Lord Tomlin described the relationship between legal academics and the judges with a couplet which went like this: "for the dons are so hard on the judges and the judges so rude to the dons". Now when I forded the stream coming from the legal world to the Press Council I found, rather to my astonishment, that that couplet could have been entirely rewritten: "that the press are so hard on the judges and the judges so rude to the press," because my impression has been that there is a considerable gulf between the two parties. In fact I was astonished at how much it was so and that does really stem, I think, from a want of understanding from each side as to the way in which the other works.

With the press my impression is that it is not just with journalists. The people I deal with on the Press Council are very senior members of the press and they are just as suspicious of judges as the hard working journalists. I think that they don't fully understand the way in which judges work. There is a lack of understanding of the intellectual demands that are made on judges. There is a lack of understanding of the complexity of the issues that judges deal with and there is a lack of understanding of the way in which courts and judges function.

It is not only Chief Justice Doyle's notion that everybody thinks that they ponce around in red robes all the time, but I had a considerable job persuading the Council not to write to the Chief Justice this year, telling him to bring his boys and girls into line on something they were ruling on. The view was quite clearly held that a Chief Justice was something akin to a secretary of a department or a CEO of an organization and he only needed to take the chaps and chapesses aside and straighten them out and everything would change.

On the other hand, I see a very substantial lack of understanding on the parts of judges and lawyers—I don't think it should be limited to the press castigating judges—on the constraints that are imposed on the press.

---

[1] "The Law Report", ABC Radio; Session 1 Panel Chair.
[2] Professor; Chairman, Australian Press Council.
[3] President, Australian Law Reform Commission.
[4] Law correspondent, *The Sydney Morning Herald*.
[5] Law correspondent, *The Australian*.

I want to throw into the pot the issues that I have noted in the year that I have been Chair of the Press Council. They have all tended to stem from the fact that we are no longer really a state-based press in Australia.

Access through the internet and the movement of people interstate have really made the press an Australia-wide publication. The effect of that, I think, has been that there is now an increased need for, what I would term, commonality in the approach of the courts. That is reflected in a number of ways. First of all, simply in the content of the law. I think that there is a want of understanding on the part of the courts that what they are pronouncing upon in one State has to be the same in another State. It is no good the judges condemning a newspaper thinking that they are only condemning it in South Australia because they are equally condemning its publication in Queensland. They have to be aware of the circumstances there as much as in the State in which they are operating.

The press clearly has a worry about equal application of the law. David Flint has referred to some examples of contempt and the press thinks, with some reason, that it is singled out in contempt cases. The press thinks that the sort of conduct that attracts condemnation from one person will be allowed to pass by but not when it comes from the press. The courts have got to contend with this worry and make sure that they are dealing with the press in an even-handed way.

The issue that comes up all the time is a general concern about uncertainty. The press sees it in relation to issues of defamation, in relation to issues of contempt, in relation to non-publication orders. The press, as I read it, wants to comply with the law but it does not have a clear knowledge of what that law is. It cannot be certain that the same principles will be applied to the same law by different courts. I think that's a major concern that the courts have to grapple with if they are to establish a working relationship with the press. If the press continues to run into these sorts of problems then the effect will be that they won't publish. They won't be bold enough to publish and that will be bad for the courts and that will be bad for the community.

ALAN ROSE:

These issues are long standing. The defamation issue, contempt, in fact those reports of the Australian Law Reform Commission and some State reform commissions are still waiting for treatment. That in itself is an indication of the difficulties legislators, the media and of course politicians who have got any interest in this matter face in dealing with the problem.

Most of the possible solutions are there on the table, but at the end of the day, it comes down to whether one can get the numbers and convince enough opinion at the time that a particular change should be made. There have been many ad hoc and worthwhile changes but I agree that what is now staring us in the face is the need for leadership on an Australia-wide basis to produce common standards of two kinds, not just in dealing with the media. But we are in danger of forgetting that the media is only an intermediary in communicating with the community.

Many of the changes that are taking place in our courts have distinct possibilities of excluding the public. I agree with the need for active communication, actively seeking out the opportunity to communicate from the courts and possibly the suggestion for a Commonwealth judicial commission. At least from the communication and education perspective, because we are one market, and there is a need for a common approach. It is a leadership responsibility which the Chief Justices in each of our jurisdictions carry, but they don't seem to be acting in concert as seen from the perspective of the public.

I will finish by referring again to the public. Many of the very worthwhile changes that have been made in the way that our courts operate, certainly as seen from the Law Reform Commission's perspective and from litigants' perspectives and the profession's perspective, have the real potential to further exclude the public.

Far more of our business now is being done, effectively, behind closed doors. Our case management systems are ensuring that much, quite sensibly in terms of eliminating delay and reducing costs in getting to the nub of the legal problem more quickly, are being done electronically in private conference. They are not being done in a public court. Many of our trials, when they do take place in court, are cryptic to say the least. There are communications between those practitioners and judges who have spent months before the trial filing down the issues so that they can be communicated in almost monosyllabic terms during a trial—reference to documents, reference to exhibits. None of this, as it would have a couple of decades ago, now comes out publicly in the court itself.

There is a way to deal with this. Most of our courts are, at this stage, going through a technological revolution. Many of the new processes, whether they are at the filing level, reducing appeal books and so forth, are now on the track to becoming fully electronic.

Young people in our community and many others of various age groups have mastered the electronic communication medium. The internet and many of the other public broadcast electronic media are capable of taking that electronic content and allowing its access across a much wider group in the community. So I come to the point that we are losing the public because the public is being increasingly locked out of courts.

We have the vehicle through new technology to bring them back to the courts but whether it is that technological development or whether it is any one of the other initiatives, it does require something of the courts which they are not particularly, from a historical background, comfortable with. And that is a corporately managed, strategically presented approach to public communication which embraces the media as one of the intermediaries but, most particularly, takes on an active communication process. This is appropriate to the particular role and responsibilities of the courts as a third arm of government, and one which can't be ignored.

That means leadership, and the Chief Justices of our courts, whether they form into a judicial commission or any other body, must necessarily act in concert because it is international in a sense. That is, the court system here, like any other part of government, is part of projecting Australia as a system of government and as an active economy.

To date I don't think we have had leadership at that level. Internationally, we have seen at the Law Reform Commission a highly valuable economic product that Australia sits at the front of. We are about as good as you get, not just in this region, but internationally, and we are not in a position to communicate that strength effectively at the moment.

It is the judges, particularly the leadership of those judges, who must get into the market, not only for ideas, but if I can use a rather crass word, for their business, because Australia has an important place for that business now and in the immediate future.

SUSANNAH LOBEZ:

I think that we can't beat around the bush—we need to discuss what is required on behalf of the media, what the needs of the practising journalists are, what difficulties do they have with the judiciary and what concerns the Attorney-General and some of the judges about the press and the media.

MARGO KINGSTON:

I would like to take up the really interesting question that the media–court relationship is an aspect of a broader, and I think a much more important, requirement that society needs to understand itself. It needs to understand its own institutions.

I followed the Pauline Hanson campaign in the federal election and the One Nation party family policy document proposed that because family law wasn't working extremely well, the Family Court and family law should be abolished and the people in your street should decide on instinct what would happen to your marriage, your children and your property. I had this vision of Madame Defarge dropping another stitch as another marital head rolled from the guillotine. I found it quite shocking that many people have so much ignorance that the rule of law is their fundamental protection when a society is going wrong. Of course, later in the campaign we had our own troubles with One Nation and it seems to me a lot of people wanted to sack the judges and arrest the journalists, so I think that is a very big problem that all of our institutions have at the moment. A lot of factors are involved.

I favour the Michael Wooldridge analysis that modern western states are dividing into a policy culture and a community culture, where the community doesn't really understand what we in the policy culture are

51

doing any more and distrusts us and doesn't think any more that we are working for them.

I also believe John Ralston Saul's view that when things go terribly wrong, as they have in this country recently with the rise of One Nation, then blame the elites, don't blame the peasants. Obviously that raises a lot of questions in this particular area. It is all very well to talk about judicial commissions for the judiciary, but where is the accountability of the media?

To my mind the institutions involved in the power structure, the Parliament, the executive, the judiciary *and* the media, have got a lot of work to do to restore their credibility. The way you do that is by taking your ethics and obligations seriously.

In the media we always carry on about how we have got a democratic right to speak on behalf of the people. But in most cases we are working for people who just want to make a profit and it is a very self serving argument. To get down to the narrow stuff of the courts and the media, of course the courts have got to accommodate us but we have to be a messenger of worth to the people. We have got to tell the truth to the people. Of course, in a self regulation sense we can't have the courts or the government interfering with the media.

We have the Press Council. Parliament has its little contempt committees and the judges, well, they don't seem to have anything really except they judge all of us. But what I would like to see is the Press Council taking a big lead in this and setting up some strict separate division to handle complaints about legal stories. It should publish information to journalists about judgments that it has made against journalists.

I would like to go even further than that. I know we all have to go to these two week sessions, every journalist, which is an in-depth seminar on what the law is and how it works and what rules we have to obey. I think that should be expanded to an industry-wide practice, almost an industry self regulation, that reporters do not report the courts unless they have training so that they cannot make mistakes. I think that is vital and, of course, that would involve some of the big companies subsidising some of the small regional newspapers who have not got those facilities and this is where the courts could get tricky.

Why should the courts go out of their way to look after us if we are not taking our responsibilities seriously, not to reveal identity, not to prejudge and all that sort of thing?

The other thing I think the media has got to do, especially the big media organizations, is to stop saying, "I am sorry, it was pressure of time, we did not know the law". That's just not on. We need big fines for those big cases when, for example, talk show hosts talk about previous convictions in the middle of a trial. It has to be made crystal clear to the media that they have their responsibilities too.

In that way we can help each other. Maybe we can lift some credibility and we can start stabilizing the enormous dissatisfaction that there seems to be in many parts of Australia about how we are operating and whether we are doing our jobs properly.

BERNARD LANE:

I thought I could illustrate a few ways in which the coverage could be improved if there could be reforms in relations between the courts and the media. Some have been touched on.

One is trying to represent more of the facets of individual cases that attract a lot of public interest, for example the *Kruger* case or the so-called *Stolen Generations Case* before the High Court. This was often reported as if it was nothing more than a moral struggle about the removal of Aboriginal children but there were other aspects to it. If these sorts of reforms in relation to the courts and the media do continue, it may be that the media can communicate more of those aspects to do with the wider significance of that case for constitutional rights.

A related aspect is getting a better balance between the outcome of a case and the reasoning that led to it, conceding of course that it is usually the first thing of interest to the media and perhaps to the general public to know the immediate impact. There is a need to get a better balance between presenting the sometimes colourful personal aspects of a case, with the general rule that emerges from the case which may ultimately have much wider significance.

Perhaps some of the reforms proposed will help the media strike a better balance. It is something that we can be optimistic about, given all the pressures, as long as these sorts of reforms do continue.

Questions and comments from the floor

PATRICK KEYZER:

I have two points. There was some consideration given to the creation of a Commonwealth judicial commission. There is already an organization called the Council of Chief Justices of Australia and New Zealand—the only organization of judges with the power to develop enforceable policies in this area. Perhaps it could authorize the creation of a commission.

The second point that I would like to make is this: it is incorrect to say that the courts are not dependent on any group or body in society, least of all the executive government. The courts are funded by the executive and the executive has an obligation to ensure that there is adequate funding of the courts so that they can inform the media about their work.

SUSANNAH LOBEZ:

I can't see any way that is going to happen. There is no money around so you have got to find more interesting ways to do it than throw money at it. In the current terminology of the government, I just can't see it. I mean, if you have got an absolute crisis in the Family Court with children not being represented and people not being represented, how can you possibly justify 50 or 60 grand to employ a PR officer?

PATRICK KEYZER:

I would support extra funding for that as well: it is a small price to pay to improve community understanding of the courts.

CHRIS MERRITT:

I don't think the issue is quite one of money, although that is important. The point that has been made by a number of people which I think is absolutely on point comes to this—leadership—and the bringing of that leadership to bear at the top end of the media. We have had lots of discussion about, if I can put it simply, the workings at the journalist level but where I think it needs to be brought to bear much more importantly on a sustained basis, quite apart from public communication, is in the area of editorial management and proprietors. That is where there is no common understanding, as I see it, of media accountability.

It is at that point where I think Chief Justice's committees, commissions, and the current Council of Chief Justices have an opinion. That's right across the media. It's not just print or electronic, it is all aspects of the media, national and regional, that there should be an understanding of the courts and the importance of the roles that both the courts and the intermediary, that is the media, play with respect to the understanding of the court's role in government and the importance of individual cases all the way down. I don't see that leadership taking place.

SUSANNAH LOBEZ:

Margo Kingston made a point about who was going to do this job of educating the journalists about what they can and can't do and looking for certainty. I know that in South Australia, I think it's a document currently being worked on, there is a booklet, a handbook for journalists who are going to be doing court coverage. Now if that were to be expanded and a federal version available, or indeed seven separate versions, I'm sure there would be people in this room who could produce a booklet like that. That might be something that would be the standard and I suppose then it comes down to people like Denis Pearce of the Press Council to actually make sure it is enforced.

WENDY BACON:

I think the courts have done a remarkably poor job in setting down the ground rules for journalists. You only have to look at the *Lange* case and the uncertainty that the journalists are left with about what might be "reasonable conduct" for a journalist reporting politics.

I have just recently had a student who has interviewed 18 fairly senior media lawyers, all of whom have made the same point. So that is not just anecdotal. I spend time contemplating with my journalism students about what might be a public interest case in 1998 that would override, that would prove a defence in, a contempt of court case. All I can do is to go back to a comment Michael McHugh made in a case that I was once involved in the New South Wales Supreme Court. I think it's quite pathetic the lack of spelling out by the courts about what some of these concepts like "public interest" and "reasonableness" might mean. I have my own view as to why it is so superficial but journalists are left with very few solid ground rules.

DENIS PEARCE:

I think this is a concern of the Press Council. We are acting as a "feeder" from various quarters. But the important point I think to bear in mind in this is that it is all very well for courts to lay down general standards but the journalist has to operate within such a tight confine that you cannot go off and get advice from a leading lawyer as to what the nuances of *Lange* or one of the other cases might be. Journalists have to be able to deal with these issues on the spot. The complexity of the judgments shouldn't operate as a barrier to publication.

SIMON RICE:

If the media does what it is supposed to do correctly and the courts, as Chief Justice Doyle called for, take part actively and reach out, I think the Attorney's point or question at the beginning identifies the divide that exists even then, which has to be accepted. That is the question of accountability.

No matter how hard and how well the courts do it, no matter how responsibly the media acts, isn't it the case that the media doesn't have the responsibility to serve the democratic cause that Justice Doyle called for? But really, the media will cut, they will edit, they will present in accordance with requirements of news presentation, entertainment and of the proprietor. It is difficult to see the media ever acknowledging an obligation to fulfil the agendas of the courts.

It seems to me that we are asking for the media proprietors to act in that way is contrary to the whole move we have towards destabilizing social relations and stripping away corporate responsibility for democratic processes. It is inconsistent. Acting at their best, the divide is there and the courts, I think, need to be smarter about what they can expect from the media and acknowledge that at the end of the day, the way it is presented is the media's call and not theirs.

DENIS PEARCE:

I think one of the difficulties, and it hovers over the entire question of relations with the courts or media, is that we live in such volatile times and it is less and less clear what an ordinary person knows, assumes or

55

expects from an institution. There has been talk of the way in which there is pressure on the traditional concept of judicial independence, to try and reconcile it without losing something essential to greater pressure on the resources and courts or to a demand for accountability.

There is a similar problem for the media in that there is an attempt to discover whether you can have what used to be called public interest journalism, serious or quality journalism, in an atmosphere where there is tremendous commercial pressure and technological change.

Behind the difficulty of both the courts and the media is this ultimate question of what the ordinary people know, expect and believe. Are they merely cynical and indifferent, or do they have what used to be the traditional value assumptions and expectations? To what degree have those been modified? So the question of how optimistic or pessimistic to be about relations between the courts and the media proposals for reform is a very difficult question to answer.

CHIEF JUSTICE DOYLE:

I agree with Simon Rice. I don't think it is the media's job to do our job. I think we have to learn to work with the media. But I also think we are entitled to talk to the media about what we think is good reporting. I don't think it is good reporting to report a sentencing decision quite inadequately in the sense of saying nothing about *why* the judge did it. I think that is just bad reporting. So I think we have to learn to work with the media and understand its constraints but I don't think it is always engaging in what I call "good journalism". That is the most we can ask of the media.

One other point: I think to some extent the media calls in as aid at times the fact that they are exercising democratic rights, if you like. So if it is going to call those rights in aid, I think it might have to accept some responsibilities going beyond profit making.

SUSANNAH LOBEZ:

One way of doing it is to get your spouse or child under another name to complain to the Press Council because the press has a responsibility to give the reasons. Otherwise, you are just throwing out the facts. I would be pretty confident that the Press Council would make quite strong rulings on that.

The thing about the Press Council is that it is wonderful for us, it is nice and cosy, but it is not the best it could be and I think a lot of people are trying to develop it. But if you get an adverse finding, it is published in the paper. I can't see any reason why that couldn't be exercised in the normal way in regards to legal reporting and get results.

DENIS PEARCE:

I have close experience of that. Yes, we are there and we do get complaints. We receive complaints from any member of the community and that is often overlooked. People do think they have to be the person who is affected to complain. But you don't—we accept third party complaints. We do insist on a degree of, and I think it is right to say a degree of, accuracy. It's accuracy that is appropriate to the form of writing and the particular item that is under consideration.

SUSANNAH LOBEZ:

Would you consider the reasons for the decision to be an essential part of the story in sentencing?

DENIS PEARCE:

Absolutely. I think that the material has to be properly presented.

SUSANNAH LOBEZ:

I would just like to make the comment in relation to those remarks made by Chief Justice Doyle and Simon Rice that it seems to me that for a long time, members of the community, whether or not the courts are acknowledged as part of their democratic process, see themselves as consumers of legal services. They are consumers of what the judge hands out and like it or not, they can say what they think and often do.

However, when it comes to the media, although those same citizens, those same members of the public are consumers of media services, perhaps we might not find that when they make their complaints, they are the same complaints that lawyers and judges would make. In other words, "you told us too much of the sexy, interesting detail about that particular defendant". I don't know that the public are going to actually, as consumers, make those kind of demands.

I think it is incumbent upon the media to explain to people why it is important, for instance, that fairness is an essential part of a criminal trial.

THE LAW AND FREEDOM
OF THE MEDIA

Richard Ackland

"Media Watch", ABC Television and Principal, Law Press of Australia.

Let me share with you some thoughts that were expressed twelve years ago by someone we know and revere. Here they are:

> Much can be said for the view that it is now reasonable to publish allegations concerning the official conduct of public officials if an ordinary person considering all the circumstances would think that the allegations were *probably true* and needed to be investigated.

> If this proposition becomes accepted by the NSW courts, the difference between First Amendment protection and the protection given by section 22 will be marginal in both cases...

> If the conduct of public institutions and officials is to be properly scrutinised, it is only to be expected that erroneous, hurtful and defamatory statements will be made...

> ...[T]he public interest in robust, wide ranging debate on matters of public concern requires that the interests of individuals in their reputations must give way to the right to make good faith statements.

> Moreover, public officials undoubtedly have greater access to the media than other citizens. They are usually in a position to correct untrue statements.

What absolutely fabulous sentiments.

The message was that a modern interpretation of journalistic reasonableness will lead to a bright new dawn for the statutory qualified privilege defence and thereafter the Australian media need no longer look enviously at the protections afforded in the United States.

And who delivered that positive message, a message that put so much hope into our hearts at the time?

Why, it was Justice Michael McHugh, then of the New South Wales Court of Appeal, writing, dare I say it, in the *Gazette of Law and Journalism* in October 1986.

Justice McHugh's elevation to the High Court is a reminder that you can never predict the outlook of an appointee to high office based on the colour of public utterances made prior to securing the elevation.

Less than three years after its birth, Justice McHugh led the High Court's move to strangle *Theophanous*,[1] the constitutional defence of free speech in matters of political and governmental·affairs. He led the charge to replace this murdered child with the so-called expanded common law defence of qualified, qualified privilege—with lashings more reasonable-ness required of journalists... At least a lot more reasonableness than is ever required on the part of most trial and appeal judges.

Apparently, Justice McHugh's beloved section 22 worked so brilliantly that its reasonableness requirements just had to be imported into the High Court's expanded ambit of common law qualified privilege.

Indeed the reasonableness requirements must have been making our American media cousins so jealous of us that the court thought it better to give the requirements another couple of twists of complexity, just to even things up a bit.

The standard cliche when discussing "The Law and Freedom of the Media" is to look to Watergate when comparing the First Amendment's public figure defence with our own impressive armoury of statutory qualified privilege, common law qualified privilege and High Court qualified, qualified privilege. As Justice McHugh said in 1986:

> Vietnam, Watergate and the apparent reluctance of Western governments of all political persuasions to investigate allegations concerning their administration have all contributed to a loss of confidence in the integrity of governmental authority.

You can see that his Honour and his colleagues on the High Court have since dedicated themselves to the cause of helping to repair that lost confidence in the integrity of government. For instance, they devised the requirement that, if common law qualified privilege is to suceed for the mass media, then journalists and publishers have to have beautiful manners.

What the High Court of Australia would have expected Woodward and Bernstein to have done was to only publish what on reasonable grounds they believed to be true, and to have taken proper steps to authenticate whatever was told to them by Deep Throat, or any other source.

They would have also expected to have telephoned President Nixon, or Attorney-General Mitchell or Messrs Dean, Erlichman or Halderman and checked each day's story with them, and published their responses as soon as practicable. Not only that. If any of the characters in the Watergate drama sued *The Washington Post* for defamation, the publisher and the journalists would be required, should the standards of the Australian High Court be applied, not to have formed a belief that any of the meanings *the plaintiffs* read into the stories were untrue.

In other words, they would have to show that they believed in the truth of the meaning that the enemy placed on the story.

The intrepid reporters would be in trouble in Australia if they wanted to establish they acted reasonably and at the same time wanted to protect the identity of their main sources.

Given the scale and scope of the damaging material in the Watergate

---

[1] *Theophanous v Herald & Weekly Times Ltd* (1994) 182 CLR 104.

scandal, it might be fair to say that if the United States were saddled with the marvellous, exciting new *Lange*[2] defence as a way forward for the media into the new dawn, the lawyers would have advised against publishing considerable slabs of the story.

Of course, we don't have a public figure defence in this country. The nearest we got to it was the *Theophanous*[3] constitutional defence.

The replacement is a nightmare for a modern media that has to respond quickly and at the same time rely on sources and documents that don't necessarily want to be exposed.

But what we prided ourselves on in this country was that at least we live in a parliamentary democracy, which is of great benefit to the media. The government could be pressed and held accountable on each day the Parliament sat, commissions of inquiry conducted as part of the executive government could search for the truth, and the courts could determine disputes between parties openly.

All this openness could be reported fairly and those reports would be protected by the law from actions in defamation. It was not quite the robustness of the American jurisprudence where *journalistic* investigations would be protected more securely by the Constitution—but it was *something*.

After the recent excursion of the High Court in *Chakravarti v The Adelaide Advertiser*, we will have to review our faith in that *something*.

This was a case where the High Court went to elaborate lengths to cause disruption to the defence of fair protected report upon which great reliance has traditionally been placed in the laudable enterprise, as Justice McHugh would have it, of publishing allegations concerning the official conduct of public officials.

Chakravarti's case concerned the reporting of proceedings of the Royal Commission into the affairs of the State Bank of South Australia. In those proceedings evidence emerged which claimed Chakravarti, an officer of a bank subsidiary, Beneficial Finance, had received an unauthorised loan which was in excess of agreed benefits. There was also evidence that the chairman of the bank agreed that the conduct of Chakravarti and others involved questions of either civil or criminal misconduct that should be looked at. All that was said in open hearings of the Royal Commission and on file notes tendered. Chakravarti sued, and the High Court took a narrow, highly technical view of the reporting by *The Advertiser*.

At one point in one of the articles sued upon, the last sentence of a paragraph was made into a new paragraph by the sub-editors, at another there was a graphic break-out on the page that highlighted the evidence that was adverse to Chakravarti. Great attention was given to those factors, to the detriment of the publisher.

I have read the relevant proceedings of the Royal Commission and the tendered document and the reports of *The Advertiser*. I cannot get a

---

[2] *Lange v Australian Broadcasting Corporation* (1997) 189 CLR 520.
[3] *Theophanous v Herald & Weekly Times Ltd* (1994) 182 CLR 104.

meaning from the newspaper report that is significantly different from that said at the Royal Commission.

After a fair amount of contortion, the High Court did.

This case also reveals some deeply disturbing ideas that lurk in the minds that compose our High Court. Justice McHugh thought that the *Polly Peck* defence was not available to defendants at common law. In other words, his Honour believes that where a publication contains a number of defamatory imputations which have a common sting and not all of the imputations can be proved separately, it is not sufficient to prove that the *sting* is true.

Gaudron and Gummow JJ found that accurate portions of an otherwise inaccurate report will not reduce the basis for damages.

And, Justice Kirby believes that publishers have to assume their readers are increasingly inattentive and that they are unlikely to read all of an article. Headlines, captions, photographs, pictures and, as Justice Kirby says, "their digital equivalents" should be the subject of special attention in the context of the actual article sued on.

What *Chakravarti*'s case does is make extremely difficult the already difficult task of summarising a day's proceedings in a court, Royal Commission, Parliament, or other protected event.

If both the South Australian Full Court and the High Court of Australia can reach opposite conclusions about the meaning of an article, and for different reasons, what hope have the lawyers in giving pre-publication advice, let alone the journalists who cover these proceedings?

After initially having found that all Chakravarti's complaint was worth was $40,000, the Full Court in following the High Court's instructions has come up with a new verdict of $796,000.

Another instance of how technicality rules can be seen in a slightly different context in the *Erskine* case. This was the case which resulted in the highest defamation verdict in Australia, $2.5 million, in March 1998.

It concerned the reporting of an affidavit in a copyright dispute before the Federal Court. However, the judge in the copyright dispute had read the defamatory affidavit in chambers, not in open court. Consequently, it was not a protected document for the purposes of a fair report defence.

Strangely, if the document had been read by a judge in chambers in the New South Wales Supreme Court, which is just 50 metres to the left in the same building, Fairfax's prospects in the case would have been considerably improved because it would have been able to plead that the document was a fair protected report.

However, if the matter had gone to the High Court, who knows what absurdity would have been invented to thwart the defence.

In Victoria also, affidavits read in chambers have been freely reported in the media where a judge says, in open court, that they have been read.

The last matter of judicial grimness that impacts on the freedom of the media and should not pass without comment is the Queensland Court of Appeal's foray into the Pauline Pantsdown injunction. This really is one great judicial whopper.

The Queensland court decided that a satirical song about Pauline Hanson is so defamatory that it should be banned from the airwaves. The effect of this injunction is wider than Queensland because the defendant, the ABC, is a national creature. The court had the temerity to say if a jury didn't find the song defamatory, that finding would be over-turned on appeal. It is one thing for conservative Queensland judges to be horrified and appalled, but this decision denies a bit of satire in the lives of the rest of humanity.

Ironically the song, "I'm a Backdoor Man", is the creative output of Simon Hunt's alter ego, Pauline Pantsdown. Simon is the son of New South Wales's best known defamation law-maker, the former Justice Hunt.

The *Backdoor Man* consists of Hanson's own voice from various speeches which have been digitally rearranged and set to a dance music beat.

> I'm a backdoor man; I'm very proud of it
> I'm a back door man; I'm homosexual
> I'm a back door man—yes I am—I'm very proud of it
> I'm a back door man; I'm homosexual...
> I'm very proud that I'm not straight
> I'm very proud that I'm not natural
> I'm a back door man for the Klu Klux Klan with very horrendous plans
> I'm a very caring potato, we will never have the chance...

Hanson is now suing the ABC and her pleadings are that the song, given its ordinary meaning, could be taken by ordinary people to mean:

> that she is a paedophile, a homosexual, a prostitute, engages in unnatural sexual practices including anal sex, engages in unnatural sexual practices including anal sex with the Klu Klux Klan, she is a member of the Klu Klux Klan, is a potato—which means that she was 'a receiver of anal sex'.

De Jersey CJ refused to lift the injunction, saying: "I consider there's no real room for debate that an ordinary listener, not avid for scandal, would find one of the imputations defamatory."

A pretty confident prediction, given that it involves suspending belief to the extent that one must understand Ms Hanson to be a male homo-sexual who indulges in anal sex and is a paedophile.

After the Court of Appeal decision, Ms Hanson said that: "freedom of speech does not extend [*sic*] by allowing people the right to defame others and tell lies." Coming from a politician who has defamed whole races of people in an utterly crude fashion, this is pretty rich.

There is much about which the media should be legitimately concerned in view of the recent spate of restrictive, uncreative, unimaginative judicial determinations.

To that extent the judges reflect the mood of the country and the time. Nervous, and unexciting.

LESSONS FROM AN IMPEACHMENT

Professor David Anderson

Thompson and Knight Centennial Professor,
University of Texas Law School[*]

C ourts are governmental agents whose actions are at least as important in our daily lives as those of the legislature or the bureaucracy. They should be subject to media scrutiny no less than the other major actors of government. In the United States, the Supreme Court has accepted this and elevated it to the level of a federal constitutional principle, holding that excluding the press and public from court proceedings presumptively violates the First Amendment.[1] This presumption is so strong that it has been held to prevent closure of courtrooms during testimonies of under-aged rape victims,[2] testimonies of undercover narcotics agents[3] and preliminary examinations of prospective jurors.[4] In Australia, the courts have not gone as far but several judgments of the High Court embrace at least the principle of "open justice".[5]

But what does "open justice" mean? It undoubtedly means that the media is allowed to attend proceedings. Does it also mean the media is allowed take photographs or even televise the proceedings? Does it mean the media is allowed to be present during discussion of matters outside the presence of the jury? Does it mean it has access to documents, tape recordings and other physical evidence? Does it mean it has free rein to interview parties, witnesses, lawyers, jurors and judges? Does it mean the media cannot be prevented from disclosing inadmissible evidence? Does it mean lawyers are free to use the media to influence outcomes?

"Open justice" in the United States has come to mean nearly all of these. American courts long ago foreswore the use of the contempt power

---

[*] The author is grateful to Michael Chesterman, Annette Marfording, Martin Krygier and Richard Bauman for comments on earlier drafts of this paper.

[1] See *Richmond Newspapers Inc v Virginia* 448 US 555 (1980); *Press-Enterprise Co v Superior Court [No II]* 478 US 1 (1986). The presumption applies not only to criminal trials, but also to pre-trial proceedings and to at least some civil proceedings. See *Publicker Industries Inc v Cohen* 733 F 2d 1059 (3d Cir 1984).

[2] See *Globe Newspaper Co v Superior Court* 457 US 596 (1982).

[3] See *People v Martinez* 82 NY 2d 436; 604 NYS 2d 932 (Ct. App. 1993); 624 NE 2d 1027 (NY 1993).

[4] See *Press-Enterprise Co v Superior Court [No I]* 464 US 501 (1984).

[5] See *Russell v Russell* (1976) 134 CLR 495 at 520 per Gibbs J; *Grollo v Palmer* (1995) 184 CLR 348 at 379 per McHugh J; *Re Nolan; Ex Parte Young* (1991) 172 CLR 460 at 496 per Gaudron J.

to control media coverage,[6] and the Supreme Court has made it all but impossible for judges to enforce orders prohibiting specific media from disclosing specific information.[7] The Supreme Court thought direct restrictions on the media infringed upon the First Amendment unnecessarily because the the Court believed, then if not now, that the integrity of the judicial process could be maintained by a combination of media self regulation, restrictions on the information disclosed by lawyers and other participants, and measures to insulate jurors from prejudicial publicity.

This faith in alternative measures has proved to be misplaced as coverage of the White House sex scandal showed. The impeachment of a president is not a typical case, of course, and I acknowledge that it presents the issues on a scale unmatched in even the most sensational criminal or civil trials. However, the issues raised by the reporting of the grand jury investigation that led to the impeachment proceedings are not fundamentally different from those that arise in any high profile case. I use this example because it illustrates (albeit with magnification) the realities of "open justice" in the United States on facts that will be familiar to Australians.

Perhaps the most obvious of these realities is that courts cannot prevent highly prejudicial evidence from being leaked to the media. Virtually all of the evidence relating to President Clinton's affair with Monica Lewinsky was leaked to the media long before the House Judiciary Committee made it public. This included not only sensational bits of evidence, such as Linda Tripp's tape recordings of Lewinsky's conversations with Tripp, the existence of the stained dress, and the use of a cigar as a sex toy, but also evaluations of the demeanour of the President, Lewinsky and other witnesses who testified before the grand jury. In many instances the information appeared in the media within hours of its discovery by special prosecutor Kenneth Starr and before its presentation to the grand jury, indicating that the source of the leaks was Starr's office.[8] In the case of information leaked after presentation to the

---

[6]See *Bridges v California* 314 US 252 (1941); *Wood v Georgia* 370 US 375 (1962). Professor Chesterman has shown that none of the Supreme Court decisions actually dealt with prejudicial publicity that might influence a jury and he argues that a tightly drawn criminal statute imposing penalties on the media for publishing such material might be constitutional even if use of the contempt power for this purpose is not. See Chesterman "OJ and the Dingo: How Media Publicity Relating to Criminal Cases Tried by Jury is Dealt With in Australia and America" (1997) 45 *American Journal of Comparative Law* 109 at 127–128.

[7]*Nebraska Press Association v Stuart*, 427 US 539 (1976) held that a judge may restrain publication only if he or she can show that there is no other means of assuring a fair trial, that the restraint will be effective to prevent prejudice and that the order prohibits no more than necessary. The Court acknowledged that these requirements would be difficult to meet in any case and, since then, few judges have attempted to impose restrictions on publication and even fewer have been upheld. Cf. [Noriega] 917 F 2d 1543 (11th Cir. 1990).

[8]See Brill, *Pressgate, Content* (July/August 1998) at 122, 131–133.

grand jury, the source could have been the special prosecutor's office or a member of the grand jury.[9] The grand jury is one of the few proceedings still secret in America. Prosecutors and jurors are forbidden to disclose evidence presented to the grand jury.[10] This prohibition applies no less to the grand jury investigating the sex scandal than to any other grand jury, yet it appears to have been violated many times in the Clinton–Lewinsky investigation.[11]

Why have there been no prosecutions? One reason is the difficulty of establishing the identity of the leaker. The suspected source cannot be compelled to confess because of the constitutional prohibition against self incrimination. The media cannot be compelled to identify the culprit, for reasons that are in part legal and in part pragmatic. In the federal courts in the District of Columbia, as in most other jurisdictions, journalists enjoy a privilege to refuse to identify confidential sources.[12] This privilege is not absolute as it can be overcome by proof that the identity of the source cannot be discovered by any other means and is critical to the success of the prosecution. In this situation it might be possible to establish these requisites and compel a journalist to disclose the identity of the leaker, but not without a major legal battle. The vagueness of the criteria, the vigour with which the media resists disclosure of confidential sources and the availability of an extensive appeals process ensure that many months will pass, and much legal effort expended, before any source is identified.

More importantly, who is going to initiate the effort? President Clinton's lawyers complained bitterly about the leaks but they had no power to initiate a prosecution. Another federal prosecutor could act but that is unlikely as most prosecutors are not eager either to do battle with the media or launch investigations of colleagues who may one day have the opportunity to reciprocate.

This brings us to the question of media influence on judges. Judges have the power to order an investigation of grand jury leaks but they rarely do so. The judge supervising the grand jury in the Clinton–Lewinsky matter did not. So far as is known, no judge made even any informal effort to stem the flow of leaks. Does media influence explain this? Not necessarily, but it is not easy to identify a more satisfactory explanation.

The courts in both Australia and the United States seem to assume that

---

[9]The leaks also could have come from witnesses and some probably did. But grand jury witnesses in the federal system are not forbidden to disclose so they would have no apparent reason to insist on anonymity.

[10]See Fed. Rule Crim. P 6(e). The secrecy provisions also bind witnesses in some jurisdictions, but not in the federal system. See *Butterworth v Smith* 494 US 624 (1990). Violations are punishable as contempt in the federal system and as a specific crime in some other jurisdictions. See, e.g., Fla. Stat. s. 905.27.

[11] Starr claimed the leaks by his office did not violate Rule 6(e) because they occurred before the information was presented to the grand jury but the relevant precedents appear to reject such a distinction. See Brill, *supra* note 9, at 132.

[12]See, e.g., *Zerilli v. Smith* 656 F 2d 705 (1981).

judges are immune to media influence.[13] The maxim in Australia is that "no judge would be influenced in his judgment by what may be said by the media. If he were, he would not be fit to be a judge."[14] The corresponding dictum in the United States is that "[j]udges are supposed to be men of fortitude, able to thrive in a hardy climate", not "sensitive to the winds of public opinion."[15] If these brave claims were ever plausible, I submit that they are no longer. We live in a media culture to which no one is immune. Monarchs and popes react to media pressures. That judges should not is a noble ideal and one we should cultivate. However, it is not a fact upon which law can safely be based. It is not lack of ambition that makes men and women become judges and elevation to the bench does not eradicate ambition. Lower judges aspire to be higher judges, justices aspire to be chief justices and they all aspire to be remembered kindly by history.

In those American states where judges are elected, the relationship between these ambitions and the influence of the media is obvious. It is less obvious, but no less real, where judges are appointed. The professional and political cultures that put forward judicial nominees are undeniably influenced by the media. Advancement through the judicial ranks is based largely on reputation, which within the profession may be acquired largely on the basis of personal knowledge, but which in the wider world is dependent on the media. And media influence on judicial advancement may be more direct. One United States federal judge openly accused colleagues of pandering to the media in pursuit of promotion.[16] Lawyers who regularly represent the media publicly evaluate Supreme Court nominees on the basis of their record on issues of importance to the media.[17] A judge who angers or disappoints the media acts against self interest. That many, or even most, are willing to do so is a tribute to the integrity of the judiciary but it does not solve the problem of those who are not.[18]

Much of the information that appears in the media is there for the

---

[13]For some notable non-judicial skepticism about this, see Chesterman, *supra* note 7, at 147; Landsman and Rakos "A Preliminary Inquiry into the Effect of Potentially Biasing Information on Judges and Jurors in Civil Litigation", (1994) 12 *Behavioral Science and Law* 113.

[14]*BLF Case* (1982) 41 ALR 71 at 90 per Gibbs CJ and at 123 per Mason J, both quoting Lord Salmon.

[15]*Craig v Harney* 331 US 367 (1947).

[16]See Judge Laurence Silberman "Judicial Activism: The Press Pulls the Strings, Address Before the Federalist Society" (13 June 1994), in *Tex. Law.*, 29 June 1992 at 15–17.

[17]See, e.g., "Souter spurs cautious optimism; 1st Amendment advocates heartened by nominee", *San Diego Union-Tribune*, (4 September 1990) at A8 (quoting several media lawyers on Supreme Court nominee David Souter's voting record in media cases while sitting on a lower court).

[18]Judges who are immune to the demands of ambition may be vulnerable to the temptations of the proverbial 15 minutes of fame. Before the start of the OJ Simpson trial, the presiding judge gave a five-part interview to the CBS television station in Los Angeles. The ground rules were that the interview was to focus on Judge Ito's life and personality rather than the case. See Achenbach, "Ito Blinks in Spotlight: Judge's Blunder Brings Long Week of Intense Publicity and Criticism", *Washington Post*, 19 November 1994, at A1.

very purpose of influencing the outcome. Occasionally, the media itself seeks a particular result[19] but usually the slant comes from those who supply the information. Those sources, whether anonymous or on the record, are rarely disinterested. They want the public to accept their version of events, their assessment of credibility, their theory of the case, their views as to culpability. In the culture that "open justice" has produced, lawyers and parties feel pressure to enter the media contest, whether they want to or not. American lawyers now have official permission to yield to this pressure. The standards of conduct that regulate lawyers' conduct now permit a lawyer to make statements to the media that will have a substantial likelihood of prejudicing a proceeding if the lawyer reasonably believes it is necessary to do so to counter prejudicial comment from the other side.[20]

The legitimacy, or at least the inevitability, of this extra-judicial contest for public opinion is now rarely questioned and it was accepted by both sides in the White House sex scandal. The White House, Hillary Clinton and the President's lawyers used the media for months in an attempt to discredit the special prosecutor, his investigation and his witnesses. Starr justified the leaks from his office on the ground that "what we are doing is countering misinformation that's being spread about our investigation in order to discredit our office and our dedicated career prosecutors."[21] The House Judiciary Committee justified its decision to make public the videotape of the President's grand jury testimony on the grounds that it needed to know how the public felt about the accusations in order to decide whether to proceed further.[22] The Committee organized release of the Starr report to maximize its impact and minimize the White House's ability to discredit it.[23] Several days later it became clear that

---

[19]See, e.g., *Sheppard v Maxwell* 384 US 333 (1966), in which newspapers angrily demanded (and obtained) the conviction of a murder defendant who was eventually cleared after spending twelve years in prison. Currently many American media are stating their belief that one or both of Jon Benét Ramsey's parents are guilty of murdering the six-year-old beauty contestant even though no one has been charged. See Riley, "Beauty and the Beast", *Sydney Morning Herald,* 24 November 1998, at 41.

[20]See Rule 3.6, American Bar Association Model Rules of Professional Conduct. This model is the basis for the official rules of conduct for attorneys in most states.

[21]See Brill, *supra* note 9, at 132.

[22]See Eilperin and Morgan, "Clinton Videotape Set for Release; House Panel Votes to Make Testimony Available at 9 AM Monday", *Washington Post,* 19 September 1998, at A1 ("... Republicans countered that they were putting the information out so the public could make the most informed judgment possible as to whether Congress should proceed with an impeachment inquiry.") The committee voted for impeachment despite polls showing that a substantial majority of Americans opposed it.

[23]The report was released to the media on a Saturday morning, allowing extensive coverage in the Sunday newspapers, which, in the U.S., are the week's most widely circulated. It also assured that the report would be the subject of the Sunday morning panel shows on all major networks. Neither the White House nor the President's lawyers were given a copy until it was released to the media so they were unable to respond in detail until after the first wave of coverage. Withholding release of the videotape of the President's grand jury testimony until the next Monday provided fresh material for another round of coverage.

the report was a selective summary of evidence that made no pretense of objectivity. But by that time the opinion polls were in and the Committee was convinced that it had enough public support to proceed with impeachment proceedings. The argument that this is inevitable in a political investigation is belied by the example of the Watergate investigation 25 years earlier. In that case, the special prosecutor delivered his report on President Nixon to the Judiciary Committee with no public comment; the Committee discussed it in private and did not release it to the public and its contents were not leaked.[24]

The argument usually advanced for "open justice" is that it enables the public to understand the operation of the judicial system and scrutinize its performance. But in the White House sex scandal, as in most other cases that attract extensive media attention, the coverage has little to do with this. In the case of a grand jury investigation, the proceeding is intended to be invisible; that is why the media is excluded and the participants are sworn to secrecy. There is little the media can tell us about its operation or performance by reporting leaks about the evidence it has heard. Even when the proceeding is open, the media often makes little pretense that it is there to report on the operation of the system or scrutize its performance. The federal courts, which are the last bastions of resistence in the United States to media demands for access by television cameras, authorized a three year experiment during which cameras were admitted to trials in selected federal courts. What they found was that, although the cameras produced few adverse effects, neither did they produce much enlightenment. Most of the broadcast images were used merely to provide a backdrop for a reporter's talking head and rarely did the coverage allow viewers to see any significant portion of the proceedings. The judges decided to retain the ban on cameras in federal courts.[25]

The media, including television, sometimes actually *covers* judicial proceedings but more often it has little interest in the proceedings itself; they are merely the mine from which it extracts gems of information that otherwise would remain hidden. Judicial proceedings are immensely important to the media as a cheap and safe source of information about people's secrets. It is cheap because the information is uncovered by others and made available to the media at little cost. It is safe because it can be reported without risk of liability for the untruths it contains.[26] Without this convenient source of information we would know a great

---

[24]See Lewis, "A degrading hysterial mockery", *Sydney Morning Herald*, 23 September 1998, at 21.

[25]See Greenhouse, L., "US Judges Vote Down TV in Courts", *New York Times*, 21 September 1994, at A11.

[26]In both Australia and the United States, the media enjoy a privilege to report defamatory falsehoods that are uttered in judicial proceedings. See, e.g., *Defamation Act* 1974 (NSW), ss 24, 25, 26, Sch 2; *NY Civ Rts*, s 74.

deal less about the sins, habits, finances and activities of our fellows. This may be reason enough to insist on "open justice." But it is not the same thing as facilitating scrutiny of the judicial branch of government and it should not be allowed to hide in the skirts of that argument.

Inevitably, much of the extra-judicial information that appears in the media turns out to be inadmissible in the courtroom. In part this is because inadmissible evidence is what best serves the interests of those who supply it. The admissible evidence will come out eventually in court and can do its work there; if the inadmissible material is to have any effect, it must come out extra-judicially. But it is also because litigation in the United States produces a great deal of inadmissible evidence. Grand juries have power to investigate virtually anything they please, call any witness, ask any question, with little regard for the ultimate relevance of the material. In civil litigation the lawyers are entitled to ask any question or demand any document that might lead to the discovery of admissible evidence. As a consequence, the amount of admissible evidence adduced in either a grand jury investigation or a civil case is often miniscule compared to the mountain of inadmissible evidence they amass.

Indeed, the answer to the question that undid President Clinton—did he have sexual relations with Monica Lewinsky—was probably inadmissible. He was asked the question by a lawyer for Paula Jones in her civil suit alleging that he made unwelcome sexual advances to her in 1991. The lawyer's theory was that similar advances toward Lewinsky five years later might show a pattern of behavior. Such evidence might or might not be admissible, depending on the judge's evaluation of its probative value balanced against its prejudicial effect. If, as we later learned, it was Lewinsky who made the advances, the episode would have little probative value as to whether the President made unwanted advances toward Jones. But that was not known at the time the question was asked and Jones's lawyers were therefore entitled to ask it on the theory that knowing that he had sexual relations with Lewinsky might lead them to evidence that he had treated Lewinsky as he was alleged to have treated Jones.

Also inevitably, some of the information in the media turns out to be wrong. Aficionados of the sex scandal may recall that one of the early leaks concerned a claim that Jones could identify a distinctive mark or abnormality on the President's private parts. Jones eventually disavowed this claim but not until it had given rise to innumerable jokes on late night television and radio talk shows and lent at least a temporary aura of irrefutability to her claims.

The media, of course, understands all of this and the conscientious among the media detest the errors, resent the manipulation and aspire to cover legal proceedings fairly. Until recently, risk of serious prejudice was reduced by the sophistication, good judgment and responsibility of the mainstream media. In many states, the media and representatives of the bench and bar worked out formal voluntary guidelines that the media generally observed.[27] Judges were often able to obtain media assent to informal restrictions in specific cases. The media exercised a good deal of self restraint, particularly with respect to use of prejudicial material from anonymous sources. But those were the old days, before the mainstream news departments came to view themselves as competitors of supermarket tabloids, Oprah Winfrey and Jerry Springer, radio talk shows and internet gossips.[28] Today the voluntary guidelines are long forgotten. A judge is unlikely to be able to even identify all of the media interested in reporting about a case, let alone obtain the co-operation of all. And self restraint has little chance against the pressures of cross-media competition.

Network news departments explained that they reported the salacious details of the special prosecutor's report against their better judgment because they knew their own network's magazine shows would do so. Leaks and rumours that the mainstream media initially deemed too dubious to use without further corroboration appeared on internet sites without corroboration and soon began appearing in the mainstream media, first as reports about uncorroborated internet gossip, then without that veneer.[29] The capacity of the media for institutional self restraint is a casualty of the evolution of "the press", which (even after it came to include broadcast news operations) had some common identity and shared values, into "the media", whose operations have very little in common.

In the United States there are no effective restraints on media disclosures about pending judicial proceedings. Many believe that is a good thing. I disagree, but my objective here is not to resolve that debate. It is only to show that prejudicial disclosures cannot be prevented without direct restraints on the media. Those are historically suspect, galling to the media, and frightfully difficult to administer. But the American attempt to control disclosures without them has failed utterly. Other legal systems, with different media traditions and different legal cultures, might do better, but they should understand that we in America have not found a way to protect the integrity of trials without direct restraints on media. Rather, we have decided that trial by media is acceptable.

---

[27] See, e.g., Nebraska Bar-Press Guidelines, quoted in *Nebraska Press Assn. v Stuart* 427 US 539 (1976).

[28] See Sachs, "Mud and the Mainstream: When the Respectable Press Chases the National Enquirer, What's Going On?" (1995) 34 *Colum. Journalism Rev* at 33.

[29] The difficulty media have in resisting these perceived competitive pressures is illustrated by *The New York Times*'s explanation of its decision to name a rape victim in contravention of its long established policy. *The Times* said its editors felt that the decision had been taken "out of their hands" because a television network had used the name in a report about an American supermarket tabloid's report that the name had been reported by a London tabloid. See "On Names in Rape Cases", *New York Times*, 17 April 1991, at A17.

MEDIA PREJUDICE DURING A CRIMINAL JURY TRIAL: STOP THE TRIAL, FINE THE MEDIA, OR WHY NOT BOTH?

Professor Michael Chesterman

Professor of Law, University of New South Wales; Acting Judge, District Court of New South Wales

The Legal System's Two "Big" Responses to Prejudice during a Trial

The topic of this paper is the publication of material by the media which may unduly influence the members of a criminal trial jury which has already been empanelled. It does not deal with publicity occurring before a trial. Although the basic principles and assumptions governing the response of Australian courts to this situation have been and continue to be subjected to scrutiny,[1] this paper will more or less take these for granted and will confine its inquiries to some specific issues.

When prejudicial publicity appears during a criminal trial, either or both of two major steps may be taken.

First, the judge may give consideration, usually on application by one or more parties, to stopping the trial and discharging the jury. He or she may decide to examine the jurors as to whether they have encountered the material and if so whether they have been influenced by it.[2] The jury should be discharged if in all the circumstances this is necessary in the interests of ensuring a fair trial.[3] In resolving this issue, the judge should bear in mind that if the trial continues he or she may give an instruction to the jurors (or repeat a prior instruction) that they must put out of their minds all publicity about the trial. A trial judge's decision not to abort the trial may constitute grounds for appeal against a verdict of guilty, but courts of criminal appeal must "accord full weight to the position of the trial judge",[4] in whose discretion the matter lies.

---

[1] For example, the NSW Law Reform Commission has recently been given a reference to inquire into the law of contempt by publication, and my UNSW colleague Dr Janet Chan and I, in collaboration with the Justice Research Centre, are conducting empirical research into (amongst other things) the reactions of former jurors to publicity relating to the case in which they were engaged.

[2] It has been specifically held in Victoria that the "unsworn word of the jurors" can be heard on this matter: see *R v Vollmer* [1996] 1 VR 95 at 138 per Southwell and McDonald JJ. In NSW, the judge may interrogate the jurors under oath: *Jury Act 1977* (NSW), s 55D.

[3] See, e.g., *R v George, Harris v Hilton* (1987) 9 NSWLR 527 at 533 (Street CJ).

Alternatively, or in addition, the Attorney-General, the Director of Public Prosecutions or some other appropriate party[5] may instigate contempt proceedings against the media organization which published the material. Other individuals (such as an editor or a reporter) who are responsible for the publication may also be made defendants. If liability is proved, the normal penalty imposed is a fine. With a few significant exceptions, the criterion of liability (which must be proved beyond reasonable doubt) is, as formulated by the High Court in *Hinch v Attorney-General for Victoria*,[6] that the publication must have had a "real and definite tendency", as a "matter of practical reality" to "preclude or prejudice the fair and effective administration of justice" in the relevant trial.[7] Mason CJ, in that case, preferred the phrase "substantial risk of serious (or real) interference", adding however that this version may not in fact differ significantly.[8]

In preparing this paper, I have investigated (so far as I could identify them) the criminal cases in Australia since 1980 in which:

• allegedly prejudicial material has been published in the media after the jury has been empanelled; and

• in consequence, discharge of the jury has been sought, or at least given consideration, within the trial, and contempt proceedings have been instituted against the media publisher(s); and

• either the jury has in fact been discharged or one or more publishers have been found guilty of contempt or both these things have occurred.

As far I can tell, there have been 21 cases, each involving two sets of proceedings (the criminal jury trial and the contempt proceedings), which fit this pattern.

It seems logical, at least at first sight, that if material put out by a media publisher during a criminal trial is sufficiently prejudicial to warrant an order discharging the jury, the publisher (if prosecuted) should usually also be convicted of contempt. The converse seems logical also: that is, if ultimately the publisher is convicted, the trial should usually have been stopped. The common concern underlying both these judicial measures is that of avoiding any significant risk that jury verdicts are improperly influenced by publicity.

An observation of Brennan J in the High Court case of *R v Glennon*[9] may seem to contradict this. He said that "it does not follow that, where

---

[4] *Murphy v R* (1989) 167 CLR 94 at 101 (Mason CJ and Toohey J).

[5] This may be the court which will hear the contempt: see e.g. *Registrar, Court of Appeal v Willesee* (1985) 3 NSWLR 650.

[6] (1987) 164 CLR 15.

[7] The quoted phrases are drawn from the judgments of Wilson J and Deane J (1987) 164 CLR 15 at 34, 46; see too Toohey J at 70, 77.

[8] *Ibid.* at 27–28. In the U.K., under the *Contempt of Court Act 1981*, s 2(2), the corresponding test is in these terms. The Australian Law Reform Commission, in its Report on *Contempt* (ALRC 35, 1987) at para 295, recommended "substantial risk of prejudice".

[9] (1992) 173 CLR 592 at 613.

a punishable contempt of court has been committed, the trial must be aborted". A reading of the surrounding passage suggests, however, that by "aborted" he meant "stayed indefinitely". The relevant issue of principle before the High Court was whether the fact that *pre-trial* publicity adverse to an accused person—in this instance, some notorious broadcasts by Derryn Hinch—has been held in contempt should more or less automatically imply that a subsequent conviction must be overruled on fairness grounds or indeed that no fair trial of the accused can *ever* occur. The majority Justices in the case rejected this proposition.[10] Mason CJ and Toohey J indicated in their joint judgment that a major reason for accepting divergent outcomes—that is, that there might be contempt liability, but no overriding of the jury's verdict of guilty and no permanent stay—was one of timing. Contempt liability was to be assessed as at the time of publication, which could be well before the trial began, whereas the fairness of the trial proceedings leading to a guilty verdict would be assessed as at the time of trial and the grounds for a permanent stay at the time when it was applied for.

This point about timing is however irrelevant to the situation which I am discussing, because the time of publication and the time when the issue of aborting the trial must be resolved are virtually the same.

Accordingly, the High Court's observations in *Glennon* do not, in my submission, preclude suggesting an assumption of convergence in cases of publicity during the trial. Unless some clear reason for divergence can be seen, the two measures which I am discussing—stopping the trial and fining the media—should either occur together or should not occur at all.

Actually, however, in the 21 cases since 1980 which I have examined, there have been only eleven "convergence cases", that is, cases in which publicity during the relevant criminal jury trial has both caused the trial to be aborted and led to a contempt conviction.[11] There have been as many as ten "divergence cases", just under 50 per cent of the total.

Is such a high proportion justified? What, if anything, justifies divergence? What, if anything, should make convergence more or less mandatory? In none of these ten cases were these questions directly addressed. Instead, following the trend of the High Court's observations in *Glennon*,[12] the judges hearing the contempt proceedings merely indicated that contempt liability depends on different principles to those governing

---

[10] See Mason CJ and Toohey J at 605–606, Brennan J at 613–617 (with whom Dawson J agreed). The minority Justices, Deane, Gaudron and McHugh JJ, did not address this issue.

[11] If the *Costs in Criminal Cases Bill* 1997 (NSW) had been enacted and the six NSW cases in this group had occurred thereafter, the convicted media publishers would have been liable to be ordered to pay the costs of the aborted trials. See M. Chesterman, "Costly Terminations" (1997) 45 *Gazette of Law & Journalism* 5.

[12] And also some dicta in "convergence cases": see ,e.g., the NSW Court of Appeal's judgment in *Director of Public Prosecutions (Cth) v United Telecasters Sydney Ltd (In Liq)* (1992) 7 BR 364 at 370.

any application for discharge of the jury.[13] The trial judges hearing these applications were of course not concerned to determine contempt liability: at most, they announced their intention to refer the matter of contempt to an appropriate prosecuting authority.[14]

A Fine for the Media to Pay even though the Trial is Not Stopped

In seven of these ten "divergence" cases, publicity put out during the relevant jury trial led to a contempt conviction even though the trial was not aborted. This group of seven can be further divided into two sub-groups, as follows:-

(A) CASES WHERE THERE WAS EVIDENCE BEFORE THE TRIAL JUDGE THAT THE JURY PROBABLY OR DEFINITELY DID NOT ENCOUNTER THE PUBLICITY

Four cases belong within this sub-group. In one of them, there was a clear finding in the criminal trial that the jury could not have encountered the publicity. This was *Registrar of the Supreme Court of South Australia v Advertiser Newspaper Ltd*,[15] where the prejudicial newspaper article was published the morning after the jurors had retired to consider their verdict. They had been locked up overnight, and early on the morning of publication the trial judge had contacted the Sheriff to make sure that no newspapers were delivered to them. He therefore rejected defence counsel's application to discharge the jury.

In the contempt proceedings, the newspaper proprietor pleaded guilty, bypassing any submission that there was no contempt because in the circumstances there was no possibility that the jury could have been influenced by the article. Bollen J stated that the contempt was a "very serious" one as in his view the jurors would have had to be discharged if the article had been published while they had access to it. But having regard to the plea of guilty and to the "moderate" nature of the contempt prosecutor's submissions, he imposed only a "small" fine of $10,000 plus costs.

In the remaining three cases in this sub-group, there was good reason to believe that the jury was not exposed to the publicity. At the criminal trial involved in *Registrar of the Court of Appeal v John Fairfax Group Pty Ltd*,[16] the judge put written questions on this issue to the jury, requiring

---

[13] Though for a relatively full elaboration of this (negative) rule, see *Attorney-General for NSW v Television and Telecasters (Sydney) Pty Ltd*, unreported, Supreme Court of NSW, Greg James J, 10 September 1998.

[14] See, e.g., *R v Zammit*, unreported, Supreme Court of NSW, Newman J, 14 February 1998 per Newman J—referral to the Court of Appeal to act of its own motion.

[15] Unreported, Supreme Court of SA, 17 May 1996 per Bollen J.

[16] Unreported, NSW Court of Appeal, 21 April 1993. An account of these steps taken to discover whether the jury had read the offending article appears in *R v Ladislaus Meissner* (unreported, NSW Court of Criminal Appeal, 27 November 1992). See too *Bayeh v Attorney-General for NSW* (1995) 82 A Crim R 270 at 281–282.

its answers under oath pursuant to the *Jury Act 1977* (NSW), s 55D. He was satisfied that the prejudicial material within the offending newspaper article had not come to the jury's notice, and therefore declined to stop the trial. In his judgment in the contempt proceedings, Sheller JA referred to the principle that the presence or absence of actual prejudice was irrelevant to liability. Mahoney JA invoked the analogy of "the driver on a public road who must take care not to injure those in his way". The court found the publisher liable, imposing a fine of $75,000 plus costs (a further fine of $1,000 was imposed on the journalist who prepared the offending article). Although substantial, this fine is well below the record in *sub judice* cases in NSW, which stands at $200,000 plus costs.

The contempt proceedings in *R v David Syme & Co Ltd*[17] arose out of a trial in which the appellate proceedings are reported at length as *Zampaglione*.[18] This report shows that after the publication of the newspaper article later found to be in contempt, the trial judge declined to abort the trial, which had been in progress for some six or seven weeks, because he believed that the jury had been attentive, that its mind would be fully focused on the voluminous evidence and that the detriment occasioned to the witnesses (some of whom were under police protection) and the public purse would be considerable. In his report to the Court of Criminal Appeal, he added two further reasons: (a) at the time when he made this ruling, he believed the Crown case to be "overwhelmingly strong" and (b) his tipstaff had subsequently gleaned from some of the jurors (who for other reasons were locked up for the rest of the hearing) that none of them had come across the article.

In his contempt judgment in *Syme*, finding the publisher guilty, Marks J did not refer to these findings of the trial judge (he may not have been aware of these last two matters, as his judgment preceded that of the Court of Criminal Appeal). He merely stated the well established principle that "[t]he tendency of the publication must be judged as at the time of publication and is not determined by the fact that for some reason no harm has resulted".[19] He rejected the publisher's defence that it did not actually know of the criminal trial, holding that this was on account of its gross negligence. The penalty which he imposed, a fine of $75,000 plus costs, is largest on record in Victoria (it has been equalled in one subsequent case, as mentioned below).

In the last case in this sub-group, *R v Pearce*,[20] the prejudicial material, which in contrast to the previous three cases favoured the accused, appeared in a television news programme broadcast only about 45 minutes after the jury had left the court for the day. Jurors would not have encountered it unless they had travelled home quickly and turned out on

---

[17] [1982] VR 173.

[18] (1982) 6 A Crim R 287; see at 290–300.

[19] [1982] VR 173 at 177, citing *R v Pacini* [1956] VLR 544 at 547.

[20] (1992) 7 WAR 395.

their TV sets, or had been told about it. Counsel for the prosecution drew it to the trial judge's attention, but neither he nor defence counsel applied for discharge of the jury.[21]

In the contempt proceedings, Malcolm CJ (with whom Pidgeon and Rowland JJ agreed) said that "there could not have been a strong likelihood" that the jury had encountered it and that this was relevant to "the gravity of the contempt".[22] But he rejected the argument of the defence that the prosecution was obliged to prove actual communication to the jury, because of having formulated the allegation of contempt in terms of a tendency to influence the jury to acquit "by communicating to them as members of the public". He held instead that the court must be:

> satisfied beyond a reasonable doubt that the publication is of a character which might be communicated to members of the jury, and so interfere with the due consideration of justice. In other words it is necessary to be satisfied beyond a reasonable doubt that the consequence might follow as a matter of practical reality.[23]

The television station, the programme producer and the person (a State Government Minister) whose statement in a press conference constituted the prejudicial material were found guilty of contempt. They were ordered between them to pay the costs of the contempt proceedings, but no formal penalty was imposed.

The judgments in these four contempt cases show divergent attitudes to the significance of the trial judges' findings that the jury did not, or probably did not, encounter the offending publicity. It seems to me that underlying these divergences is a crucial contradiction within the accepted test of liability for *sub judice* contempt. This test speaks first of a "real and definite *tendency*" to prejudice the relevant trial, suggesting that this relatively abstract concept of a "tendency" inherent in the publication is the key element in liability. But the later qualifying phrase, "as a matter of *practical reality*" shifts attention to the actual circumstances of the publication, including the factual likelihood of its reaching the attention of the jury. The Mason formulation of "substantial risk of serious (or real) prejudice" does this too.

In contempt cases involving material published before the relevant trial, this second element has at times been prominent. In *Attorney-General for NSW v John Fairfax & Sons and Bacon*,[24] for instance, the fact that the defendant newspaper had a relatively small circulation in the region from which the jury in the relevant trial would be drawn was a significant factor in the New South Wales Court of Appeal's finding that no contempt had

---

[21] See *Ibid.* at 429–430.

[22] *Ibid.* at 425.

[23] *Ibid.* at 425–426. See *Director of Public Prosecutions v Wran* (1986) 7 NSWLR 616 at 627.

[24] (1985) 6 NSWLR 695: see at 697 (Glass JA), 713 (McHugh JA).

occurred. Yet in the first two of these four cases of publicity during trial which I have just outlined, the "practical reality" of the jury's lack of contact, or probable contact, with the publicity did not, it would seem, matter greatly to the court hearing the contempt. In the third, *Syme*, the judge was seemingly unaware of it. That this should have happened for purely procedural reasons seems unfortunate.

In the South Australian *Advertiser* case, the issue was bypassed because the defendant publisher pleaded guilty, letting slip the opportunity to argue that because the jury had been locked up overnight and their access to newspapers was controlled, publication of the article was, in terms of "practical reality", highly unlikely to cause harm. In *Syme*, Marks J's only brief reference to the issue whether the jury encountered the publicity emphasised the "tendency" element in the test of contempt liability. He did not refer to the judge's decision to proceed with the trial as a factor which might mitigate the penalty,[25] although the converse situation of a jury being discharged has subsequently been treated as a ground for increasing a contempt fine.[26] He saw no contradiction between the judge's decision not to abort the trial and his own decision to impose a record fine. The *John Fairfax* judgments displayed a similar pattern of responses, though by New South Wales standards the penalty was a good deal less serious.

Only in the fourth case, that of *Pearce*, did an argument based on the "practical reality" of the jury not coming into contact with the publicity cut much ice. While it did not protect the publisher from a finding of liability, Malcolm CJ's statement of principle placed the onus on the contempt prosecutor to prove beyond reasonable doubt that the jury "might" have seen the programme or been told about it. According to Mason CJ"s alternative formulation of the basic test, as noted above, this would presumably mean that there should have been a "substantial risk" of this happening. Also, appropriately in my view, Malcolm CJ treated the absence of any "strong likelihood" of jury exposure to the programme as a mitigating factor in considering any penalty.

On the major issue of liability in this context, I consider Malcolm CJ's approach to be preferable to that of the other cases. It does not exonerate the publisher from liability merely because the contempt prosecutor cannot prove affirmatively that the jury encountered the publicity. But if, as arguably occurred in the *Advertiser* case, it was clear that the jury could not have done so because they were isolated from contact with media output, the publisher would not be liable.

I am interpreting Malcolm CJ's statement as meaning that what matters

---

[25] His judgment listed a number of other factors: see [1982] VR 173 at 180.

[26] See, e.g., *R v Thompson, Parry and TVW Enterprises* [1989] WAR 219 at 225; *Attorney-General for Victoria v Gordon, Cronin and Herald & Weekly Times*, unreported, Supreme Court of Vic., 12 July 1985 per Brooking J: contra *Hinch v Attorney-General for Victoria* [1987] VR 721 at 731, 748.

is the objective likelihood, as at the time of publication, of the jury encountering the publicity, not the degree of probability which the relevant members of the publishing organization might have estimated (if they had thought about the matter) in the light only of the circumstances which they knew or should have known. This must surely be correct. To adapt the analogy to *sub judice* contempt suggested by Mahoney JA in the *John Fairfax* case,[27] if a driver on a public road with a speed limit of 100 km/h is in fact driving at this speed, she does not become guilty of dangerous driving by virtue of excessive speed merely because her speedometer was overstating her speed and she therefore thought it was 140 km/h. The alternative interpretation imports a strong element of fault into what according to the authorities is a species of contempt based on strict liability.[28]

(B) CASES WHERE THE TRIAL JUDGE MADE NO SPECIFIC FINDING AS TO WHETHER THE JURY ENCOUNTERED THE PUBLICITY

As far as I can tell, three cases answer this description, in which the contempt proceedings were, respectively, *R v Truth Newspaper* (1993),[29] *R v Nationwide News, Ex parte DPP of WA* (1997)[30] and *R v Nationwide News* (1997).[31]

This pattern of events may raise the concern that judicial reluctance to incur the costs and inconvenience of aborting a trial could have led to a suspect verdict, in the light of a finding in the associated contempt proceedings that the jury may well have been exposed to publicity which was sufficiently prejudicial to sustain a contempt conviction. In the last of these three cases, for instance, the trial judge described the relevant newspaper article about the accused, Brian Quinn (who was at the time giving evidence), as "absolutely appalling" and he agreed with the epithets "woefully inaccurate", "malicious" and "poisonous" suggested by defence counsel. In his contempt judgment, Gillard J used the phrase "character assassination on a grand scale" and he specifically found that "there was a real possibility that the article did come to the attention of a juror". Describing the contempt as "serious", he imposed fines of $75,000 (the record figure in Victoria, as already mentioned) plus costs on Nationwide News and $10,000 on the journalist responsible. Yet the trial, which at

---

[27] Compare the analogy between *sub judice* contempt and industrial safety offences—with which I agree—suggested by the Australian Law Reform Commission in its Report on *Contempt* (ALRC 35, 1987) para 259.

[28] See, e.g., the discussion of this question in *Registrar, Court of Appeal v Willesee* (1985) 3 NSWLR 650.

[29] Unreported, Supreme Court of Vic., 16 December 1993 per Phillips J.

[30] Unreported, Full Court of the Supreme Court of WA, 16 May 1997.

[31] Unreported, Supreme Court of Vic., 22 February 1997 (liability) and 18 February 1998 (penalty), per Gillard J.

the time of publication was in its 31st day, was not aborted. The matter was considered, but no formal application for discharge was made.

Alternatively, of course, the decision to continue the trial in these circumstances may be warranted because the contents of the publication are thought not to raise a sufficient risk of influence, or because, as the *Syme* case illustrates, factors such as the judge's estimate of the strength of the Crown's case appear to justify continuance. But if no such factors are apparent, how can a contempt conviction be justified?

On any view, where there is reason to believe that the jury may have come into contact with the publicity, contradictory outcomes of this nature will often be difficult to reconcile.

No Liability (and So No Fine) for the Media even though the Trial Was Stopped

In the remaining three divergence cases, the converse occurred. The jury trial was aborted as a result of the publicity, but the contempt proceedings against the publisher failed.

In two of them, an established principle of contempt law provides a ready explanation. In *Registrar, Court of Appeal v Willesee*[32] and *Sun Newspapers Pty Ltd and Murray*[33] a television broadcast and a newspaper article (respectively) were held to have the requisite tendency to prejudice the relevant jury trial, which was aborted in consequence. But they did not attract contempt liability by virtue of the superior public interest in dissemination of information about, and public discussion of, the general matters of public importance with which they dealt.[34]

The third case is the very recent one of *Attorney-General for NSW v Television and Telecasters*.[35] Here, an item in an evening television news programme informed viewers that, following an incident during a criminal trial that day leading to immediate removal of the jury, defence counsel had made an unsuccessful application for the trial to be aborted. At the time of the incident, the jury would have realized simply that some sort of application had been made in their absence. If however the broadcast that evening came directly or indirectly to their notice they would have discovered what the application was for. For this reason, on the next day, the trial judge held, pursuant to a second application, that the trial should be aborted.

Contempt proceedings against the broadcaster were, however, unsuccessful. Greg James J, invoking Mason CJ's formulation in *Hinch* (see above), considered that for the jury to obtain this information did

---

[32] (1985) 3 NSWLR 650.

[33] (1992) 58 A Crim R 281 (SC Qld).

[34] That is, the *Bread Manufacturers* principle applied, as confirmed in these terms by the High Court in *Hinch v Attorney-General of Victoria* (1987) 164 CLR 15.

[35] Unreported, Supreme Court of NSW, 10 September 1998 per Greg James J.

not create any "substantial or real risk of serious prejudice to a fair trial". He could not see that it would influence any juror one way or the other. He stressed that it was not for him to express a view on the trial judge's decision to abort the trial. His judgment suggests, however, that he may have thought it unnecessary.

An alternative explanation for divergence in a case like this may be that even before the prejudicial publication occurred the trial judge had concerns about the fairness of the trial, and the publication, though not particularly prejudicial in its own right, was, in effect, the "last straw". In such a case, it would seem appropriate for this to be explained in the judge's reasons for discharging the jury.

The Issue of Admissibility

An interesting aspect of the judgment of Greg James J in the *Television and Telecasters* case is his determination that the terms of the successful application for discharge and the judge's ruling upon it were not admissible in the contempt proceedings. In so holding, he declined to follow an observation of Gobbo J, dealing with similar issues in the contempt case of *R v Day and Thomson*,[36] that "the fact that a mistrial occurred is not wholly irrelevant; it at least indicates that the risk [of prejudice] was not a fanciful one". He pointed out that the issue of admissibility was not argued in *Day and Thomson*.

As I interpret Greg James J's ruling, it was simply that for the purposes of the contempt case before him the tendered material relating to the termination of the criminal trial was not relevant and was therefore inadmissible. He did not seek to establish a general rule that similar material from the transcript of an aborted trial should always be inadmissible in associated contempt proceedings. But if he did, I would submit that such a rule would be unfortunate, for reasons that should be clear from this paper. If for instance the criminal trial is *not* aborted because, as occurred in the Adelaide *Advertiser* case, the judge finds that the jury was shielded from the publicity, this should be admissible in the contempt proceedings because, according to my arguments, it should provide a basis for successfully defending them. In other less extreme situations, counsel's arguments and the judge's ruling on the issue of jury discharge may well provide guidance to the court hearing the associated contempt proceedings, at least on the issue of penalty if not on liability. The issue of admissibility should therefore depend on the particular circumstances.

---

[36] [1985] VR 261 at 264.

Conclusion

In summary, my conclusions are as follows:

1. Unless some clear reason for divergence can be seen, there should be at least an assumption that the two responses to prejudicial publicity during a criminal jury trial which I am discussing—stopping the trial and fining the media—should either occur together or not at all.

2. A clear reason why a trial may legitimately be stopped without the publisher being liable for contempt may be that the publication, although prejudicial, contributed to the public interest in dissemination of information about, and public discussion of, some general matter of public importance.

3. The judge's ruling on any application to abort a trial on account of prejudicial publicity should so far as possible indicate any factors other than the publicity which the judge took into account.

4. The transcript of this ruling, and of counsel's submissions in the application for the trial to be aborted, should in general be admissable in any associated contempt proceedings.

5. Rather than speaking only in terms of a general "tendency" to prejudice a trial, the criterion of contempt liability should include a specific requirement of proof that there was a real risk that the jury would encounter the relevant publicity. A possible formulation, based on the suggestion by Mason CJ in *Hinch v Attorney-General for Victoria*,[37] would be that "there was a substantial risk that the published material (a) would come to the attention of one or more members of the jury in the relevant proceedings and, through so doing, (b) would cause serious (or real) prejudice to the fair conduct of those proceedings".

6. Where such a risk was present, but the evidence suggests that the jury did not in fact encounter the publicity (implying that the publicity alone provided no grounds for aborting the trial), this should mitigate any penalty imposed for contempt.

7. Judges and trial lawyers should make further endeavours to ensure greater consistency in decisions on whether or not to abort a trial on grounds of publicity, though it must be recognized that this is a difficult goal to achieve and there must always be a strong element of judicial discretion in each decision.

---

[37] (1987) 164 CLR 15 at 27–28.

THE COURTS, PARLIAMENTARY PRIVILEGE AND THE MEDIA

Professor Sally Walker

Hearn Professor of Law, University of Melbourne, Law School

It is widely known that parliamentarians are immune from liability in respect of anything said by them forming part of the proceedings of the House. What is not so widely understood is that the scope of this privilege of freedom of speech may have an impact on the media. This article concerns two ways in which the ambit of the parliamentarians' privilege of freedom of speech may affect the media. First, in relation to the protection from liability for defamation in respect of fair and accurate reports of parliamentary proceedings and, secondly, in relation to defamation proceedings instituted by a Member of Parliament against a media organization. In both cases, the way that the courts define the limits of parliamentary privilege, or interpret legislation dealing with it, may affect what media organizations can publish without fear of liability for defamation.

Before investigating the two issues mentioned in the previous paragraph, it is necessary to outline the parliamentarians' privilege of freedom of speech.

1. The Parliamentarians' Privilege of Freedom of Speech

Article 9 of the *Bill of Rights* (1688) provides that:

> the freedom of speech and debates or proceedings in Parliament ought not to be impeached or questioned in any court or place out of Parliament.

This privilege of freedom of speech is enjoyed by Members of all Australian Houses of Parliament pursuant to legislation which adopts the privileges of the House of Commons,[1] pursuant to legislation which provides that the *Bill of Rights* is part of the law[2] or, at common law, on the basis of

---

[1] Commonwealth Constitution, s 49; *Constitution Act* 1867 (Qld), s 40A; *Constitution Act* 1934 (SA), s 38; *Constitution Act* 1975 (Vic), s 19; *Parliamentary Privileges Act* 1891 (WA), s 1; *Legislative Assembly (Powers and Privileges) Act* 1992 (NT), s 4 (adopting the privileges of the House of Representatives). See also *Sankey v Whitlam* (1978) 142 CLR 1 at 35 per Gibbs ACJ; *Holding v Jennings* [1979] VR 289 at 290–291; *Australian Broadcasting Corporation v Chatterton* (1986) 46 SASR 1 at 17–18 per Zelling ACJ, 30 per Prior J.

[2] *Imperial Acts Application Act* 1969 (NSW), s 6.

necessity.[3] It is interesting to note that Houses of Parliament see the privilege of freedom of speech as an aspect of their right to control their own proceedings.[4]

One consequence of the privilege of freedom of speech is that no civil or criminal proceedings may be instituted against a Member of Parliament in respect of anything said or done by the member in the House in her or his capacity as a Member of Parliament. Most significantly, no action for defamation brought against a Member of Parliament can be founded on anything said by the Member in a speech or on anything said or done by the Member in any other part of the proceedings in Parliament.[5] The absolute privilege from liability for defamation in respect of statements made in parliamentary proceedings enables Members of Parliament to speak freely, making assertions and allegations which they could not otherwise have made without the risk of liability for defamation. The relationship between this parliamentary privilege and the publication of material by the media will now be considered.

2. The Protection of the Media from Liability for Fair and Accurate Reports of Parliamentary Proceedings

Legislation in each Australian jurisdiction accords qualified privilege to fair and accurate reports of parliamentary proceedings.[6] Thus, a media organization is protected from liability for defamation in respect of the publication of a fair and accurate report of parliamentary proceedings unless the plaintiff can establish that, in publishing the report, the media organization was actuated by malice.[7] In *Wason v Walter* it was explained that the protection reflects the paramount public importance attached to the communication of proceedings of Houses of Parliament to the public.[8]

---

[3] *Gipps v McElhone* (1881) 2 LR (NSW) 18 at 21–22 per Martin CJ, 24 per Manning J, 25–26 per Windeyer J; *Chenard and Co v Arissol* [1949] AC 127.

[4] Sir Charles Gordon (ed.), *Erskine Man's Treatise on The Law, Privileges, Proceedings and Usage of Parliament* (1983) at 77.

[5] *Gipps v McElhone* (1881) 2 LR (NSW) 18; *Holding v Jennings* [1979] VR 289; *Australian Broadcasting Corporation v Chatterton* (1986) 46 SASR 1 at 18 per Zelling ACJ, 36 per Prior J; *Beitzel v Crabb* [1992] 2 VR 121 at 125; *Prebble v Television New Zealand Ltd* [1995] 1 AC 321 at 328. In some jurisdictions the Members' immunity for defamation is reinforced by legislation, but this is restricted to defamatory remarks made in speeches: *Defamation Act* 1889 (Qld.), s 10(1); *Defamation Act* 1957 (Tas.), s 10(1); *Criminal Code* (Tas.), s 202(1); *Criminal Code* (WA), s 351.

[6] In some cases the protection extends to the publication in the jurisdiction of a report of proceedings of the Commonwealth Parliament or other State or Territory Parliaments: *Defamation Act* 1974 (NSW), s 24, Sch 2 cl 2 (1) and s 26; *Wrongs Act* 1958 (Vic.), s 3A(1); *Criminal Code* (WA), s 354(1); *Defamation Amendment Act* 1909 (ACT), s 5(a). In other jurisdictions it seems that the privilege applies only to reports of proceedings held in the jurisdiction in which the report is published: *Defamation Act* 1889 (Qld.), s 13(1)(a); *Wrongs Act* 1936 (SA), s 7(1)(ab); *Defamation Act* 1957 (Tas.), s 13(1)(a); *Defamation Act* (NT), s 6(1)(ba). For the purpose of the criminal law see also *Criminal Code Act* 1924 (Tas.), s 205(1)(a).

[7] *Wason v Walter* (1868) 4 LR QB 73 at 85, 94.

[8] (1868) 4 LR QB 73 at 89.

In 1987 the Commonwealth Parliament enacted legislation giving the protection of what appears to be absolute privilege to reports of proceedings of the Senate, the House of Representatives or a committee or sub-committee of either or both of those Houses.[9] Similar legislation operates in relation to reports of the Northern Territory Legislative Assembly and its committees.[10]

In all cases, this legislation is directed at reports of proceedings in Parliament. In this respect it mirrors the parliamentarians' privilege of freedom of speech based on Article 9 of the *Bill of Rights*, set out in section 1 above, which also applies to proceedings in Parliament. What falls within the ambit of "proceedings in Parliament" is, however, unclear.[11] This issue is of significance to the media because, the wider the ambit of "proceedings in Parliament" for the purpose of the privilege of Members of Parliament, the wider the operation of the protection accorded to media reports.

The courts' interpretation of the scope of "proceedings in Parliament" will now be examined.

2.1 THE COURTS' INTERPRETATION OF "PROCEEDINGS IN PARLIAMENT"

It has generally been accepted that the Member's absolute privilege does not protect her or him from liability in respect of the publication by the Member outside the House of a speech made in the House.[12] In the Full Court of the South Australian Supreme Court in *Australian Broadcasting Corporation v Chatterton*, Zelling ACJ did, however, hold that a Member who simply repeated outside the House what he or she said in the House was protected by absolute privilege.[13] This was rejected by Prior J.[14] The other member of the Court, Jacobs J, did not deal with this question. In the same case Zelling ACJ suggested, without deciding, that it is possible that it is part of the proceedings of Parliament to answer questions in a television interview;[15] again, this was rejected by Prior J[16] and was not mentioned in Jacob J's judgment.

Support for extending the meaning of "proceedings in Parliament" can be found in two Canadian cases. In *Roman Corp Ltd v Hudson's Bay*

---

[9] *Parliamentary Privileges Act* 1987 (Cth), s 10.
[10] *Legislative Assembly (Powers and Privileges) Act* 1992 (NT), s 13.
[11] See Australian Parliament, *Joint Committee on Parliamentary Privilege Final Report* (October 1984) PP No 219 chapter 5; SA deSmith, "Parliamentary Privilege and the Bill of Rights" (1958) 21 *Modern Law Review* 465; Sir Charles Gordon (ed.), *Erskine May's Treatise on The Law, Privileges, Proceedings and Usage of Parliament* (1983) at 92.
[12] *R v Abingdon* (1793) 1 Esp 226 [170 ER 337] at 228 [338]; *R v Creevey* (1813) 1 M and S 273 [105 ER 102] at 278 [104], 279–280 [104], 280–281 [104–105]; *Beitzel v Crabb* [1992] 2 VR 121 at 126–127.
[13] (1986) 46 SASR 1 at 18–19.
[14] (1986) 46 SASR 1 at 29–36.
[15] (1986) 46 SASR 1 at 19.
[16] (1986) 46 SASR 1 at 34–36.

Oil and Gas Co Ltd it was held that the sending of a telegram by the Prime Minister and the issuing of a press release by a Member of Parliament were part of parliamentary proceedings; both the telegram and the press release set out statements previously made in the House.[17] In *Re Clark and Attorney-General of Canada* it was held that the protection extends to a Member releasing information to the media.[18] Furthermore, in the English case of *Rost v Edwards* it was held that letters written by an Opposition Member to two Members of Parliament in relation to questions which he subsequently raised in the House were protected by parliamentary privilege;[19] note, however, it was held that a Register of Members' Interests did not form part of the proceedings of Parliament.[20]

So far as the Senate and the House of Representatives are concerned, s 16(2) of the *Parliamentary Privileges Act* 1987 (Cth) defines "proceedings in Parliament". It provides:

> For the purposes of the provisions of Article 9 of the *Bill of Rights* (1688) as applying in relation to the Parliament, and for the purposes of this section, "proceedings in Parliament" means all words and spoken acts done in the course of, or for purposes of or incidental to, the transacting of the business of a House or of a committee, and, without limiting the generality of the foregoing, includes:
> (a) the giving of evidence before a House or a committee, and evidence so given;
> (b) the presentation or submission of a document to a House or a committee;
> (c) the preparation of a document for purposes of or incidental to the transacting of any such business; and
> (d) the formulation, making or publication of a document, including a report, by or pursuant to an order of a House or a committee and the document so formulated, made or published.[21]

The fact that this legislation defines "proceedings in Parliament" so as to include words spoken, not only "in the course of", but also "for purposes of or incidental to" the transacting of the business of a House or of a committee may be interpreted as extending the protection accorded to statements made by federal Members of Parliament beyond statements made in the House or in committee proceedings. In *O'Chee v Rowley*[22] a Member of Parliament was able to rely on this expanded definition of

---

[17] (1971) 23 DLR (3d) 292 at 298–300 (Ontario Court of Appeal); the Supreme Court of Canada dealt with an appeal on a broader issue "without dissenting from the views expressed in Courts below as to the privilege attached to statements made in Parliament"—(1973) 36 DLR (3d) 413 at 419.

[18] (1977) 81 DLR (3d) 33 at 56–58 (Ontario High Court of Justice); cf. *Stopforth v Goyer* (1978) 87 DLR (3rd) 373 at 381–382 (Ontario High Court of Justice; the Court of Appeal did not deal with the question of absolute privilege—(1979) 97 DLR (3d) 369).

[19] [1990] 2 QB 460 at 476.

[20] [1990] 2 QB 460 at 476–478.

[21] Section 6(2) of the *Legislative Assembly (Powers and Privileges) Act* 1992 (NT) is in similar terms.

[22] (1997) 150 ALR 199.

"proceedings in Parliament". The case concerned defamation proceedings brought against a Senator in relation to statements made by the Senator in a radio broadcast. In his defence, the Senator disclosed that he had various documents in his possession which were relevant to whether his statements were published in good faith. Some of the documents ante-dated and others post-dated speeches in the Senate made by the Senator on the topic discussed in the radio broadcast; none of the documents had been tabled in either federal House of Parliament or had been submitted to a committee of either House. The Senator claimed privilege from disclosure of the documents. He asserted that the documents "were created, prepared, brought into existence or came into … [his] possession for the purposes of or incidental to the transacting of the business of the Senate".

A majority of members of the Full Court of the Supreme Court of Queensland held that s 16(2)(c) of the *Parliamentary Privileges Act* 1987 (Cth), taken together with Article 9 of the *Bill of Rights*, operated so that the Senator could not be required to produce the documents.[23] Fitzgerald P dissented, holding that the Senator's claim "would expand the boundaries of parliamentary privilege to limits which are…unnecessary, excessive and unsupported by authority and not within the statutory language."[24]

The pressure for the courts to extend the ambit of "proceedings in Parliament" will come from an argument that the law should recognize that the work of a Member of Parliament is not confined to activities which take place as part of the debates in the House. The judge in *Roman Corp Ltd v Hudson's Bay Oil and Gas Co Ltd* was influenced by "the complexities of modern government" and the development and employment in government business of greatly extended means of communication; it was held that the object of the privilege of freedom of speech is to protect members from harassment in carrying on the business of the House which must encompass sending a telegram and issuing a press release where the telegram and the press release contained information about decisions made in the House.[25]

Until what falls within the ambit of "proceedings in Parliament" is resolved in Australia, reliance should not be placed on these extended interpretations. Indeed, it is suggested that a narrow approach should be taken to what is encompassed by "proceedings in Parliament". It is suggested that "proceedings in Parliament" should be confined to statements and action which form part of the formal transacting of the business of the House or in a properly constituted committee. There are two reasons for this. First, it provides certainty regarding what is encompassed

---

[23] (1997) 150 ALR 199 at 207–212, 215 per McPherson JA (with whom Moynihan J agreed).
[24] (1997) 150 ALR 199 at 204.
[25] (1971) 23 DLR (3d) 292 at 299.

by "proceedings in Parliament" for the purpose of the absolute privilege enjoyed by Members of Parliament and the qualified, and perhaps sometimes absolute, privilege accorded to fair and accurate reports of parliamentary proceedings.

Secondly, the making of an allegation by a Member of Parliament, while protected by parliamentary privilege and the reporting of the allegation by the media, has the potential to cause great damage to an individual who is the subject of the allegation. It is in the public interest that Members of Parliament and media organizations should have freedom to discuss political and government matters. Nonetheless, it is suggested that an appropriate balance is struck between public interest and the private interests of individuals whose reputations are affected by such publications, if, in cases falling outside the narrow definition of "proceedings in Parliament" suggested above, Members of Parliament and media organizations are protected only by the *Lange* form of qualified privilege. The qualified privilege established by the High Court in *Lange v Australian Broadcasting Corporation*,[26] which applies in relation to the publication of material "concerning government and political matters that affect the people of Australia",[27] requires that the publisher establishes that it was "reasonable" to publish the material.[28]

3. Defamation Proceedings Instituted by a Member of Parliament against a Media Organization

This section examines the courts' approach to the application of parliamentary privilege when defamation proceedings have been commenced against a media organization by a Member of Parliament. The scope of parliamentary privilege may arise as an issue for the courts in the following circumstances: a media organization publishes material which criticizes the actions of a Member of Parliament (often the criticism may allege that the Member misled the House); the Member of Parliament institutes defamation proceedings against the media organization; the media organization relies on certain defences which require it to produce evidence of the actions or statements of the Member in parliamentary proceedings; the Member of Parliament objects to the admission of the evidence on the ground that this would infringe parliamentary privilege. *Prebble v Television New Zealand Ltd*[29] referred to later in this section, *Allason v Haines*[30] and, in broad terms, *Hamilton v Guardian Newspapers*[31] mentioned in section 3.2 below, fall within this category.

---

[26] (1997) 145 ALR 96. See Walker, "*Lange v ABC*: the High Court rethinks the 'constitutionalisation' of defamation law" (1998) 6 *Torts Law Journal* 9.

[27] (1997) 145 ALR 96 at 115.

[28] (1997) 145 ALR 96 at 116.

[29] [1995] 1 AC 321.

[30] [1995] TLR 438.

[31] (1995) 139 Sol Jo 772.

A more particular example would occur in the following circumstances: statements are made by a Member of Parliament in the House which are critical of a person who is named in the parliamentary proceedings; the statements are reported in the media; the media also interviews or publishes a statement made by the person who was the subject of the statements made in the House; the person's reply asserts that the Member of Parliament's allegations are untrue, that is, that the Member has lied; the Member of Parliament then institutes proceedings for defamation against the media organization. In these circumstances, the media organization may seek to rely on the defences of truth or, as it is more properly known, justification, fair comment and qualified privilege. In order to rely on these defences, the media organization will want to adduce evidence of what the Member of Parliament said in the parliamentary proceedings. The issue then arises, will the court permit the evidence of what was said in Parliament to be put into evidence or will it refuse to do so on the ground that to admit the evidence into the court proceedings in these circumstances would infringe parliamentary privilege? Broadly, *Wright and Advertiser Newspapers Limited v Lewis,*[32] which is examined later in this section, falls into this category.

It has been noted that the question of whether the courts should admit evidence of parliamentary proceedings in the circumstances referred to in the previous paragraph involves a conflict between three public interests: first, the need to ensure that the legislature can exercise its powers freely on behalf of its electors, with access to all relevant information; second, the need to protect freedom of speech generally; third, the interests of justice in ensuring that all relevant evidence is available to the courts.[33] The courts' approach to the conflict to which these interests give rise may have a profound impact on the outcome of defamation proceedings and, ultimately, on what the media can publish without fear of liability for defamation.

As Article 9 of the *Bill of Rights*, which is the basis of the parliament-arians' privilege of freedom of speech, is part of Australian law, it follows that the courts will uphold the privilege. Nonetheless, the interpretation of Article 9 has been a matter of dispute between the Houses of Parliament and the courts; the outcome of this dispute will affect the media.

In Australia, the question of the proper interpretation of Article 9 of the *Bill of Rights* came to a head in litigation involving Mr Justice Lionel Murphy. In *R v Murphy*[34], acting on instructions from the President of the Senate, counsel argued that Hunt J should disallow certain questions which might be asked of witnesses who had given evidence before, and

---

[32] (1990) 53 SASR 416.

[33] *Prebble v Television New Zealand Ltd* [1995] 1 AC 321 at 336.

[34] (1986) 5 NSWLR 18.

[35] Submissions had also been made to Cantor J who presided at the first Murphy trial, see *R v Murphy* (1986) 5 NSWLR 18 at 22.

made statements to, Senate Select Committees.[35] Hunt J held that it would not be a breach of privilege to ask a witness in court proceedings whether he or she made a statement to a parliamentary committee even where the purpose was to invite the court to disbelieve the witness's evidence given in the court proceedings by reason of inconsistency between the statement to the committee and the witness's later evidence to the court. His Honour reasoned that, in these circumstances, there is no attack on what was said before the Committee, but the attack is on the honesty of what was subsequently said by the witness in the court proceedings.[36] Hunt J held that parliamentary privilege operates only to prevent the questioning of statements made in Parliament in proceedings which seek to assert legal consequences against the maker of the statement for making that statement; according to Hunt J, what is meant by Article 9 of the *Bill of Rights* is:

> that no court proceedings ... having legal consequences against a Member of Parliament (or a witness before a parliamentary committee) are permitted which by those legal consequences have the effect of preventing the Member (or committee witness) exercising his freedom of speech in Parliament (or before a committee) or of punishing him for having done so).[37]

In its application to defamation proceedings brought by a Member of Parliament against a publisher in respect of material which alleges that the actions or words of the Member of Parliament in the House were inspired by improper motives or were untrue or misleading, this interpretation of Article 9 would permit the media to produce evidence of parliamentary proceedings:

- to establish that published material is true and therefore protected by the defence of justification;
- to establish that it has published a fair and accurate report of proceedings in Parliament and that therefore it is protected by the qualified or absolute privilege referred to in section 2 above or by the *Lange* form of qualified privilege, which is also mentioned in section 2; or
- to prove a parliamentary speech as a fact upon which a fair comment was made.

In none of these cases does this use of the proceedings assert legal consequences against the maker of the statement for making the statement. This is illustrated by *Wright and Advertiser Newspapers Limited v Lewis*.[38] The plaintiff was a Member of the South Australian House of Assembly. He instituted defamation proceedings against the defendants in respect of a letter written by the first defendant and published by the second defendant. The letter accused the plaintiff of making unfounded

---

[36] *R v Murphy* (1986) 5 NSWLR 18 at 26–27.
[37] *R v Murphy* (1986) 5 NSWLR 18 at 30; see also at 34.
[38] (1990) 53 SASR 416.

and defamatory statements in Parliament about the first defendant and, in effect, abusing his position as a parliamentarian. The defendants filed a joint defence which raised the defences of justification, qualified privilege and fair comment. The plaintiff sought to strike out particulars in relation to those defences on the ground that they infringed parliamentary privilege. The Full Court of the Supreme Court of South Australia held that the parliamentary privilege did not operate so as to prevent a defendant who wishes to rely on these defences from referring to statements made by the plaintiff in Parliament. Adopting an approach similar to that of Hunt J in *R v Murphy*,[39] in *Wright and Advertiser Newspapers Limited v Lewis* King CJ said:

> Freedom of speech and deliberation in the Parliament is the primary value sought to be protected by Parliamentary privilege. To accord to a defendant the right to defend himself against an action for defamation by proving truth, would not impinge upon such freedom. A Member would not be inhibited in the exercise of free speech or of his parliamentary duties by fear of legal consequences, because he would be aware that his actions and motives could not be examined in court unless he instituted the proceedings which rendered such examination necessary. Only the Member's action in launching proceedings alleging a false imputation could lead to an examination in court of the issue of the falsity of the imputation, and therefore of the Member's statements and conduct. I cannot think of any other public or parliamentary interest which could be impaired by such an examination in such circumstances.

> I do not think that a defendant, so defending himself, can be regarded in any real sense as impeaching or questioning the freedom of speech, debates or proceedings in Parliament as forbidden by Article 9; nor can the courts be fairly regarded as doing so if they permit a defendant to so defend himself. It would not be sought to visit any legal consequences on the Member, nor to examine his actions or motives except so far that examination might be rendered necessary by the Member's own action.[40]

Similar reasoning was adopted by White J[41] and Olsson J.[42] Chief Justice King made the point that, if the view argued for by the plaintiff were correct, the result would be remarkable:

> A Member of Parliament could sue for defamation in respect of criticism of his statements or conduct in the Parliament. The defendant would be precluded, however, from alleging and proving that what was said by way of criticism was true. This would amount to a gross distortion of the law of defamation in its application to such a situation ... If the defendant were precluded from proving the truth of what was alleged, the Member of Parliament would be enabled to recover damages, if no other defence applied,

---

[39] (1986) 5 NSWLR 18.
[40] (1990) 53 SASR 416 at 426.
[41] (1990) 53 SASR 416 at 436.
[42] (1990) 53 SASR 416 at 446.

for an imputation which was perfectly true. Moreover as the defence of fair comment would often be unavailable, as in the present case, because it would not be permissible to prove the factual foundation for the expression of opinion. The defence of qualified privilege might be seriously inhibited because the defendant would be prevented from answering an allegation of express malice by proving facts as known to him. If this is the true legal position, it is difficult to envisage how a court could apply the law of defamation in a rational way to an action by a Member of Parliament in respect of an imputation relating to his statements or conduct in the House, or could try such an action fairly or adjudicate upon it justly.[43]

The approach of the courts to this matter is, however, uncertain. Both *R v Murphy*[44] and *Wright and Advertiser Newspapers Limited v Lewis*[45] were criticized by the Privy Council, on appeal from a New Zealand decision, in *Prebble v Television New Zealand Ltd*.[46] This case also concerned defamation proceedings brought by a Member of Parliament against a media organization, this time in respect of a television programme. The plaintiff asserted that the programme carried a number of defamatory imputations, including an imputation that he conspired to sell state-owned assets on favourable terms in return for donations in his political party from business leaders. One defence relied on by the media organ-ization was justification. It sought to demonstrate the truth of what it had published by reference to statements and actions, some of which took place in Parliament. It was common ground that Article 9 of the *Bill of Rights* was in force in New Zealand.[47]

There were two types of allegations in the particulars of the defence which the Privy Council identified as having the potential to infringe parliamentary privilege. First, allegations that the plaintiff and other ministers made statements in the House which were misleading in that they suggested that the government did not intend to sell off state-owned assets when, in fact, the spokesperson was, it was alleged, conspiring to do so. The second type of allegation said to infringe parliamentary privilege was that the conspiracy was implemented by introducing and passing legislation in the House.[48] The New Zealand Court of Appeal upheld a lower court's decision, striking out those particulars of the defence which infringed parliamentary privilege.[49] Nonetheless, by a majority, the New Zealand Court of Appeal held that, in view of the inability of the defendant to deploy all the relevant evidence in support

---

[43] (1990) 53 SASR 416 at 421–422. See also at 436–437 per White J and 448 per Olsson J.
[44] (1986) 5 NSWLR 18.
[45] (1990) 53 SASR 416.
[46] [1995] 1 AC 321.
[47] [1995] 1 AC 321 at 332.
[48] [1995] 1 AC 321 at 330.
[49] *Television New Zealand v Prebble* [1993] 3 NZLR 513 at 520 per Cooke P, 534 per Richardson J, 536 per Casey J, 539–540 per Gault J, 545 per McKay J.

of the plea of justification, it would be unjust to allow the plaintiff to continue with his action; a stay of the plaintiff's action was ordered unless and until the parliamentary privilege was waived.[50] The case went on appeal to the Privy Council. The Privy Council's attitude to the staying of proceedings will be examined in section 3.2 below. At this point, the decision of the Privy Council regarding the scope of parliamentary privilege will be analysed.

As previously noted, in *Prebble v Television New Zealand Ltd* the Privy Council criticised both *R v Murphy*[51] and *Wright and Advertiser Newspapers Limited v Lewis*.[52] So far as the approach to Article 9 taken by Hunt J in *R v Murphy*[53] is concerned, the Privy Council's main criticism was that Hunt J based his analysis on a narrow construction of Article 9 derived from the fact that the object of Article 9 was to ensure that a member of Parliament could not be liable for what he or she said in Parliament. According to the Privy Council:

> This view discounts the basic concept underlying Article 9, *viz* the need to ensure so far as possible that a member of the legislature and witnesses before committees of the House can speak freely without fear that what they say will later be held against them in the courts.[54]

So far as *Wright and Advertiser Newspapers Ltd v Lewis*[55] is concerned, the Privy Council could not accept that the fact that the maker of the statement is the initiator of the court proceedings can affect the question whether Article 9 is infringed. It was said:

> The privilege protected by Article 9 is the privilege of Parliament itself. The actions of any individual Member of Parliament, even if he has an individual privilege of his own, cannot determine whether or not the privilege of Parliament is to apply.[56]

It is the Privy Council's attitude to *R v Murphy*[57] which reveals a major difference of approach regarding the scope of parliamentary privilege. It is, however, suggested that regardless of whether Hunt J is right that the object of Article 9 is to ensure that a Member of Parliament cannot be liable for what he or she said in Parliament, or the Privy Council is right that the aim is to ensure that members can speak freely without fear that

---

[50] [1993] 3 NZLR 513 at 520–522 per Cooke P, 534–535 per Richardson J, 536–537 per Casey J, 540 per Gault J. McKay J dissented in relation to this aspect of the decision (at 545–546).

[51] (1986) 5 NSWLR 18.

[52] (1990) 53 SASR 416.

[53] (1986) 5 NSWLR 18.

[54] *Prebble v Television New Zealand Ltd* [1995] 1 AC 321 at 334.

[55] (1990) 53 SASR 416.

[56] [1995] 1 AC 321 at 335.

[57] (1986) 5 NSWLR 18.

what they said will later be held against them, the test established by Hunt J in *R v Murphy*[58] is correct. That is, that parliamentary privilege operates to prevent the questioning of statements made in Parliament only where it can be said that the court proceedings seek to assert legal consequences against the maker of the statement for making that statement. It is only where this test is satisfied that it can be said that the Member would have any fear that what he or she has said will be held against the member.

There is a qualitative difference between, on the one hand, a case in which what was said in parliamentary proceedings is the subject of litigation and, on the other, a case in which a statement made in Parliament is put into evidence in proceedings which are directed at material which is not part of proceedings in Parliament. If a Member of Parliament thought that defamation proceedings could be brought against them in respect of what they said in Parliament, of course this might affect their willingness to speak freely in the House.

This should, however, be contrasted with the position where all that happens is that evidence of parliamentary proceedings is put into evidence in the course of defamation proceedings brought *by* the Member of Parliament. The decision to commence proceedings lies in the hands of the Member of Parliament. The Member of Parliament knows that no consequences will follow so far as he or she is concerned from anything said in the House unless he or she chooses to institute proceedings.

Indeed, the same could be said of those cases where a Member of Parliament reaffirms, outside the House, usually in a media interview, what he or she has said inside the House and someone sues the Member of Parliament in respect of what he or she said outside the House on the basis that the Member has adopted the statements made in the House.[59] Admitting evidence of what was said in the House in these circumstances could not be said to detract from the Member's capacity to speak freely in the House. Evidence of what was said in the House would be admitted, in this case, only where the Member of Parliament has taken the step of affirming what he or she said in the House, outside the House.

So far as the criticism of *Wright and Advertiser Newspapers Ltd v Lewis*[60] by the Privy Council in *Prebble v Television New Zealand Ltd* is concerned,[61] the suggestion that the actions of any individual Member of Parliament cannot determine whether or not the privilege of Parliament is to apply seems to be contrary to legislation which was subsequently enacted permitting a Member of the United Kingdom Parliament to waive parliamentary privilege. This legislation, which will be referred to in section

---

[58] (1986) 5 NSWLR 18.
[59] See, for example, *Beitzel v Crabb* [1992] 2 VR 121.
[60] (1990) 53 SASR 416.
[61] [1995] 1 AC 321 at 335.

3.3 below, assumes that the actions of an individual Member of Parliament can determine whether the privilege of Parliament is to apply, at least when the waiving of her or his privilege is permitted by legislation.

3.1 FEDERAL (AND NORTHERN TERRITORY) LEGISLATION

The Commonwealth Parliament reacted to Hunt J's decision in *R v Murphy*[62] by enacting the *Parliamentary Privileges Act* 1987 (Cth).[63] Section 16 of the Act declares what is the effect of Article 9 of the *Bill of Rights* in its application to the Commonwealth Parliament. Section 16(3) states:

> In proceedings in any court or tribunal, it is not lawful for evidence to be tendered or received, questions asked or statements, submissions or comments made, concerning proceedings in Parliament, by way of, or for the purpose of:
> (a) questioning or relying on the truth, motive, intention or good faith of anything forming part of those proceedings in Parliament;
> (b) otherwise questioning or establishing the credibility, motive, intention or good faith of any person; or
> (c) drawing, or inviting the drawing of, inferences or conclusions wholly or partly from anything forming part of those proceedings in Parliament.

The Northern Territory has enacted legislation in the same terms as s 16 of the federal Act.[64]

The validity and effect of this legislation was questioned in *Laurance v Katter*[65]. In this case, the plaintiff sued a Member of the Commonwealth Parliament in respect of statements made by the Member of Parliament in radio and television interviews which, it was alleged, adopted and reaffirmed statements made in Parliament by the Member imputing impropriety to the plaintiff. The three members of the Court of Appeal of the Supreme Court of Queensland adopted quite different approaches to the question whether s 16 of the *Parliamentary Privileges Act* 1987 (Cth) operated so that the plaintiff's action must fail. Pincus JA held that s 16(3) was incompatible with the implied freedom of political communication.[66] Following the High Court's decision in *R v Richards; Ex part Fitzpatrick and Browne*,[67] Fitzpatrick P held that s 16 could not be invalidated or read down to accommodate the implied freedom of political

---

[62] (1986) 5 NSWLR 18.

[63] The background is outlined in *Amann Aviation Pty Ltd v Commonwealth of Australia* (1988) 81 ALR 710 at 715–717. The Second Reading Speech makes it clear that the purpose of the legislation is to avoid the consequences of Hunt J's approach in *R v Murphy* (1986) 5 NSWLR 18; see Commonweath, Senate, *Parliamentary Debates* (Hansard), 7 October 1986 at 892–895.

[64] *Legislative Assembly (Powers and Privileges) Act* 1992 (NT), s 6.

[65] (1996) 141 ALR 447.

[66] (1996) 141 ALR 447 at 486. The implied freedom of political communication, and the cases which established at, are outlined in Walker, "*Lange v ABC*: the High Court rethinks the 'constitutionalisation' of defamation law" (1998) 6 *Torts Law Journal* 9.

[67] (1955) 92 CLR 157.

communication.[68] Davies JA read down s 16(3); in his view, the section was enacted merely to make it clear that parliamentary privilege applies not only where a member or witness is sued but also where evidence is sought to be tendered; in both cases, the privilege applies only where the parliamentary proceedings would be impeached or questioned.[69] Davies JA then held that this was not the case in these proceedings.[70]

The High Court granted special leave to appeal from the decision of the Queensland Court of Appeal, but the case was settled before the appeal was heard. It is possible that an appeal to the High Court in *O'Chee v Rowley*,[71] which is mentioned in section 2.1 above, may resolve one of the questions which arise from *Laurance v Katter*;[72] that is, are laws dealing with parliamentary privilege amenable to challenge on the ground that they are inconsistent with the implied freedom of political communication? Courts have been reluctant to come into conflict with Houses of Parliament in relation to matters relating directly to the privileges of the Houses and it is not unlikely that the High Court will adopt an approach similar to that of Fitzgerald P in the Court of Appeal of the Supreme Court of Queensland.

3.2 THE "STAYING" OF PROCEEDINGS

When Article 9 is relied on by a plaintiff to preclude a defendant from putting into evidence what was said in Parliament, the court may take the view that the inability of the defendant to deploy all the relevant evidence so prejudices the defence that the proceedings should be stayed. As explained in section 3 above, in the *Prebble* case, the New Zealand Court of Appeal had stayed the plaintiff's action unless and until the privilege was effectively waived by the House and the individual member concerned. On appeal to the Privy Council, the stay was lifted; it was made clear that a stay could be granted only in extreme circumstances, such as where the whole subject matter of the allegedly defamatory material relates to the plaintiffs conduct in the House so that the effect of parliamentary privilege is to exclude virtually all the evidence necessary to rely on the defence of justification.[73] For this reason, the Privy Council appears to have been of the view that *Wright and Advertiser Newspapers Limited v Lewis* was a case in which a stay should have been ordered,[74] but the New Zealand case did not fall into this category as much of the material relied on by the defendant to make out the defence of justification related to action outside the House.[75]

---

[68] *Laurance v Katter* (1996) 141 ALR 447 at 451–453.

[69] (1996) 141 ALR 447 at 489–490.

[70] (1996) 141 ALR 447 at 490.

[71] (1997) 150 ALR 199.

[72] (1996) 141 ALR 447.

[73] *Prebble v Television New Zealand Ltd* [1995] 1 AC 321 at 337–339.

[74] [1995] 1 AC 321 at 338.

[75] [1995] 1 AC 321 at 338.

In *Allason v Haines*[76] a defamation action was, in fact, stayed. In 1991 the plaintiff, a Member of Parliament, had tabled a motion naming a journalist who he alleged had betrayed to Israeli authorities an Israeli who had divulged Israeli atomic secrets. The journalist's paper published an article claiming that the plaintiff had hidden behind parliamentary privilege and behaved in a cowardly and dishonourable way. The plaintiff brought a defamation action against the newspaper which was settled.

In 1994 the plaintiff tabled a motion about Members of Parliament who were "agents of influence" of the KGB, but did not name the Members concerned. The defendants published an article commenting on the fact that the plaintiff had been banned from naming the Members of the House of Commons even though he had not been banned "from making similarly unproven allegations against a journalist in a Commons motion in 1991". The plaintiff brought an action for defamation in respect of this publication. Owen J held that to enforce parliamentary privilege in this case but to refuse a stay of proceedings would be unjust to the defendants as it would deprive the defendants of what was probably their only defence "while allowing the plaintiff to continue on an unsatisfactory and unfair basis". Defamation proceedings were also stayed in similar circumstances in another English case, *Hamilton v Guardian Newspapers* because the media organization's defence rested largely on statements made by the plaintiff in the House of Commons.[77]

While a stay would protect the media organization from defamation proceedings in cases of this kind, this outcome is problematic: whether what has been published was defamatory and, if so, whether a defence operates, is not resolved and there is no public airing of the relevant issues.

3.3 WAIVING PARLIAMENTARY PRIVILEGE

It would seem that, in the absence of legislation authorizing it, the parliamentary privilege of freedom of speech cannot be waived by an individual Member of Parliament and perhaps not even by a House of Parliament.[78] Following the staying of the proceedings in *Allason v Haines*[79] and *Hamilton v Guardian Newspapers*,[80] s 13 of the *Defamation Act* 1996 (UK) was enacted.[81] This provides that, where the conduct of a person in, or in relation to, proceedings in Parliament is in issue in defamation

---

[76] [1995] TLR 438.
[77] (1995) 139 Sol Jo 772. See also Sharland and Loveland, "The Defamation Act 1996 and Political Libels" [1997] *Public Law* 112.
[78] *Prebble v Television New Zealand Ltd* [1995] 1 AC 321 at 335 (on the common law); *Hamsher v Swift* (1992) 33 FCR 545 at 564 (on s 16 of the *Parliamentary Privileges Act* 1987 (Cth)); see also, Barlin (ed.), *House of Representatives Practice*, 3rd edn., (1997) at 688; Limon and McKay (eds.), *Erskine May's Treatise on The Law, Privileges, Proceedings and Usage of Parliament*, 22nd edn., (1997) at 66–67, 171–172.
[79] [1995] TLR 438.
[80] (1995) 139 Sol Jo 772.

proceedings, he or she may waive the protection of parliamentary privilege. The waiver does not affect the protection of parliamentary privilege in relation to any other Member of Parliament who has not waived it. Although this will, in practice, make a difference only in those cases where the Member of Parliament takes the view that he or she is likely to succeed in defamation proceedings instituted by the Member of Parliament, it does not mean that in those cases where the Member does waive his or her privilege, the courts will be able to address the real issues which should arise in defamation actions rather than being concerned with whether there is a breach of parliamentary privilege. Nonetheless, it would be better if the need for a waiver did not arise. It would be better if the courts defined parliamentary privilege in such a way that it was not necessary to stay proceedings. It would be better if the courts defined the limits of parliamentary privilege in the way that they have in *R v Murphy*[82] and *Wright and Advertiser Newspapers Limited v Lewis*[83] so that the need to stay proceedings did not arise.

---

[81] It might be argued that s 13 of the United Kingdom *Defamation Act* 1996 is part of the law in Queensland and Western Australia. This is because the Queensland and Western Australian legislation adopts the powers and privileges of the House of Commons and its Members but does not refer to those powers and privileges as at a certain date but, instead, to those exercisable by the House of Commons and its Members "for the time being" (*Constitution Act* 1867 (Qld.), s 40A, *Parliamentary Privileges Act* 1891 (WA), s 1)—see Walker, *Contempt of Parliament and the Media*, Adelaide Law Review Research Paper No. 4 (1984) at 25 (Queensland), 29–30 (Western Australia).

[82] (1986) 5 NSWLR 18.

[83] (1990) 53 SASR 416.

PANEL DISCUSSION

The Honourable Justice Tony Fitzgerald AO[1],
Associate Professor Wendy Bacon[2], Julie Eisenberg[3],
Andrew Kenyon[4] and Judith Walker[5]

JUSTICE FITZGERALD:

I will try briefly to provide a broad context for this discussion. There seem to be two overlapping major issues when considering the law and freedom of the media. One is the balancing of competing public interests, freedom of communication, fair trial and privacy. For example, that of the victim and the accused in criminal proceedings. The other is the relationship between media power and privilege on the one hand, and media responsibility on the other. How much can be left to self regulation and at what point must the law interfere?

In that broad context, the issues which I understand the speakers to have raised, and upon which I hope the panellists will comment, include the law of contempt's restrictions on reporting of court proceedings, suppression orders, an obligation to disclose a confidential source and, of course, publications which injure reputation.

JULIE EISENBERG:

I would like to pick up on a point that Richard Ackland made right at the very beginning, which is a really good illustration about a case involving media content law. I think it has implications that trickle down to some of the issues between the media and the courts. That is the *Chakrovarti* case. I am just going to elaborate a little further beyond what Richard said.

I sometimes have difficulties in explaining to working journalists some of the technicalities of defamation law. The *Chakravarti* case is a classic example of where I give them the extract from the Royal Commission and I give them the article and we sit down and actually try and work out firstly, where those defamatory meanings came from, and secondly, why it wasn't a fair report.

At least in the case of one of the two articles that was sued over, all the quotes that the journalists used were accurate. The problem came

[1] AC, Judge of Appeal, New South Wales Court of Appeal; formerly President of the Queensland Court of Appeal; Session 2 Panel Chair.
[2] Associate Professor of Journalism, University of Technology, Sydney.
[3] Media Lawyer, Communications Law Centre.
[4] Visiting Fellow, University of Melbourne.
[5] General Manager, ABC Legal and Copyright Department.

not from the accuracy in the reporting but in the juxtaposition, as Richard Ackland pointed out.

One of the issues in that case was the fact that the article was dealing with a transcript which covered statements made about four executives of the State Bank of South Australia subsidiary, which then moved on into a discussion about two of the executives. Mr Chakravarti was one of the people who accidentally got caught up in the allegations made about two other executives.

It was a very complicated case. It was messy. Even if you read the article, it is not entirely clear what happened in the Royal Commission and obviously the journalists did their best to try and make it clear for the readers.

What it illustrated were really two problems. One is the difficulty for the media in going into a court and summarizing something very complex that has happened during a very long day, or during weeks of evidence, and putting it into a digestible form. That is the first part of the problem. The second part of it is then having an understanding of what actually happened in the courts.

Just to illustrate this, one of the tests for whether or not something is regarded as a fair report, for the purposes of defamation law, is whether or not it gives the same impression to readers that they would have got had they been sitting in court that day.

Now having looked at the article in the *Chakravarti* case, I'm sure there were many lay people sitting in court that day who may have been just as confused when the evidence switched from talking about four executives to talking about two executives. It illustrates, I suppose, a fundamental problem of interface between the courts and the media. Obviously the courts are there to do justice and the processes are there to suit the parties in the particular case and not to suit the media. But at the same time, they present considerable difficulties for the media, even in understanding what barristers are talking about or what the judges are saying. I'm not alone in complaining about this.

I recall a speech that Justice Kirby made a couple of years ago when he was talking about the introduction of cameras into the courtroom. One of the things he complained of was how some of it would make really bad television because you have mumbling barristers and he actually named two exceptions to the mumbling barristers. I thought by doing that, he probably defamed the rest of the class of barristers in Australia. But it does illustrate a fundamental problem and one which is not easy to resolve.

That judgment also illustrated another difficulty which again is problematic and I know the courts are trying to address. The High Court judgment in *Chakravarti* was probably about 60 or 70 pages long. There were five judges. They gave three judgments and even as a trained lawyer, I had some difficulty trying to work out which ones were agreeing on which particular points, because that decision covered eight or ten points of considerable legal significance. For journalists, trying with deadlines to get across the essence of that judgment to the public in a way which is comprehensible, it raises a lot of issues.

So the *Chakravarti* case I see as an illustration, not only of the difficulty in giving guidelines to the media about what they can and can't report, but also the fundamental difficulties in the way that courts are run and their user-friendliness, not only to journalists but also to members of the public. At the end of the day, the media is an interface between the courts and the public who can't turn up and sit in court every day. I think that case highlighted those.

ANDREW KENYON:

To start off with Richard Ackland and again *Chakravarti*, a different area of the case that has created uncertainty is in connection with pleading. If the defendant says: "what I published doesn't mean what you have said to the plaintiff, it means something else and I have a defence". It is now unclear at what point of the litigation process the defendant will be able to or have to say that.

State or territory courts are just now beginning to deliver judgments following *Chakravarti* and there is a divergence in what the judges are saying should now happen. There were already divergences in the Australian states and this hasn't helped.

I'm glad the *Pantsdown* decision was mentioned. I thought it was a very interesting decision. It's very short. It deals with what is undoubtedly extremely offensive material to the plaintiff. I was somewhat surprised that the Court was so short but enough of the meanings arose for the jury to find it defamatory in the context of something that was intended to be satirical comment. The judgment itself doesn't explore those issues at great length. It may be that other commentary will look into that more.

One of the themes that David Anderson raised is something that has been left inarticulated so far about what the media's role is. They are the "fourth estate"—how does the law conceive of that and how should it?

David Anderson mentioned that perhaps it is better to think judges aren't influenced by the media in America. Judges may play to the media. Perhaps it is possible that in those instances, the judicial office is not being used in the best possible way. The media has certain privileges under law but also does not always use them in the best possible way. I think there is unexplored territory for legal writers and courts to think about how the media can be encouraged to use its privileges better and if it should get the benefit of the doubt.

A very simple example: witnesses or people involved in a court case have absolute privilege for what they say. It is understood as being necessary in the interests of justice that they can speak in court and give their evidence. Judges have long noted that this privilege is given with the knowledge that it could be abused. People could get up and say malicious falsehoods but the privilege is seen as necessary within our constitutional system. It is much easier to base that privilege and the need for it than it would be to give any vaguely comparable privilege to the media.

The media invokes its role as the fourth estate, its role as a useful messenger to the public, but it is also a commercial entity. The commercial influence on media content is something that hasn't been explored much yet. Both the combination of the role of the editor-in-chief and the publisher in certain newspaper entities needs to be raised, and the way that may change how the media is understood internally, how journalists think of their role and perhaps how the court should think of it.

JUDITH WALKER:

One instance where the media is going to find it very hard is where it is broadcasting interviews with other people, as to whether they are reliably reported. A journalist may well not have any belief as to the truth or otherwise of what has been said, and overall it might be quite a balanced report, but it puts in doubt very much whether we can rely on *Lange*. That is just one instance of its difficulty in application.

Regarding Pauline Pantsdown, the ABC is seeking special leave to appeal the decision. We may well not get special leave and even if we do, we may not get the decision we want. However, we think it is important to go ahead and try and get special leave at least.

In relation to *sub judice* contempt, you are undoubtedly aware that the New South Wales Law Reform Commission is undertaking a review. The ABC will provide submissions to that review but there are three issues I would like to see the Law Reform Commission look at in particular. That is, consideration being given to abolishing *sub judice* contempt in civil cases where there is no jury; preventing private individuals bringing proceedings for contempt of court, which they can do at this stage in New South Wales. In fact, the ABC was prosecuted by the Civil Aviation Authority a couple of years back for publication on "Background Briefing". We were successful and were not convicted of contempt. The other issue which is always alive is the time at which proceedings are said to be pending. Particularly in situations like extraditions, arrests and questioning by the police. I find it is much easier to give pre-publication advice in relation to defamation than it is in relation to contempt.

In relation to what Professor Walker was saying about the Parliaments and the courts, there is another issue too, which is not related but does arise. If a Member of Parliament during a court case makes statements in the Parliament that could be in contempt of those proceedings and the media reports those statements, is the media liable? I think it probably could be prosecuted for contempt whereas the Member would be immune from such proceedings.

They are just some brief issues. Some of you may recall the ABC, a few years ago, broadcasted a programme called "Joh's Jury". We would not be able to make that program in Queensland now because of the restrictions that have been imposed in Queensland on approaching jurors. Queensland has probably the most restrictive provisions in Australia. I think it was a good programme and it would be a shame, as is the case now, that it could not be made again.

WENDY BACON:

I want to say one thing about judges wanting the public to have better access to the courts. While I think it is admirable and I agree with the sentiment, the best people to talk to in this respect are really the public relations and communication management, a huge growth industry. As journalists, while reporting fairly and accurately (whatever exactly we mean by that), in the end we have a critical role and one that must include criticism of the courts.

I saw there could be a career in critical reporting on the High Court when, as a young student journalist, I found myself in the courts on censorship charges and went to a High Court judgment called *Crowe v Graham*. I found that, when it came to judging the "modesty of the average person", the High Court felt it was best to leave that question not to evidence, but to judges and magistrates. I realized at that moment there were grave problems in legal thinking and these needed to be explained to the public.

I thoroughly endorse what Chris Merritt said about the need for a judicial commission. Underlying a lot of what journalists are saying is a grave concern about our ability to report, to do our jobs properly, in the current economic situation of the media. Adding to this concern about economic constraints is concern about the threatening and unsympathetic judicial attitudes displayed towards the media by Australian courts.

Another notion that we need to look at is what we mean by "freedom of the media". Both as journalists and lawyers, this idea of freedom of expression is one that goes to the heart of the way we think, but rarely do we unpick it and look at the contradictions within it. There is a lot of fine political philosophy which does this. I just refer to two people. Professor Schauer of Harvard University has come to Australia and examined some of the contradictions underlying the development of the notion of freedom of expression. Also Professor John Keane has traced back different strands of thinking around freedom of expression and the contradiction in linking "freedom of expression" with the notion of a "marketplace of ideas".

For me, freedom of the media is connected with giving people access to a voice, and I think this goes to the heart of journalism. We all agree that the media is obviously an important part of modern democracy. All citizens need to feel that they have a voice, that they are able to speak. This is not the situation in which we find ourselves. Freedom of the media is also connected with freedom of access to information and access to the courts.

That is why if we actually look at the ways in which our freedoms are constrained, it is important to analyze particular decisions. Our High Court has had muddled thinking about the meaning of freedom of expression. But if we don't have a framework for our media which can provide a public sphere for freedom of communication, then there is a disjuncture between the freedoms we like to think we have and what in practice we have. I think journalists and the public are confronting these contradictions daily.

How we sort our way through the economic constraints and the commercial imperatives that are overwhelming our ability to report is a very tricky question. Somewhere, I think, in the meeting of law and politics and journalism we have to resolve those questions more clearly as a society. I think we need to go back and unpick some of these notions we throw around, for example "public interest". What do we mean by that in relation to freedom of expression?

JUSTICE FITZGERALD:

There is a very troubling mood swing against the judiciary and I'm going to call on Mr Ackland to defend the judges. Is there anyone in the audience who wants to make a comment at this stage?

SPEAKER:

I feel that we need here not only "Media Watch", which Richard Ackland presents on the ABC, but what we need is a "Court Watch". There used to be some journalists in Australia, in New South Wales, *The Sydney Morning Herald*, who actually had a role in mentioning the courts and felt that they were doing their job properly. I was grateful to John Slee. He worked for *The Sydney Morning Herald* and he was probably the right hand to newspapers and he was very critical of the courts. Unfortunately, Mr Slee was sued twice for defamation and I think that pushed him out of the market. Since he's gone, there is very little going on here now. Are journalists actually looking into this area, to see that the judges are doing their job properly? After all, justice not only has to be done, it has also to be seen to be done.

I know in Sweden they have a person whose role is actually looking at the courts to see that they do their job properly. He actually sits in court to watch what is going on and to make sure the judges are acting properly in light of the money the government puts into the courts.

JUSTICE FITZGERALD:

I think the general trend of your observations is probably reflected in a suggestion that one of the other speakers made this morning about a federal equivalent to the New South Wales Judicial Commission. But that may not be quite as effective as having Mr Ackland conduct "Court Watch".

I think what we are doing is very useful at the moment but there does seem to be one thing missing. This isn't just an attempt to deflect attention away from criticism of the judiciary. I'm really almost out of the judiciary so there is no personal interest in it but one of the things I don't think anybody has really discussed yet, and perhaps Andrew was going to do it when I cut him off, is that given that there is probably an enormous commitment to freedom of speech to the maximum permissible extent, and I think that is a view which would be shared surprisingly to some of you perhaps by the judges as well as the journalists, at what if any point should there be control by the law? How can we, if at all, curtail freedom of speech?

It is not much good just telling us of the imperfections in the present system unless someone has some positive suggestions as to what the new controls ought to be.

MICHAEL CHESTERMAN:

In the previous cases dealing with the implied freedom, the issue of compatibility of the constitutional freedom with contempt law has been mentioned. But I'm afraid that the general tenor of those comments has been to say that contempt laws should be seen as certainly surviving the implied freedom, although in the *CAA* case, Justice Kirby in the NSW Court of Appeal, as he then was, said the implied freedom certainly must impel the courts to scrutinize very carefully any excesses with the contempt law. So, I think the answer has to be that the core of the thing will remain and the *Lange* case probably still remains as providing an important incentive to judges at all levels to ask, when they apply the contempt law: "Is this repression going further than is necessary to protect the fair administration of justice?"

SALLY WALKER:

I agree with everything that Michael said but I will just add a proviso that I think the area of contempt law that is wrong, under *Lange,* is contempt by scandal. I have a feeling that is the area that is much more likely to be inconsistent with implied freedom. But I don't think an argument about *sub judice* contempt would get up.

JUSTICE FITZGERALD:

Julie, earlier you had a question that you wanted to ask one of the speakers. Do you want to pursue that?

JULIE EISENBERG:

It was really just to get a view from other members of the panel on the implications of *Chakravarti*, what they thought of them? Whether they thought there were any severe practical problems that arose from it and what really went from there?

WENDY BACON:

I don't want to cut across what anyone else wants to say but I think it is a very worrying decision. If I look back to when I was reporting in the 1980s I faced a contempt of court charge as a result of writing an article called "Roger Rogerson and the Barbecue Set". That was really a compilation of different material that we had gone out and gathered from different privileged reports and put together. As Michael McHugh who was on the Court then said, it was superficially one of the most defamatory articles he had seen but much of it was covered by parliamentary privilege, as we saw it then.

Now in that situation, what we faced was a cover-up of a police investigation. Once the media was on to it, the tactic was to get Roger Rogerson before the courts. Then discussion would be limited. It didn't turn out to be that long but then more cases were *sub judice*.

I happen to agree with the contempt of court protection of the right to a fair trial. In that case we were certainly testing the limits, but we were relying on "fair and accurate reporting" of the courts and parliamentary provision. I must admit that occasionally since then I have wondered if it was a bit like it is with satire and defamation. That is, that there is a principle of sort established by practice, but perhaps it would be very rocky if it were tested in the courts.

SPEAKER:

I would like to ask Michael Chesterman a question. Today at this forum we are represented by the ABC, *The Sydney Morning Herald*, *The Australian Financial Review*, and *The Australian*. I was wondering how many of your 21 cases actually involved media who aren't represented today, i.e. the commercial broadcasters in radio and television, in particular the popular newspapers, and whether they may account for the majority of contempt cases? On the other hand, whether perhaps the quality media who are represented here today may account for the majority of defamation cases?

MICHAEL CHESTERMAN:

I wouldn't agree in terms of the contempt cases actually, although as you asked, I quickly scrolled my eyes down the list of the titles. John Fairfax features fairly regularly. Nationwide News features in a couple of cases I had up on the screen. The television commercial broadcaster in issue was Channel 10 in the most recent case I have referred to. 2UE, as we know, has been there.

Then some of the most serious and significant ones like David Syme back in Victoria in 1982 is by *The Age*. I don't think you can generalize in terms of saying "it is the commercial media who get contempt trouble and are responsible" or, if you like, "the national broadcasters who don't".

RICHARD ACKLAND:

Could I just ask Michael Chesterman a question, what does he think of the New South Wales Attorney-General's decision not to prosecutor Alan Jones for contempt? This arose in the Neddy Smith trial, where Jones said, in the middle of Mr Smith's evidence, that Mr Smith was not to be believed, to an audience that Jones seemed to appeal to, mostly in New South Wales. Do you see this as an encouraging breakthrough or is it more to do with the fact that there is a New South Wales election coming up and Mr Carr doesn't want to lose Mr Jones?

MICHAEL CHESTERMAN:

It all depends on your point of view, Richard. I thought it was certainly well within the boundaries of the contempt for him to be prosecuted. He was attacking the credibility of the accused while the trial was running. Put it this way, if he had been prosecuted, I wouldn't have been surprised.

SPEAKER:

I put a question to Michael, David, Sally and Richard, whoever wants to answer it. A topic that has come up, really only briefly today, in a different context, is the internet. I was at a conference earlier this week run by the ACCC where there were hundreds of people and the buzz word and the graphics that were put up on overhead projectors showed this absolutely exponential increase in the use of the internet. Now a lot of that was in commerce but I think it has to inevitably follow that a lot of that will be media as well and people will increasingly turn to other sources for their media. Obviously that is going to have a big impact, not only on the ability of people to enforce defamation laws where the person who is defaming them is off in Tonga or Ghana or wherever, but also in the area of contempt. I just wanted to get maybe Michael's thoughts and in view of the Starr investigation, David's thoughts on it.

MICHAEL CHESTERMAN:

I think there is a very real issue for contempt law. There is some interesting work being done in terms of research at the University of Leeds by a fellow called Clive Walker. Of course he has also taken on board the problem that they have more there than here of material simply coming over from Europe through mainstream television which you can't really block out from an English audience. The geographical proximity makes it cheaper.

I think in the longer term there will have to be a look at the extent to which material coming out through the internet really does permeate potential jurors and if the stage is reached where you have to feel whatever you do in terms of mainstream prohibitions against our media, you are not going to prevent the spread of that material. We may have to rethink how we deal with this whole situation.

JUSTICE FITZGERALD:

Professor Anderson, this goes back I think to your earlier theory that material gets into the public arena no matter what attempts are made to prevent that. Would you like to add something?

DAVID ANDERSON:

Yes, I would. I think this is part of a much, much bigger issue and maybe soon to be the biggest issue of all and that is cross-media competition. If you just take the subject of a fair trial, for example. I think in the past the principal protection against the effects of prejudicial publicity have been the restraint and good sense of the mainstream media in many different ways. Judges can often get the media to agree to different particular restrictions. There have been voluntary guidelines adopted that were at one time widely followed throughout the United States. Guidelines agreed upon by the media and the judiciary about how to handle these problems.

Those are all dead in the United States. The main reason they are dead is because of the effects of cross-media competition of which the internet is just a part. But there are many others and one of the problems is that when you have a gathering like this, the people who are going to be the problem aren't in this room. They are the people out there with the websites; they are the people doing the satirical magazines; they are the people doing the radio talkback shows. Those are the real sources of the problem, at least in the future.

In the past, we have had what we always call "the press". We continued to call it "the press" even after it included broadcasting. I think it is more the notion that you all describe as the "fourth estate" which is a body that has some shared values and some common interests. That has evolved into the media. The media has no shared values and no common interests. At least if you include in the media everybody who needs to be included.

Now if you think about just a few of the ways in which this affects the issues we have been talking about. When the Special Prosecutor's report was delivered to the House Judiciary Committee and then made public by that Committee, the network news organizations in the United States, the executives and the producers sat down and said, well, we're not going to use this material. It's not the kind of stuff we can use on a network newscast and so on and that lasted about 30 seconds. They then realised that wait a minute, 30 minutes from now our own network's magazine show is going to come on and they are going to use all this stuff. So what the hell are we talking about suppressing it for? We can't. The decision is taken out of our hands effectively.

Another example is early in the events when these internet websites began appearing with uncorroborated rumours and so on. That was their draw card, that they would publish any rumour that came along. Well, first the mainstream media ignored them. Then pretty soon there got to be so much talk about this and so much popularity of these things that the mainstream media then began reporting that the internet was reporting these unconfirmed rumours. Pretty soon they began reporting these things without even that veneer. The standards of that aspect of the media just take over. It is the lowest form of common denominator. We now have around 30 magazine shows on television in the United States, ranging from Oprah Winfrey to Jerry Springer. Believe me, there are no restraints. Self restraint is not a phrase in their vocabulary. As we think about these problems, it is one thing to think about what would we do, those of us in this community in this room, but I'm afraid we are not going to have control over it.

JUSTICE FITZGERALD:

Anyone wish to comment?

SPEAKER:

I think it's a little disappointing that in some ways we started out talking about how the courts could communicate more effectively with the public and we are now talking about how much we are going to stop communication so that we avoid contempt, so that we avoid defamation, et cetera.

I thought the question about the internet may lead us back to a remark made by Alan Rose this morning about the new media. Courts have websites too. The High Court of Australia publishes its judgments on the web very speedily. Courts use CD-Roms and other forms of electronic record of evidence which make the evidence extremely accessible within the courtroom and to the lawyers involved. All of these channels of communication seem to me to open up a new dimension for the courts which perhaps might take them back to those days that we all look at with misty and nostalgic eyes, when the community could come through the door of the courtroom and understand what was going on and see justice being done. Surely this should be something of our aim in terms of talking about the courts and the media.

How can the courts communicate? I don't like to think of it just as getting the public relations officer in to put the right spin on it. I think some of the public relations officers do that more than others and I think the Federal Court has been a wonderful example of how that has not been done but it has in fact got the message across very directly.

So how can the courts communicate directly, as they used to when people could walk in the door of the court, so that people can understand what is going on and not be continually trying to work out how they can block media giving the wrong impression or fouling up the case?

MICHAEL CHESTERMAN:

We have a very active website. The judge can go on the web virtually instantly and he could browse through it and find a fair bit about the court. Improving it will make it a lot better but it is frequently accessed. When there is a high interest case, there are an enormous number of accesses. Our latest project actually is to develop a quiz for school children on the website.

JUSTICE FITZGERALD:

I thought you were going to say for judges.

MICHAEL CHESTERMAN:

That will be interactive and you can get pictures of the courts, pictures of the judges. Australia actually was one of the leaders. There were two models. Australian courts through AUSTLII (the Australian Legal Information Institute) were effectively the leaders in getting on to the web and you will find judgments.

JUSTICE FITZGERALD:

My sense is there is a much greater consensus about the desirability of interaction between courts and the media in the provision of information about the workings of the courts, and the cases that come before the courts, than there is about any controls there ought to be upon the media's behaviour in what is reported. That is the hard bit. I don't really think we are grappling with it. I think we are tending to go back to the motherhood issues just a little bit. Motherhood is important.

Do we accept Professor Anderson's position? It may be a desirability position. Because it can't be prevented, we should forget all about these problems and make it open slather.

DAVID ANDERSON:

I was attempting to show you the horrible side of it.

JUSTICE FITZGERALD:

I didn't mean you were advocating it but I thought you were saying it was upon us, or would be soon upon us. Are you suggesting we should do something about it or should we lie back and enjoy it?

DAVID ANDERSON:

You can decide for yourselves how much you enjoy it. I guess my point would be you are much better equipped to deal with the problem here because you have direct means of restraint. If you are attempting to rely, as we do, largely on these indirect means of restraint, it is never going to work within an area of intense cross-media competition.

ANDREW KENYON:

I think most of the things I was going to raise have been raised by Professor Anderson and another. Let me say briefly about the points Judith Walker raised and then some of the speakers commented on which is the uncertainty of contempt law and the difficulty of giving advice.

Fairly extensive research in Britain has looked at how defamation law affects the media, print, national, local, radio, television, et cetera. One of the interesting findings from that was that in terms of national newspapers certainly, many people involved volunteered the fact that contempt was a bigger concern to them than defamation.

I support your comments and in terms of the defamation research, we also had a query relating to maybe investigative journalism or popular press, I think more defamation suits in certain areas. I don't think that research in Britain necessarily found strong trends except one that occurs to me and that was the Sunday papers in Britain. They had a strong tradition of investigative journalism, and had a much higher issue of complaint and writs than the dailies. A much higher rate and in fact a higher number overall, even though there are six times the dailies nationally printed for each weekly. I think that is all I need to add.

JUSTICE FITZGERALD:

Any of our speakers have something they wish to add? Mr Ackland?

RICHARD ACKLAND:

Might I just say this, at a practical level, and this is where I think websites can play a real part because all journalists are cruising these sites now constantly, but this is what arose in the *Erskine* case which of course ended up in a terribly expensive verdict against *The Herald*. A journalist going down in the lift of the court is handed an affidavit by the person who swore the affidavit file. He thinks "oh, that's a court document, that's fine". Off we go and stick it in the paper.

The lawyers at the newspaper can't literally check everything. It just seemed a reasonable sort of assumption for a lay journalist to make— "here is something from the court, therefore it is protected". Journalists don't really know all the time what is off limits, whether you can report a Statement of Claim or not. No one is really sure about that half the time, as far as I'm aware.

The jury is out of the room. There is all sorts of vagueness surrounding the stuff journalistically and it can lead to enormous trouble. In a practical way I think courts can actually do quite a bit about educating on this sort of thing. The media lawyers of the main publishers run courses and Julie runs courses and they are all terrifically beneficial, but I think in a whole lot of very obscure little areas—court rules and things like this—are just a minefield for journalists in what can be reported. Not even the lawyers know about them necessarily, or if they do, they have conflicting advice about them. It is just something that could go up on the website, you know, a little sort of education department.

SPEAKER:

Picking up that point, the one consistent message I keep getting from journalists' criticism is the idea that it is insular, it is clubby between the judges and the Bar Table. The barristers and the judges know the documents they have approved because they have read them, but the journos sitting nearby do not have a clue because they have not seen any documents. It does make it awfully difficult for journalists.

WENDY BACON:

I would just like to say one thing about going even further on the internet. One of the difficult things for reporters can be just getting access to court transcripts. My impression is that since transcripts are electronic, it is more difficult. Now, I think I have seen one court put up some transcript, but I think it would be very helpful to have as many electronic transcripts up on the internet—after all, they are part of the public record. Also, why not some exhibits and affidavits and other things?

This would really enable journalists to do thorough overviews of court cases, and to go back into the evidence, which you really need to do in order to write a summary of the case. To pick up on a point of Barry Hart's, journalism also has a real function in scrutinizing miscarriages of justice. How many of our miscarriages of justice would have been investigated if it had not been for the media playing a very proactive role?

ALAN ROSE:

That was the point I was trying to make this morning. The technology is there now. The difficult part of it was ever getting enough to get access to it. That is now no longer a problem. The electronic brain can sort all of this, all of those hand-up briefs, all of those outlines of arguments.

JUSTICE FITZGERALD:

Would any other panel member like to make a comment?

MICHAEL CHESTERMAN:

I just wanted to make the comment that we are a long way at the moment from publishing electronic transcripts of District Court proceedings. It is still going into a tape recorder and being transcribed as and when necessary, but not otherwise. There is a big court resources issue. I quite agree with the theory of what you are saying, that once the document has got into a court proceeding, admitted into evidence, forming part of the proceeding as much as what is said verbally then, of course, it should be open for reporting, but we have a little way to before we can produce an electronic system which enables access to this information.

ACCESS TO THE COURTS AND ITS IMPLICATIONS

The Honourable Justice Bernard Teague

Justice of the Supreme Court of Victoria

It's time the electronic media engaged more with the courts about increasing its access to the courts. It's time the courts engaged more with the electronic media. It would be easier if the print media were to be left out of that engaging.

I have spent most of this year presiding over trials of accuseds charged with murder. Here, two points of relevance have been brought home to me in that time. The first is that at present, the electronic media requests are easy to say no to. The second is that, while the courts are using the new technologies, they are shunning the media that uses the new technologies. During the year I have made various orders affecting the media. I have also delivered the occasional warning. At one time, I even made an order denying the public access to my court. That was after a telephoned death threat, and I did except the press. I have made at least one suppression order limiting what the media can print or put to air. I have warned persons, whose actions might have prejudiced a fair trial, of the possibility that they might be dealt with for contempt of court.

During most of the year, I have had two video cameras in my courtroom. It is state of the art technology. The cameras were in use yesterday to enable evidence to be taken in Melbourne from a doctor in Canberra. There was no possibility that what was recorded would be broadcast.

During the year, I have had a number of requests from court reporters put to me in my chambers. I have had no requests to permit the use of a video camera. The reporters are aware that the answer would have to be "no". Tape recorders are a bit different. Some years ago, I approved the use of tape recorders when I am handing down a sentence. However, I only allow such use by reporters who undertake not to broadcast the tape. I have had requests for the use of a tape recorder with part of the tape being broadcast. The answer to date has been "no". I have also had requests to make myself available for interview. The answer to date has been 'no'. Whenever I am asked to clarify orders affecting the media in court, I do so.

Generally, my polite declining of requests made to me in chambers is done through my associate or the Courts' Information Officer. No reporter has yet asked that I treat a request as more than a polite request. That is, as an application to be dealt with in open court. I assume that this position is the same with other judges. I am suggesting today that it might be time for that kind of move to be made. I would much prefer that it be made in some other judge's court.

Such an application would have to be taken more seriously if the right preparation were taken. If the right kind of collective action were to be taken, there are potentially major gains for the electronic media. Let me outline what I have in mind with reference to developments in three other areas of access by the media to the courts. I will then come back to the position of the electronic media.

The first area concerns suppression orders. Courts often make orders restricting what can and cannot be published in the media. Such orders may relate to the closing of the court, the suppression of names or the suppression of evidence. Thirty years ago, when I started out as a media lawyer, there was a resigned acceptance by reporters that such orders would often be made inappropriately. Sometimes it would be enough, for some judges, that counsel made the request and there was no opposition. Nowadays, if opposition is warranted, it is much more likely that opposing views will be presented to the court.

In Melbourne, between the early 70s and the late 80s, Tony Smith (now Judge Smith) and I acted for clients in the print and electronic media. However, our instructions to challenge the inappropriate making of suppression orders generally came from the print media. It is my opinion, albeit unsupported by any hard evidence, that there has been a considerable reduction in the volume of inappropriate orders over the past 30 years. There has also been a continuing refinement in the terms of such orders. More attention is now paid to the criteria in statutes, to making orders which are focused rather than being overly broad and to providing for time limits on the operation of orders. This is an area where Court Media Liaison Officers can, and do, make an invaluable contribution. With continuing vigilance, there should be even less likelihood of orders being made, in the future that are inappropriately restrictive.

The second area, which is linked to the first, relates to standing. When I started out as a media lawyer, there were problems establishing that the press had standing to put its position as to suppression orders. Court reporters just gritted their teeth and "lumped it" when a suppression order was made. There then came a period when a decision of Lord Denning, supporting the standing of the media, was much flourished. A disgruntled reporter called the editor. The editor called the solicitor. The solicitor rushed to court. The judges had to listen to a different perspective. Today, no judge would challenge the right of journalists to be heard by the courts on issues affecting publication. Reporters should be encouraged, and perhaps trained, to do so more often. There are still issues as to standing to be resolved relative to tribunals, but they can be considered on another occasion.

The third area is that of contempt of court. The basic principles of the law as to contempt have not changed. There are continuing concerns on the part of journalists about the uncertainty of how the law impacts on their work. As a media lawyer, I shared that concern, if only because at times journalists were effectively setting me up as the person who would have to be answerable if there was a contempt. This is one of many areas where there is fascination in the different approaches in New South Wales and Victoria. There has always been much more "remedial" work for media lawyers mopping up after gung-ho writers and broadcasters in Sydney than in Melbourne.

In Victoria there have been significant changes in legislation since our most recent notorious case. That was when Derryn Hinch chose, in 1986, to broadcast Michael Glennon's convictions not long before he was due to stand trial. Fewer prosecutions have been initiated since the power to do so was taken from the DPP in 1994. In my opinion, the appointment of a Courts' Information Officer is the single most important reason why contempt is much less of a concern in Victoria these days. I can only think of one recent prosecution. That was after the Brian Quinn (Coles-Myer) trial, which did result in convictions and fines of a journalist and publisher. The John Elliott trial might have caught out our beloved Premier had he not chosen to go into Justice Vincent's court and apologize. Generally, the changes which have been made, at least in Victoria, can be seen as having, for journalists, increased capacity to be critical and reduced the risk of being dealt with for potential transgressions.

The fourth area concerns the practices and policies of the courts in relation to the use of equipment such as tape recorders, still cameras and video cameras. It is about sound and vision. The courts have adapted relatively readily to the use of new technology where it improves the quality of trials. I mentioned earlier the use of video cameras for taking evidence from witnesses in remote locations. Computer screens and lap tops sit on the Bench with judges as well as on the Bar Table. In one of my recent murder trials, a long one, the jury asked for its own computer so that members could keep summaries of the evidence. After taking certain safeguards, I arranged for a computer to be provided.

However, the courts have adopted a very different attitude to the use of any kind of replacement for the journalists' pen. Some courts have experimented with practices devised to provide better access to electronic media court reporters. Most have opted to act very conservatively.

Before I proceed further, I would raise a *caveat*. I have avoided any public or semi-public comment on the subject of television in the courts for the last three years. The main reason for that lies in the ethical restraint against a judge commenting on any decision beyond the reasons handed down at the time. I intend to hold to that line so far as what I did and said in 1995. However, I feel only a little restricted now in commenting about what the future course, as to televising the work of the courts, might be. It seems to me that, in the last three years, there has been a shift away from whether the work of the courts should be televised. The debate is now how should televising be regulated?

I also think that the release in August of a report from New Zealand will help us in Australia to focus more clearly on the issues that now have to be addressed. The report was on "Media Coverage of Court Proceedings". It dealt with trials over the last three years of guidelines for such coverage devised by the courts in New Zealand. That report makes very interesting reading. Of significance is that both the Chief Justice and the President of the Court of Appeal have been quite heavily involved in the work of the Consultative Committee. Also significant is that the Committee has had its work "backed up" with market surveys.

One matter addressed in that report is of particular relevance here. It concerns the significance of the electronic media, as against the print media, as a source of information about the work of the courts. The recent Australian Institute of Judicial Administration study on "Courts and the Public" written by Professor Parker, referred to two studies, one in the United States and one in Queensland. His comment on those studies was that they showed that the *majority* of the general public receives its information about the court system through the electronic media. The New Zealand report also started with the premise that the newer forms of media are the *primary* means by which the public now receives information. Professor Parker went on to make two further comments. The first was that there must me a strong argument for employing the electronic media more fully in disseminating information about the courts. The second related to the need for appropriate guidelines and safeguards.

There are various indications that the courts might be likely to encourage greater access in the near future. More judges in more juris-dictions are accepting that there is a need to build the level of confidence that the community has in the work of the courts. Sir Gerard Brennan, in a lecture he gave in Ireland as Chief Justice, said: "...the courts should facilitate media access to whatever is on public record or in the public domain".[1] There are various signs that some judges may be becoming less reluctant to explain the work of the courts through the media.

An example of how it can be done superbly was the interview in 1996 of Gleeson CJ on "Lateline" explaining principles of sentencing. Other examples which went to air this year were "The Highest Court" on the ABC and Davies JA from the Queensland Court of Appeal on the "Sunday" programme. For some years the two Chief Justices who have spoken today, Chief Justice Doyle from the Supreme Court of South Australia and Chief Justice Black from the Federal Court of Australia, have been supportive of measures aimed at better informing the

---

[1] "The Third Branch and the Fourth Estate", second lecture in the series "Broadcasting, Society and the Law", Faculty of Law, Radio Telefis Éireann, University of Dublin, 22 April 1997.

community of the work of the courts. Three months ago, Sir Ninian Stephen gave further impetus towards change. He urged the High Court of Australia to consider measures which included permitting the televising of its proceedings.

Various measures could be taken to attempt to achieve or accelerate further change. I suggested earlier the potential value of some collective action on the part of electronic media reporters. The courts might be pressed to define their practices as to various aspects of access by the media. Where avenues are opened, the media might devise ways of making optimum use of them. It may be difficult to imagine some courts publishing any policy statement in this area. A more *particular* approach might be better than a *general* one.

Some courts do have guidelines for particular situations. I cite the Supreme Court of South Australia guidelines for radio. That might provide a good starting point. Why not take the South Australian guidelines to the Federal Court and politely ask that they, or similar guidelines, be approved and implemented in that Court or that reasons be given why that should not be done. If the Federal Court could be persuaded to accept the South Australian guidelines on radio, pressure could be put on other courts around the country to do likewise. Perhaps early next year, the New Zealand television guidelines will be available. They will be freshly "polished up" after four years of extremely thorough piloting and consultation. What better place to urge that they be piloted in this country than in South Australia? Of course, care would have to be taken subsequently to maximize the prospect that any applications under the guidelines were handled in the right way. That means not only selecting the right cases, but making the application in a way that would minimize the prospect that they could be refused informally and easily.

The notion of collective action may not come easily to competing electronic media reporters. However, my background in Law Society work revealed how competitors could sometimes become allied closely in a common cause. Perhaps Susannah Lobez would only need to get a handful of others together to make up a powerful group? Perhaps there is scope for some media lawyers or media law academics to get involved?

I would add some cautionary comments about television. I have been impressed by the way the New Zealanders went about their exercise. I am still in two minds about the wisdom of them trying to work through as many problems as they took on. The results of their work to date suggest that there is no clearly right way to go. For my part, I would suggest that progress is likely to be easier if there were to be a grading of the occasions when television cameras might be used in the courts. For want of more sophisticated titles for the gradings, I suggest "soft", "hard", "too hard", and "much too hard". I believe that it would not be difficult to maximize the "soft" occasions when cameras would be welcomed as they already are at times.

Under "soft" occasions, I would include the welcome and farewelling of judges, the opening of new courts, the opening of trials in which there is a special "public interest", like *Pyramid* and *Estates Mortgage*, the filming of footage for documentaries like "The Highest Court", and interviews of Chief Justices on subjects such as sentencing and law reform issues, particularly as to evidence and procedure. Under "hard" occasions, I would include the handing down of decisions in civil cases of particular community interest and the handing down of sentences on pleas of guilty. In relation to the "hard" occasions, the preparation of guidelines would be necessary. Under "too hard" occasions, I would include civil witness trials and the handing down of sentences other than on a plea of guilty. Under "much too hard", at least for the few years, I would put criminal jury trials. With the benefit of hindsight, I wonder whether more might have been achieved in New Zealand if the project had not taken on criminal jury trials. The problems which they pose are relatively immense.

At the start of my paper, I implied criticism of the print media. I like to think that I have helped newspapers enough in the past that they won't mind too much. Because the papers are in competition with the electronic media, any advantages gained by the latter will disadvantage the papers. We can't expect the print media to be objective in assessing the merits of televising what happens in the courts. Print journalists and editorials can be expected in the future, as in the past, to marshal more effectively the arguments against additional televising of the courts that those in the electronic media favour.

There are a few other aspects of my subject which I only have time to flag and not to elaborate on. I mention. Firstly, Court Media Liaison Officers. I have referred to them briefly. I ought to have given them more praise. I cannot understand how any court can be expected to get by without one. I expect them to continue to do their invaluable "foot slogging" work. I also expect them to be doing more ground-breaking work, particularly in conjunction with the electronic media court reporters.

Secondly, I mention the matter of judgment summaries. This is one area of expansion which I can see benefiting the courts and the media. There has to be a refining of techniques. This is an area being looked at closely by Prue Innes, the Victorian Courts Information Officer. At present, she is in the United States on a Churchill Fellowship.

Thirdly, the matter of judges being accessible for media interviews, is an area where I think conservatively. I believe Chief Justices will have to do more and more interviews. Lesser judges should only give interviews when pressed to do so by Chief Justices in areas of special expertise.

Finally, I mention the matter of leadership. To be a Chief Justice these days, one must have an extraordinary range of skills. Whether the pace of change in the areas I have discussed remains very slow or accelerates to become just slow, will depend, more than anything else, upon the leadership and vision of Chief Justices.

IN DEFENCE OF THE ADMINISTRATION OF JUSTICE: WHERE IS THE ATTORNEY-GENERAL?

The Honourable Robert McLelland

Shadow Attorney-General for the Commonwealth of Australia

The Honourable Daryl Williams QC MP, the Australian Attorney-General, maintains that it is not the role of the Attorney-General to defend the judiciary against personal criticism. This paper will ask the question: if it is not the role of the Attorney-General whose role is it and what are the consequences of the Attorney-General's inaction?

In a paper presented on 11 November 1994,[1] prior to becoming Attorney-General, Daryl Williams expressed the view that "there are good practical reasons why neither judges nor the public should look to the Attorney-General to take up cudgels for judges in media debate". His reasoning was based on his analysis of the current role of the Australian Attorney-General.

That analysis was, in turn, substantially based on conclusions contained in a Report by the Electoral and Administrative Review Commission chaired by Mr David Solomon. Mr Williams argued that the Australian Attorney-General is first and foremost a politician and not the chief law officer of the nation as is arguably the case in the United Kingdom.

Mr Williams relied heavily on the fact that, in Australia, the Director of Public Prosecutions (DPP) has independent statutory authority to supervise criminal and contempt of court proceedings. While Mr Williams acknowledged the power of the Australian Attorney-General to give directions to the DPP, he indicated that this power is rarely exercised. Mr Williams also acknowledged that the Attorney-General retains the right to grant or refuse a fiat for the bringing of a relator action. However, he argued that the Attorney-General is seldom requested to do so because of a general broadening of situations in which litigants are granted standing to commence proceedings in their own name.

Essentially, Mr Williams argued that to have a politician defending the judiciary would, in itself, further politicize the issue in controversy.

It is noteworthy that David Solomon who chaired the Administrative Review Commission, which Mr Williams relied upon for his analysis, expressed the opinion that Mr Williams reasoning was flawed. He said:

---

[1] Paper presented to the National Conference, Courts in a Representative Democracy, on 11–13 November 1994.

I think it highly desirable that Attorneys should regard the defence of the judiciary as being among their functions. Judges cannot be expected to become involved in exchanges with politicians. In effect the Attorney is their only protection. It is only very rarely that anyone else, such as a journalist, is prepared to defend them.[2]

Mr Williams' analysis has also been criticized by Gerard Carney.[3] Mr Carney argued that while the Attorney-General in the United Kingdom does perhaps have greater independent standing than in Australia, the Australian Attorney-General nonetheless has significant duties and responsibilities which are derived from both the executive prerogative power at common law and from statute. He noted that those powers included the power to:

- initiate and terminate criminal prosecutions;
- advise on the grant of a pardon;
- grant immunity from prosecution;
- issue a fiat in relator actions;
- appear as *amicus curiae* or contradictor;
- institute proceedings for contempt of court;
- apply for judicial review;[4] and
- provide legal advice to the Parliament, Cabinet and the Executive Council.[5]

Gerard Carney notes that, as a result of having those powers bestowed, the Attorney-General is often described as the "chief law officer of the Crown".

In his 1994 paper, Daryl Williams argued that, while the community could not expect the Attorney-General to defend the judiciary, the judiciary should look to organizations such as the Council of Chief Justices and the Australian Judicial Conference for their defence. The flaw in Mr Williams' argument is its total impracticality. Those bodies meet irregularly and would require any response to criticism of an individual judge or court to be by a majority decision. It is akin to arguing, for instance, that a solicitor or a barrister should not respond to personal criticism but allow such response to be through the Law Society or by the Bar Council.

The impracticality of Mr Williams' suggestion is demonstrated by recent incidents in which the judiciary has been criticized, regrettably, for political purposes as the following examples show.

Tim Fischer's Attack on the Competence of the High Court

The most notable incident was, of course, the Deputy Prime Minister's

---

[2] *Ibid.*
[3] Associate Professor of Law, Bond University.
[4] *Judiciary Act 1903* Section 78 A (1).
[5] *Kidman v The Commonwealth* (1925) 37 CLR 233 at 240.

attack on the Court prior to the handing down of the *Wik*[6] decision. Mr Fischer stated on 27 November 1997 that: "I am frustrated and angered by the delay in handing down of the decision by the High Court of Australia with regard to the *Wik* decision."

This criticism was rightly rejected by the then Chief Justice of the High Court, Sir Gerard Brennan AC KBE, in a letter to Mr Fischer dated 3 January 1997. Sir Gerard said:

> You will appreciate that public confidence in the constitutional institutions of government is critical to the stability of our society...I ask you to bear this in mind and to consider whether the making of attacks on the performance by the Court of its constitutional functions is conducive to good Government, even if an attack can gain some temporary political advantage.

Mr Howard defended Mr Fischer's attack on the High Court when the correspondence from the Chief Justice was disclosed on 28 February 1997 by saying: "There is nothing wrong with criticizing judgments, people frequently criticize the judgments of the courts."

However, Mr Fischer's attack was not a criticism of a judgment of the Court. It was a direct attack on the competence of the High Court and the diligence with which it carries out its functions.

Mr Fischer continues to this day to deny that his remarks were a personal attack on the Court. On 28 February 1997 Mr Fischer stated that: "I have never attacked an individual judge other than to make reference to their written judgments and I've got a right to do that in a responsible way recognizing the separation of powers." However, his words of criticism belie that contention.

Other Criticisms

Yet, Mr Fischer's comments represent just some of the abuse that has been hurled at the Court.

For example, Victorian Premier Jeff Kennett said on 20 February 1997 that: "We are all concerned that the High Court is not giving the clarity of leadership that this country requires."

But by far and away the worst offender has been the former Queensland Premier, Rob Borbidge. Mr Borbidge said on 28 February 1997 that: "The current High Court, across large parts of Australia, is increasingly being held in absolute and utter contempt." But most infamously he said on 1 March 1997 that: "Some of the High Court judges are dills about history."

These criticisms cannot, in any way, be said to be valid. They are clear and unequivocal attacks on the credibility and professionalism of the Court.

---

[6] *Wik Peoples v Queensland* (1996) 187 CLR 1.

Judicial Activism

A broader attack has also been waged by conservatives against what is known as "judicial activism". Critics of judicial activism argue that the courts should merely interpret the law and should not make the law.

The most public criticism made in this regard was that made by the Attorney-General Daryl Williams who stated on 7 February 1997 that:

> Just as the Executive should not expect judges to play advisers in the political process, as evidenced in the recent *Wilson* case in the High Court, so judges need to refrain from intruding into the legislative function.

Likewise, Queensland Premier Rob Borbidge stated on 10 February 1997 that: "If the High Court is embarking on a course of judicial activism, the High Court itself disregarded the principle of the doctrine of the separation of powers."

The New South Wales National Party Leader Mr Armstrong also stated on 28 February 1997 that: "I think that the High Court has in some of its statements on the *Wik* decision gone beyond the powers of separation that the courts have under the Constitution."

Mr Howard supported these views when he stated on 21 February:

> I can understand why people are saying more about this than they used to, because we have had a few emanations from the judicial area to the effect that really what the role of the courts is to give the Parliament a hurry on and to fill the gaps that the politicians don't fill by their actions. If that is the view of some people in the judiciary, well it's a very mistaken view and it's a view that goes beyond the writ of the judiciary in our system of government.

He repeated his view on 24 February 1997 when he told the Federal Parliament that:

> The role of the High Court is to interpret the law, the role of the Parliament is to make the law, and the laws governing Australians ought to be determined by the Australian Parliament and by nobody else.

The view that judges do not make the law ignores over 1,000 years of Australian and British legal history. The Common Law—the very basis of our legal system—is, by definition, judge-made law. The Common Law is fundamental to the operation of the Rule of Law in our society.

As Justice McHugh succinctly put it during argument on the *Lange*[7] and *Levy*[8] cases on 4 March 1997: "Anybody who doesn't believe that judges make the law doesn't live in the real world."

In his more reasonable moments the Prime Minister has recognized

---

[7] *Lange v Australian Broadcasting Commission* (1997) 71 ALJR 818.
[8] *Levy v Victoria* (1997) 146 ALR.

this. On 28 February 1997, Mr Howard stated that Australia did not need a Bill of Rights because the Common Law was adequate to protect our rights. However, the protection of rights in this way is a relatively modern exercise and has inevitably involved judges in modifying the Common Law. This is the epitome of judicial law making at work.

Likewise, the Australian Attorney-General, Daryl Williams, has recognized a legitimate role for judicial law making. He stated on 25 October 1997 that it was inevitable the High Court would make some decisions: "...not based on any attempt to declare the existing law. If there is no relevant statute law or relevant precedent, the Court will have to look to other sources..."

He further went on to recognize that the High Court clearly does exercise some restraint: "when in unchartered waters, sometimes saying 'this is not a matter for judicial law-making, it is a matter for Parliament.'"

Mr Williams said that when the courts were in "an activist phase" the need to leave matters to Parliament was likely to be given less weight. As he openly recognized:

"I suspect this is due to Parliament not dealing with all its workload."

There is, of course, a valid academic and legal debate about the extent to which judges should be "judicially active". Regrettably, many conservatives have chosen not to engage in that debate. Rather, they have used the slogan "judicial activism" for political purposes as a means of discrediting legal decision making without actually engaging in a considered response to the particular decision. It has become the legal equivalent of being described as "politically correct".

Independence of the Judiciary

The concern expressed by conservatives about "judicial activism" has principally transpired because of their discontent with the effect of a number of High Court decisions. This is best seen in their reaction to cases such as:

* the native title cases such as *Mabo[No.1]*[9], *Mabo [No.2]*[10] and *Wik*;[11]
* the cases implying rights and protections into the Constitution such as the *Theophanous*[12] and *Stephens*[13] decisions; and
* the use of powers, such as the external affairs power, to expand the legislative scope of the Commonwealth as occurred in the *Tasmanian Dams*[14] case and the *Seabed*[15] case.

Some, such as Senator Lightfoot from Western Australia, still rail

---

[9] *Mabo v Queensland [No 1]* (1988) 166 CLR 186.
[10] *Mabo v Queensland [No 2]* (1992) 175 CLR 1.
[11] *Wik Peoples v Queensland* (1996) 187 CLR 1.
[12] *Theophanous v Herald and Weekly Times Ltd* (1994) 182 CLR 104.
[13] *Stephens v Western Australian Newspapers Ltd* (1994) 182 CLR 211.
[14] *Commonwealth v Tasmania* (1983) 153 CLR 1.
[15] *New South Wales v Commonwealth* (1975) 135 CLR 337.

against the *Engineers*[16] case and long for the return of the reserved powers doctrine.

Most of these criticisms are based on dissatisfaction with the political implications of the decision rather than genuine academic or legal criticism of the reasoning of the Court.

As Mr Williams correctly noted on 1 May 1997:

> Where criticisms of a decision of the Court is based not on an analysis of the legal argument supporting the decision, but on other personal or political considerations, the criticism is likely to be unfair.

An interesting counterpoint to Mr Williams reasoned statement is the basis for the Prime Minister's criticism of the *Wik*[17] decision. On 2 June 1997, Mr Howard said in the Parliament that:

> [The 10 Point Plan] endeavours to address the fact that in the view of the Government the High Court's decision in *Wik* pushed the pendulum too far in one direction and the proper role of the Parliament so to bring the pendulum back to the middle.

And again he stated in the Parliament on 16 June 1997 that:

> The truth is that the *Wik* decision pushed the pendulum a long way from the centre. The debate essentially was about what measures were necessary in order to bring it back to equilibrium.

The Prime Minister's criticism of the *Wik* decision has regrettably always been one based purely on politics. Put simply, he thought the balance of rights should have been drawn differently by the Court and in a manner that was of great disadvantage to indigenous Australians. He has never mounted a legal critique of the decision. Instead, he has engaged in a political campaign and enacted legislation that was designed to achieve much the same effect.

In response to all these improper criticisms, the High Court has remained largely, and appropriately, silent. For it to have done otherwise would have required it to directly engage in the political process. Meanwhile, the criticisms have become increasingly vociferous and personal. And, because of his policy, they have gone unchecked by the Attorney-General.

In summary, criticism of the judiciary and in particular political criticism requires an immediate and effective response. It is not an understatement to say that our very system of government and the fundamental freedoms enjoyed by all citizens are at stake if the role of the judiciary is not properly protected.

---

[16] *Amalgamated Society of Engineers v Adelaide Steamship Co Ltd* (1920) 28 CLR 129.
[17] *Wik Peoples v Queensland* (1996) 187 CLR 1.

The Consequences

Justice Kirby said in a speech delivered on 15 August 1997:[18]

> I have seen countries where the power of the Courts has been eroded by unrelenting political attack. Let me tell you, when you take the independence of the judges away all that is left is the power of guns or of money or of populist leaders or of other self interested groups.

Justice Kirby's warning is not novel. It has been the warning of more enlightened statesmen throughout the centuries. In 1925 Charles Hughes, the President of the American Bar Association, warned that "[d]emocracy has its own capacity for tyranny". He said:

> Some of the most menacing encroachments upon liberty invoke the democratic principle and assert the right of the majority to rule. Shall not the people—that is, the majority—have their heart's desire? There is gainsaying this in the long run, and our only real protection is that it will not be their heart's desire to sweep away our cherished traditions of personal liberty. The interests of liberty are peculiarly those of individuals, and hence of minorities, and freedom is in danger of being slain at her own altars if the passion of uniformity and control of opinion gathers head.[19]

In that context Mr Hughes said that:

> an honest, high minded, able and fearless judge is the most valuable servant of democracy, for he illuminates justice as he interprets and applies the law, as he makes clear the benefits and the shortcomings of the standards of individual and community right among a free people.

More recently Sir Frank Kitto warned:

> Every judge worthy of the name recognizes that he must take each man's censure; he knows full well as a judge he is born to censure as the sparks fly upwards; but neither in preparing a judgment nor in retrospect may it weigh with him that the harvest he gleans is praise or blame, approval or scorn. He will reply to neither; he will defend himself not at all.[20]

The Honourable Sir Gerard Brennan AC KBE, while still Chief Justice of Australia, said on 22 April 1997:

> Should a judge be accountable to the government of the day? Certainly not. Should the judge be accountable in some way to an interest group or to the public? The rule of law would be hostage to public relations campaigns or majoritarian interests. Should a judgment be fashioned to satisfy popular sentiment? That would be the antithesis of the rule of law.[21]

---

[18] *Sydney Morning Herald*, 16 August 1997.

[19] Presidential address to the American Bar Association, September 2 1925, *ABA Journal* September 1925.

[20] "Why write judgements?" (1992) 66 *Australian Law Journal* 787 at 790.

Those principles, which are at the heart of our Westminister system, have been recognised and applied in decisions of the High Court. In *Clunies-Ross v the Commonwealth*[22] the High Court said:

> It would be an abdication of the duty of this court under the Constitution if we were to determine the important and general question of law...according to whether we personally agreed or disagreed with the political and social objectives which the Minister sought to achieve...as a matter of Constitutional duty, that question must be considered objectively and answered in this Court as a question of law and not as a matter to be determined by reference to the political or social merits of the particular case.

The fundamental error made by those who have more recently criticized the judiciary is their misunderstanding of who are the custodians of power in our system of government. As Sir Gerard Brennan aptly said, "...sovereignty is vested in the people and the courts give practical effect to that doctrine".[23]

Sir Gerard Brennan's deep understanding and passionate commitment to our system of government lead him to take the extraordinary step in January 1997 of writing directly to the Deputy Prime Minister as I have already described.

One wonders whether Chief Justice Brennan, as he was then, would have taken that extraordinary course of writing such a letter to the Deputy Prime Minister had he been confident that the nation's Attorney-General would have adopted the traditional role of defending the judiciary against politically motivated criticism.

This issue is far more than academic. During the course of the last federal election campaign the One Nation Party, for instance, advocated the introduction of legislative controls on the judiciary. Clearly its policy was based on a fundamental misunderstanding of our system of government.

Nevertheless, the ill informed comments of political leaders (which include the Deputy Prime Minister and the two State leaders) have clearly lent encouragement to those more ignorant elements of society who do not understand and respect the role of the courts in protecting our fundamental institutions. These institutions guarantee our freedoms from the unchecked and arbitrary control of the majority of the day.

I have argued that the judiciary cannot be protected by a Judicial Council or Judicial Conference or any similar forum. What are the alternatives? Should judges adopt the role of, not only administering

---

[21] "The Third Branch and the Fourth Estate" second lecture in the series "Broadcasting, Society and the Law" presented at the Faculty of Law, Radio Telefís Eireann, University College Dublin, 22 April 1997.

[22] (1984) 155 CLR 193 at 204.

[23] "The Third Branch and the Fourth Estate" second lecture in the series "Broadcasting, Society and the Law" presented at the Faculty of Law, Radio Telefís Eireann, University College Dublin, 22 April 1997.

justice, but also defending the role of the judiciary by politically promoting their decisions? Should the courts engage public relations consultants to strategically leak snippets during the preparation of judgments to test the public mood? Should they hold doorstop interviews to simplistically describe their judgements by one line grabs? Should they instigate a campaign of vilification of the party they will find against in their decision?

Clearly they should not. However, these are all common and accepted political tactics. If our courts are to defend themselves against political attacks, at what point do you draw the line regarding the extent of that defence? At what point is respect for our judicial administration so diminished that the courts will be forced to adopt such self promoting tactics?

The answer is that they should never be in a position where they need to resort to those tactics because the judiciary should be vigorously defended by an objective and considered Attorney-General. That is not to say that an Attorney-General is obliged to defend judicial decisions *per se*. Rather, the Attorney-General has a clear obligation, as chief law officer of this country, to defend the institution of the judiciary.

If the attitude of our current Attorney-General is not reversed then it will be a significant turning point in the history of our system of government. Individual judges will be forced to defend themselves in order to defend the very institution of the judiciary. That situation would be not only regrettable but extremely dangerous for the administration of justice in this country.

ACCESS TO THE COURTS AND ITS IMPLICATIONS

Roderick Campbell

Legal Reporter, *The Canberra Times*

"Access to the courts and its implications." Fortunately, perhaps, those seven words could embrace almost anything. After much floundering about on the PC, I picked out a couple of "anythings" to address today, to wit, the stark realities of the relationship between the third branch of government and the Fourth Estate, and the adequacies, or otherwise, of the relationship between one court in particular, the High Court, and its broader constituency.

When we ponder the relationship between the courts and the media, I don't think we're too fussed about the relationship between the clerk of the Local Court at Dubbo and the reporter from *The Daily Liberal*. They undoubtedly have a fine working relationship and are probably in the same cricket or netball team. What we are really talking about is the relationship between the superior courts and the metropolitan media. That relationship is, I suggest, strained and often combatant, and will remain that way unless and until both sides are a little more honest about themselves.

What I am about to say might appear at times to relate more to barristers and solicitors than it does to judges and magistrates. There are two things to be said about that. First, all judicial officers were once practising lawyers and, to some extent at least, once a lawyer always a lawyer. Second, a journalist's experiences with the court system often have more to do with his or her relationship with the lawyers who practise there than they do with the judges or the bureaucrats. So, it is not simply a matter of how the court as an institution relates to the media that we need to consider.

It is hard to think of two more opinionated and holier-than-thou professions than the law and journalism. Both camps engage in considerable nonsense about their respective Holy Grails, invoking "the public interest" or "the interests of justice" as they charge into the fray. A lot of it is posturing, of course, but it is also the way many others see both groups. The media claims to do what it does for the benefit of the public, because the public has a right to know, et cetera, et cetera. If only it were true. The legal system claims that it does right by all, without fear or favour, and acts always in the interests of justice, et cetera, et cetera. If only it were true.

Gatherings like this, while all very nice, will be a waste of time unless both sides start owning up to their sins. It will only be then that we can move beyond the name calling and work at developing an effective relationship.

The respective roles of the courts and the media are obviously very different but remain very much interwoven. The courts are there to sort out the legal rights of litigants and to dispense justice. The media is interested in the news. The courts make news and so the media is interested. The courts need the media so the public can be informed about what they are doing and how they are administering justice, otherwise they would be operating in a vacuum.

The media needs the courts because they are a rich source of human drama. Some of them also make the law, and that is rather important. And they provide the referees in some of the best stoushes around.

To a degree, some of the courts might be seen as having an almost symbiotic relationship with the media. Certainly some judicial figures are more media-friendly than others. Some are very astute at using the media when they have a barrow to push, whether it is something as grubby as money or as lofty as judicial independence.

We need to recognize who it is we are dealing with here. It is primarily lawyers and journalists. There are fundamental differences in outlook and thinking that can and do create an enormous gulf, despite the fact that some of the theoretical strengths of both groups are the same. Lawyers and, these days, journalists, are well educated, and we all tend to be inquisitive, questioning, analytical, objective, not prone to jumping to conclusions, and occasionally passionate. In theory, we have a lot in common. I guess that is why some lawyers and some journalists get along extremely well. But that is a rather small "some", I'm afraid.

Only a handful of judges and lawyers seem to have any real knowledge of how the media operates. Of course, when you have months to write a reserved judgment, or 28 days in which to prepare an appeal, a world of daily deadlines, and deadlines which are approaching at the speed of light by the time court adjourns for the day, is probably hard to comprehend. When the High Court hands down six judgments on one day, do the judges consider the fact that a lone journalist will have to read through all six, cogitate some tens of thousands of words, work out which ones are newsworthy, explain it all to the legally-ignorant chief of staff or news editor, and write several hundred, maybe 1,000 or more, succinct and accurate words about it all, and all in a few hours? If such things ever occurred to the judges, they might not do it any more. No, I don't think judges think about things like that. With a few exceptions, I don't think they really consider journalists' needs, otherwise one of them might, by now, have formulated a suppression order that makes sense.

But journalists are little better. Journalism in Australia in the late 1990s is largely focused on the drama, the colour, the trivial and the salacious.

It rarely has the patience for the serious and truly important issues...
except, of course, for those media outlets represented here today. That is
why, in Canberra just over a fortnight ago, there were more than a dozen
journalists from all over the eastern seaboard gathered like bees around
a honey pot at the Abbott and Costello show, otherwise known as the
Peter Costello and Tony Abbott defamation action against Random House
and Bob Ellis. Twenty metres away, just three journalists were covering
the Michael Cobb travel rorts fraud trial. Next door, three local journalists
and one inter-stater were interested in a rather bizarre murder trial. And
in the neighbouring Coroner's Court, only a couple were following a
coronial inquiry into a death in custody. None of these was as "sexy" as
Abbott and Costello but they were all far more important.

It must also be remembered that the average court reporter is young
and inexperienced, with little if any knowledge of the law and the rules
of the game. They have never met a *functus officio* in their life and would
not recognise an *obiter dictum* if it bit them. Even bread and butter expres-
sions such as "liberty to apply" and "declaratory relief" bamboozle them.
When the High Court announced its decision in the *Patrick Stevedores*
case earlier in the year, the words "liberty to apply" had several senior
journalists thinking there was another avenue of appeal there for the
asking.

I should make a few more observations on the legal half of this equation.
Steeped in the adversarial culture, lawyers are by nature and training a
combatant breed. In some miraculous way, something akin to St Paul's
experience on the road to Damascus, judges are expected to cast off
those cultural shackles the moment they don the ermine or the black
gown and pole vault the Bar Table to the Bench. The strengths of the
legal mind can sometimes be its owner's downfall, at least to the eyes of
the outsider. A fetish for detail, for strategies, for pedantry, for determined
loyalty to the client's cause. All these are right and proper and essential,
in moderation.

I know a lawyer's first loyalty and duty is meant to be to the court. I
know it because I read it in a High Court judgment on why barristers
cannot be sued, but I'm not sure I believe it. Despite the lofty rhetoric,
it's as plain as a pikestaff that most lawyers understand that their first
duty is to the person or corporation paying their fees. A lawyer friend of
mine does not agree. He claims a lawyer's first duty is to oneself.

If I remember correctly, that same High Court judgment spoke of the
virtues of a legal profession whose members did not chase every rabbit
down every burrow because to do so is not in the best interests of the
justice system. With the greatest of respect, that is nonsense.

I have sat through many hundreds of court hearings and read thousands
of court judgments over the years, and no one can tell me that lawyers do
not regularly file outrageous ambit claims in personal injuries cases, do
not construct oppressive sets of interrogatories, do not mount insupport-

able defences, do not coach their clients, and do not conduct terribly unfair cross-examinations. The judges know perfectly well that this is going on but too rarely do they do much about it. The more astute journalists know it, too.

The big problem lawyers from both sides of the Bench have is that they see the world through a lawyer's eyes, not through the eyes of the mythical man on what is now, I presume, the Bondi Junction train. An ability to painstakingly extract, over many months, several dozen contextual imputations from a newspaper article is undoubtedly highly prized in Macquarie Street, and the training is very useful for when one becomes a judge. However, try explaining it to the guy next to you *en route* to Bondi Junction. I might add here that precious few journalists have ever travelled with our mythical passenger either. But we may have had a drink with him (or her) somewhere.

The theory, at least, is that lawyers and judges place great emphasis on the gathering and presentation of facts, in a logical, ordered and coherent way. Once appraised by learned counsel of those facts (of which there are at least two definitive versions) and the relevant law (of which there are at least two definitive versions), the learned judge or magistrate will apply the weightiest version of the law to the preferable version of the facts and come to the correct conclusion... until, of course, the Court of Appeal intervenes and decrees the very opposite. But in the meantime, heaven help the journalist who misreports those facts or misunderstands whichever version of the correct legal principle it was that the judge decided was the right one at the time.

Journalists often get it wrong because lawyers and judges do not seem to know how to say in less than 2,500 words what they ought to be able to say in 250 words. Many journalists get it wrong because, like their readers, their attention span does not extend to anything like 2,500 words.

The legal mind tends to be ponderous and long-winded. The journalistic mind is always impatient.

We are supposedly in the age of instant communications where the vast majority of people get their news from television. But television is preoccupied, to the point of obsession, with visual images. Only SBS would consider putting a news item to air without accompanying footage to distract the viewer. Commercial television will not touch a court- or law-related story if it does not have a visual image, matching or otherwise, no matter how important the story. The television journalist invariably has less than two minutes, or 300 words, in which to communicate a lengthy High Court judgment or six hours of courtroom drama. Newspapers aren't much better sometimes. Even the more highly regarded broadsheets have a fetish for the picture story and some of them look more like lifestyle liftouts than the journals of record they once proudly claimed to be. Just a few weeks ago, I had to talk one of the executives at my newspaper out of pursuing a local stroke victim for a picture because he wanted to "humanize" a story about an appeal court's ruling on what constituted a personal injury, as opposed to a disease, in workers' compensation law. The story was a legal one, not a human interest one, but that didn't seem to carry much weight. The truth is we were just short of pictures that day.

And every media outlet in Australia these days seems to have a lemming-like attraction to overkill. Cast your minds back to the Port Arthur massacre, the Thredbo disaster and, worst of all, the death of Princess Diana, and you'll recall the media hysteria which accompanied those events. The hysteria is often followed by a determination to explore every conceivable angle on the story within 48 hours and, if there's a sniff of criminal conduct, to solve the case a day later. The fact that a police investigation might be jeopardised, or criminal charges might have been laid, or a coronial inquiry has been established, are irrelevant. Last month's murder in Canberra of a Saudi diplomat is a good case in point.

Isn't it about time that the media acknowledged some of these self evident facts and stopped being so pompous and self righteous? Neither side has a mortgage on wisdom and it is, I suggest, about time that both acknowledged that fact and climbed down from their respective ivory towers and high horses. So this is what we—and you—are up against.

As I said before, we need each other. But at the end of the day, I suggest it is the courts which need the media in a more fundamental sense because it is through the media that the courts acquire their credibility and account to the wider community. As the late Sir Richard Blackburn, a former Chief Justice of the ACT Supreme Court, once said to me, "I don't care if you ignore almost everything the judges say and write, as long as you report as fairly and fully as possible our reasons for sentencing offenders". What he was saying was that is where the court's credibility sank or swam. Sir Richard was acutely aware of what the court's public was most vitally interested in.

Professor Stephen Parker said in his preface to the Australian Institute of Judicial Administration's "Courts and the Public" report in September 1998, that the relationship between Australian courts and their public is "clearly in need of improvement if the public are to retain confidence in the judicial branch of our system of government".

Leaving aside the unfortunates who actually have to go to court, the only way the courts can maintain any sort of relationship with the public is through the media. I agree with Professor Parker's view that the appointment of media officers and the opening up of courtrooms to microphones and cameras, while wholly to be commended, will not cure some of the more deep-seated problems. He refers to the need, largely unmet, for the courts to mount "proactive educative programs". Educative of whom, he does not spell out. Of journalists? Well, that might help. But the only ones who attend forums like this probably aren't the ones who need educating. Very often, it is the anonymous bosses in the newsroom who need it. Of the general public? When somebody gets around to introducing civics to the Australian education system, something might be achieved, a generation or two hence. Of judges and court staff, perhaps?

Certainly. But once again, it is generally those who are interested in media issues, and who are appreciative of the judicial–media relationship, who attend the conferences.

Just over a year ago, during his State of the Judicature address to the Australian Legal Convention in Melbourne, the then Chief Justice, Sir Gerard Brennan, said of judicial accountability: "The real problem of accountability for the exercise of judicial power is not the giving of the account, it is the reporting and critical appreciation of the account that is given."

He referred to the fact that some of Australia's courts had appointed Public Affairs Officers to assist the media in the reporting of cases. But, he warned:

> A media officer is not an advertising agent, seeking to influence favourable publicity or issuing releases designed to put a favourable spin on court decisions. The prerogative of and the responsibility for reporting and offering interpretation and criticism of court decisions must rest with the media. That is one of the great services that the media perform.

> It is the means by which the judiciary's account for the exercise of their powers reaches the people. So regarded, legal reporting and comment are necessary elements in our constitutional arrangements.

And, he added: "By employing an informed and critical faculty, the media justifies its freedom; conversely, ill-informed criticism abuses that freedom."

I'm inclined to agree. However, during the same address, and while discussing the competence and independence of lawyers, Sir Gerard warned:

> A recently emerging phenomenon occasions some misgiving. Some advocates have assumed the role of public relations officers for their clients, making their client's case to the media and offering comment on the court's judgment. That role is inconsistent with the advocate's duty to the court. The court can have no confidence that such an advocate will fairly and candidly assist the court on both fact and law. And the accolade or lament that the advocate presumes to express about the court's judgment belittles the court's authority. It is commendable for advocates to provide journalists with information to assist in the accurate reporting of a case, so far as the material is on the public record, but if court proceedings were the postscript or the prelude to counsel's media release or court door interview, the courtroom becomes a mere backdrop to counsel's media performance.

Alas, I do not go along with all of that, particularly that stuff about the lawyer's duty to the court. This is hardly surprising, given that I'm a journalist who hangs around courts. In fact, I think a far bigger problem is the unwillingness of lawyers to speak out at all.

With the greatest respect to the former Chief Justice, I have to say I am more attracted to the view of Justice Robert French, of the Federal Court and the National Native Title Tribunal. While recently discussing the limits on judicial review, he wondered how the issue of public confidence in the courts was to be handled when a media report might "show to all the world an apparently harsh decision being apparently endorsed by the court". This is known to the rest of us as "the law is an ass" phenomenon. Justice French thought the judge in such a case should be at pains to make clear the limitations imposed by law upon his or her role. He was prepared to countenance something Sir Gerard apparently would not, namely, that this could be reinforced by "a suitably briefed media office".

The Australian Institute of Judicial Administration has recommended that all jurisdictions have media liaison officers. In cases where an imminent decision or sentence is likely to excite public controversy, the judicial officer should consider providing the media go-between with a statement about the case to assist in conveying a fair summary to the public. The purpose of this would be to neither encourage nor discourage the controversy but to inform any debate that does occur.

I mentioned before the *Patrick Stevedores* case in the High Court earlier in the year. There were great hordes of reporters covering that case, more than 20 on the final day. Only two of them were specialist legal reporters; the rest were political and industrial relations experts who understood the factual background perfectly but, with a couple of notable exceptions, didn't have a clue about the legal aspects. Most of them had trouble identifying a single member of the Bench. Now, if the High Court had a Public Affairs Officer, he or she might have guided those journalists through some of the basics, instead of a couple of their colleagues, myself included, having to provide a running commentary of what was really being said and by whom.

Other courts which have media officers, most notably the Family and Federal Courts, have, I am informed, been known to publish summaries of some of their decisions. Unfortunately, few of them have ever filtered through to Canberra. Perhaps I should spend more time surfing the net.

The High Court dabbled with the summary concept in the *Patrick Stevedores* case, much to the relief of the electronic media. It is a trend which is to be applauded and ought to be greatly expanded upon.

The reasons why many of the extremely busy workhorse courts of Australia have employed media officers are pretty obvious. Even the tiny handful of dedicated legal reporters in this country could not begin to keep up with the enormous output of the courts. Those few of us who try can keep on top of what the High Court is saying, but I doubt if anyone in the media has any idea of what is coming out of the Federal and Family Courts on a weekly basis, given that both have a large number of judges scattered across the country. But there is, I might add, more to making the courts' activities accessible than feeding the internet.

Of all the courts in the land most in need of beefing up their PR effort, the High Court stands out. The recent unprecedented and often ignorant attacks by politicians and conservative academics has probably done the Court's image no good at all. Claims that the Court has been usurping the role of Parliament and embarking on law making frolics of its own have largely gone unanswered. The federal Attorney-General does not see it as his job to defend the federal judiciary from attack, so who will? The Court itself is very reluctant. A biennial speech to the Australian Legal Convention from the Chief Justice is simply not enough. The Australian Institute of Judicial Administration seems to agree. Justice Michael Kirby, the Court's most outspoken member, does his best but can't carry the baton on his own.

There are more fundamental reasons for having a Public Affairs Officer at the High Court.

There are several hundred thousand visitors to the Court each year, or at least there were until budgetary constraints led the Court to close its doors on weekends and public holidays.

A fair proportion of those visitors, including a large number of school students, manages to be on hand when the Court is actually sitting. From my observation over more than a decade, almost all of them sit there for the obligatory 20 minutes with blank looks on their faces, comprehending almost nothing. What must they think of it all? What do they tell their friends and family back in Gympie and Mt Gambier? I shudder to think...and so should the Court.

Although almost none of those visitors probably walked away any the wiser they were, in fact, witnessing history. What was going on was probably every bit as important, and possibly more so, than what they heard during the 20 minutes they spent a kilometre or so away in the Senate.

Unfortunately, the High Court does very little to make those 20 minute bites of history more fruitful for the recipients. It probably doesn't have the resources to do so, but maybe it needs to find them. While visitors can never be expected to understand the niceties of senior counsel's discourse on statutory construction or constitutional theory, they might have a chance of understanding something of what they're hearing and seeing if they are provided with a one page summary of the case which explains who all those black-robed people are representing, why the case has reached the High Court, and the basic facts. One might even throw caution to the wind and mention the legal issues involved.

But will the appointment of a Public Affairs Officer at the High Court be the magic wand the judiciary needs if it is to win over the hearts and minds of the public? I cannot see that similar appointments in other jurisdictions have had any profound impact on public perceptions. It certainly has not worked for the Family Court, and probably never will. Nor will it work if the incumbent has neither the time nor the resources to do much more than respond to the media. Communicating with journalists is only part of the story.

The real problem is that almost no one truly understands the role of the courts in Australian society. Even the well-educated and more aware among my friends and acquaintances have trouble coming to grips with the concept of the judiciary as the third arm of government, with a constitutional status broadly on a par with that of the executive and the legislature. Mention Chapter III of the Constitution and you've lost them. When a politician starts bleating about the High Court usurping the role of Parliament on issues like native title and free speech, they wonder if the politician might have a point. When I try to explain that judges have been making law for an awfully long time, and when I refer to the Star Chamber and the emergence of the common law, I get blank looks. The trouble is—as the Constitutional Commission discovered some years ago—Australians are blissfully ignorant about such matters. Most journalists are just the same.

It is not so much that the courts are barking up the wrong tree. The reality is that there is more than one tree in the forest. But only one—the one with a few journalists in it—seems to be getting much attention.

THE HIGH COURT AND THE MEDIA

George Williams

Barrister, ACT Bar; Fellow, Law Program,
Research School of Social Sciences, Australian National University*

A ustralians know very little about their system of government. The 1994 report on citizenship by the Civics Expert Group[1] found that only 18 per cent of Australians have some understanding of what the Constitution contains, while only 40 per cent could correctly name both Houses of the Federal Parliament. It is not surprising then that the role and composition of the High Court are a mystery to many in the community. In fact, more than a quarter of those surveyed nominated the Supreme Court, rather than the High Court, as the "top" court in Australia.[2]

There are many reasons for such ignorance. Some responsibility lies with both the media and the High Court. For much of this century, media scrutiny of the High Court has been rare. Attention has shifted to the Court only when political debate has become enmeshed with litigation before the Court or when a decision promised significant political ramifications. This explains the coverage given to the *Bank of NSW v Commonwealth* (the "Bank Nationalisation Case")[3] in 1948, *Australian Communist Party v Commonwealth* (the "Communist Party Case")[4] in 1951 and *Commonwealth v Tasmania* (the "Tasmanian Dam Case")[5] in 1983. In the mainstream media, the judges responsible for such decisions have been almost completely unknown and the role of the High Court in Australian democracy has been frequently misunderstood, as shown by the public debate in 1997 over whether the judges of the High Court have a law-making function.

More recently, there has been a shift in coverage of the High Court. It is true that recent cases such as *Kartinyeri v Commonwealth* (the "Hindmarsh Island Case")[6] and *Patrick Stevedores Operations No 2 Pty Ltd v Maritime Union of Australia* (the "Patrick Stevedores Case")[7] have con-

---

* I owe thanks to Geraldine Chin for her research assistance and to Emma Armson for her comments on an earlier draft.
[1] Civics Expert Group, *Whereas the People: Civics and Citizenship Education* (1994) at 133.
[2] *Ibid.* at 133. See also the survey statistics reproduced in Black, "Letting the Public Know—the Educative Role of the Courts" (1994) 1 *Canberra Law Review* 165 at 166–167.
[3] (1948) 76 CLR 1.
[4] (1951) 83 CLR 1.
[5] (1983) 158 CLR 1.
[6] (1998) 152 ALR 540.
[7] (1998) 153 ALR 643.

tinued to be a focus of attention. However, the Court itself has also come to be recognized as an important player in Australian government. The media and the Australian public have demonstrated an interest in the High Court and its judges as participants in the development of Australian law. For example, there has been a high interest in recent appointments to the Court and how this might affect the approach of the Court.

This paper explores changed understandings of the High Court and the effect this has had on the relationship between the Court and the media. It suggests reform and means of improvement, with the aim of bringing benefits to the community as a whole. The focus is on reform by the High Court, rather than by the media. This is not to suggest that the greater responsibility lies with the Court. However, it does reflect that it is in the High Court's own interest to foster accurate and informed reporting of its work. In this area, the Court has the most to lose.

Changes at the High Court

The judges of the High Court give meaning to the Constitution and develop the common law in serving an Australian community that continues to experience massive social, economic and political change. As Lord Porter stated in the *Bank Nationalisation* case: "The problem to be solved will often be not so much legal as political, social or economic. Yet it must be solved by a court of law."[8] Legalism has played an important part in maintaining the legitimacy of the High Court in the face of having to make decisions about intensely political matters.[9] Hence Sir Owen Dixon's statement in 1952 upon becoming Chief Justice of the High Court that: "There is no other safe guide to judicial decisions in great conflicts than a strict and complete legalism."[10] By legalism it is meant the trappings of formal legal argument and reliance upon technical legal solutions rather than considerations of policy.[11] By adopting a legalistic approach, judges of the High Court fostered the notion that policy and values do not influence their decision making.

Sir Owen Dixon himself did not strictly adhere to the legalism he advocated. As Leslie Zines has shown, in reaching his decisions Dixon frequently took account of extra-legal factors, including considerations

---

[8] *Commonwealth v Bank of NSW* (1949) 79 CLR 497 at 639.
[9] Galligan, B., *Politics of the High Court* (1987) at 40 where it is stated "[l]egalism has enabled the dignity and independence of the law to be maintained while allowing the Australian High Court to perform a delicate political function in a society that has been divided over important aspects of political ideology and political economy."
[10] (1951) 85 CLR xi at xiv. cf Sir Gerard Brennan, "A Critique of Criticism" (1993) 19 *Monash University Law Review* 213 at 213 where it is stated "[t]he rhetoric based on strict and complete legalism masked the truth of the judicial method."
[11] Gageler, S., "Foundations of Australian Federalism and the Role of Judicial Review" (1987) 17 *Federal Law Review* 162 at 176; Zines, L., *The High Court and the Constitution*, 4th edn. (1997) at 424–426.

of social and political policy and value judgment.[12] As Dixon stated in *Melbourne Corporation v Commonwealth*:

> In the many years of debate over the restraints to be implied against any exercise of power by Commonwealth against State and State against Commonwealth calculated to destroy or detract from the independent exercise of the functions of the one or the other, it has often been said that political rather than legal considerations provide the ground of which the restraint is the consequence. The Constitution is a political instrument. It deals with government and governmental powers. The statement is, therefore, easy to make though it has a specious plausibility. But it is really meaningless. It is not a question whether the considerations are political, for nearly every consideration arising from the Constitution can be so described, but whether they are compelling.[13]

Sir Garfield Barwick, who was Dixon's successor as Chief Justice from 1964 to 1981, also argued for a legalistic approach[14] while having recourse to questions of policy.[15] More recently, as Chief Justice from 1987 to 1995, Sir Anthony Mason differed from Dixon and Barwick. Like his predecessors, Mason applied policy considerations, and even "community values".[16] However, unlike them, he admitted to doing so. Mason, in his published writings and speeches,[17] and the Mason Court through decisions on topics such as native title[18] and freedom of political communication,[19] swept away the popular notion that the Court was engaged in a purely legalistic endeavour that did not involve making law or recourse to policy factors. This made it clear that the law-making process was not confined to Parliament.

Legalism cannot remove the need for policy and value judgment in the work of the High Court. Judges do more than apply and interpret the

---

[12] Zines, L., *The High Court and the Constitution*, 4th edn. (1997) at 429–430.

[13] (1947) 74 CLR 31 at 82.

[14] *Attorney-General (Cth); Ex parte McKinlay v Commonwealth* (1975) 135 CLR 1 at 17 per Barwick CJ.

[15] Zines, L., *The High Court and the Constitution*, 4th ed (1997) at 430-432.

[16] According to Sir Anthony Mason, "The Role of a Constitutional Court in a Federation: A Comparison of the Australian and the United States Experience" (1986) 16 *Federal Law Review* 1 at 5: "...it is impossible to interpret any instrument, let alone a constitution, divorced from values. To the extent they are taken into account, they should be acknowledged and should be accepted community values rather than mere personal values. The ever present danger is that 'strict and complete legalism' will be a cloak for undisclosed and unidentified policy values." See also Sturgess and Chubb, *Judging the World: Law and Politics in the World's Leading Courts* (1988) at 345.

[17] See, for example, Sir Anthony Mason, "The Role of a Constitutional Court in a Federation: A Comparison of the Australian and the United States Experience" (1986) 16 *Federal Law Review* 1; Sir Anthony Mason., "Should the High Court Consider Policy Implications when Making Judicial Decisions?" (1998) 57 *Australian Journal of Public Administration* 77.

[18] *Mabo v Queensland [No.2]* (1992) 175 CLR 1.

[19] *Nationwide News Pty Ltd v Wills* (1992) 177 CLR 1; *Australian Capital Television Pty Ltd v Commonwealth* (1992) 177 CLR 106; *Theophanous v Herald & Weekly Times Ltd* (1994) 182 CLR 104; *Stephens v West Australian Newspapers Ltd* (1994) 182 CLR 211.

law. They also make it. Over 25 years ago, in England, Lord Reid of the House of Lords dispelled the notion that judges do not make law by stating "we do not believe in fairy tales any more".[20] The High Court, in particular, is charged with a law-making function. Indeed, this is its central role. The Court's own procedures regarding special leave ensure that it deals with only the most important and problematic areas of the law. The cases that come before the High Court do so because there is no law on the topic or because the existing law does not provide adequate answers.[21]

Wik Peoples v Queensland (the "Wik Case")[22] is a clear example. Accordingly, the job of the Court is not merely to apply existing law, but to develop the law by, for example, filling in the gaps that have become apparent in the coverage of the law. This is how the common law has grown and been refined in England and Australia over centuries. It is an inescapable aspect of the judicial role that has been undertaken by the High Court since its inception in 1903. What has changed in recent years is not that judges have starting making law, but that they have owned up to doing so. This is one of the most important legacies of the Mason Court. As a consequence, High Court judges are now more likely to recognize their role as law makers and explicitly bring to light the policy choices confronting them.

Old notions about the High Court have been stripped away. Recognition of the Court's law-making role has not been the only major change. The Court has also demonstrated sympathy for the protection of human rights against governmental power. While Australia does not possess a Bill of Rights, a majority of the Mason Court was prepared to imply a freedom of political communication from the Constitution,[23] and individual judges even found that the Constitution might imply a guarantee of legal equality[24] or a freedom from retrospective criminal laws.[25] As a result, many Australians turned to the High Court rather than the ballot box to protect their liberty. This was particularly true for those Australians with little political power, such as Australia's indigenous peoples.[26]

These changes have incurred a significant cost. The tension between the High Court and the other arms of government has increased markedly. It is no coincidence that at the same time as the decline of legalism and

[20] Lord Reid, "The Judge as Law Maker" (1972) 12 *Journal of the Society of Public Teachers of Law* 22 at 22.

[21] McHugh, M., "The Law-making Function of the Judicial Process" (1988) 62 *Australian Law Journal* 15 (part I); 116 (part II) at 116 lists four situations in which judges commonly make law.

[22] (1996) 187 CLR 1.

[23] See note 19 *supra*.

[24] *Leeth v Commonwealth* (1992) 174 CLR 455.

[25] *Polyukhovich v Commonwealth* (*War Crimes Act Case*) (1991) 172 CLR 501.

[26] See, for example, *Kruger v Commonwealth* (1997) 190 CLR 1; *Kartinyeri v Commonwealth* (1998) 152 ALR 540.

the rise of its rights jurisprudence, the High Court attracted increasing controversy and the legitimacy of its decision making came under direct challenge, including from Australia's political leaders. Indeed, from the handing down of the *Wik* case on 23 December 1996, the Brennan Court experienced one of the most difficult periods since the High Court's creation in 1903. The judges were attacked as a "pathetic ... self-appointed [group of] Kings and Queens", a group of "basket-weavers" and even the purveyors of "intellectual dishonesty".[27]

Legalism no longer offers the High Court a refuge from controversy and scrutiny. There is no turning back to the Dixon era of "strict and complete legalism". The Court will inevitably face difficult cases raising unresolved issues of law that will expose its reliance upon matters of policy and value judgment. As a result, even where it adopts a legalistic or black-letter approach, as in decisions such as *Wik*, this will not insulate the Court from public controversy.

The High Court and the Media

The Australian community is almost totally dependent upon the media for explanation and analysis of the work of the High Court. Hence the relationship between the High Court and the media is crucial to public confidence in the Court. This is particularly true at a time when the High Court has acknowledged its law-making role, and has exercized it in protecting fundamental rights and freedoms against governmental action. If the Court is unable, through the media, to maintain the confidence and trust of the community, it risks a similar level of cynicism as is found in the views of many Australians about their elected representatives and Australia's system of representative government.

In some respects, the media is effective in its coverage of the High Court. In the tradition of David Solomon at *The Australian*, and now at *The Courier-Mail*, other Australian newspapers have journalists who write extensively about the High Court, such as Rod Campbell at *The Canberra Times*, Margo Kingston at *The Sydney Morning Herald*, Bernard Lane at *The Australian* and Chris Merritt at *The Financial Review*. Many newspapers have also been willing to publish opinion pieces by lawyers and academics explaining and commenting upon decisions of the Court or its workings.

Nevertheless, the media often betrays little understanding of the High Court, and presents a distorted, or at best superficial, view of the Court to the public. The subtleties of decision making by seven independent judges are ill suited to the ten second grab of the nightly news. Reporters can also fail to appreciate the significance of the work of the Court, and the distinctive nature of the Court as opposed to the other arms of govern-

---

[27] Quoted in Kirby, M., "Attacks on Judges—A Universal Phenomenon" (1998) 72 *Australian Law Journal* 599 at 601.

ment. Despite the opening of the High Court Building in Canberra in 1980, there is no High Court press gallery, and the Court is frequently reported *ad hoc* by journalists who would otherwise cover the political events of the day.

The High Court must be active in seeking to promote accurate and informed coverage of its work. It has too much at stake to do otherwise. In particular, it must accept a higher degree of responsibility for the communication of its findings to the community through the media. At present, there is an unfortunate disjunction between the public's inability to comprehend decisions of the High Court and the use by members of the Court of notions such as "community values"[28] and popular sovereignty.[29] While the Court has set up its own web site,[30] and is a world leader in this regard, its decisions remain largely impenetrable to anyone but the initiated. Judgments of the High Court are generally inaccessible to the media, and can take an expert several hours to fully digest, let alone a journalist with a tight deadline and no legal training.[31] Even with a law degree the job of covering one or more decisions of the High Court for an hourly news bulletin or the morning paper can be a herculean task.

The inaccessible nature of the work of the High Court has several negative consequences. Reporters often fail to convey an accurate or precise account of a High Court decision. There has been inaccurate reporting even where the Court has made an attempt to explain a decision to the public. To take a small but important example, at the handing down of its recent decision in the *Patrick Stevedores* case, journalists were clustered in the Court and outside, and the major networks and the ABC had set up satellite feeds to go live to television and radio with the result. Inside the Court, Chief Justice Brennan, who presided from 1995 to 1998, read out a short statement, which was available to the media and the public.

The statement explained the effect of the orders and went on to outline

---

[28] See n. 16 *supra*.

[29] Several judges of the High Court have now accepted such a doctrine. For example, Deane J argued in *Theophanous v Herald & Weekly Times Ltd* (1994) 182 CLR 104 at 171 that the "present legitimacy of the Constitution…lies exclusively in the original adoption (by referenda) and subsequent maintenance (by acquiescence) of its provisions by the people", while in *McGinty v Western Australia* (1996) 186 CLR 140 at 230 McHugh J found that: "Since the passing of the *Australia Act* (UK) in 1986, notwithstanding some considerable theoretical difficulties, the political and legal sovereignty of Australia now resides in the people of Australia." See Kirby, M., "Deakin: Popular Sovereignty and the True Foundation of the Australian Constitution" (1996) 3 *Deakin Law Review* 129 at 143 where it is stated "[i]f the Australian people, and not the notional legality traced back to an Imperial statute, are the ultimate source of constitutional authority in Australia, may it not be the duty of the courts in their mode of reasoning to be more accessible to the people?"

[30] Http://www.hcourt.gov.au/. This site even contains a "virtual tour" of the Court.

[31] The High Court is not alone in this regard. Linda Greenhouse, "Telling the Court's Story: Justice and Journalism at the Supreme Court" (1996) 105 *Yale Law Journal* 1537 at 1559 has said of the United States Supreme Court: "I see a Court that is quite blithely oblivious to the needs of those who convey its work to the outside world, and a press corps that is often groping along in the dark, trying to make sense out of the shadows on the cave wall."

that the appeal had been allowed in part and how the various paragraphs of the order made by Justice North of the Federal Court were to be altered. Despite this, the media was left in disarray, with few journalists having any understanding of the majority ruling, let alone any appreciation of the altered position of the administrator at the centre of the dispute. The media was able to report which side had won, but little else. Even the alignment of the bench was misconstrued, with two reputable news outlets incorrectly reporting the decision as a 5:2, rather than 6:1, decision in favour of the Maritime Union.

The inaccessibility of High Court decisions means that journalists sometimes place too much reliance upon commentators. Commentators are an appropriate source of guidance and information for journalists. However, they are used too often to merely state what the High Court has decided, as opposed to expressing an opinion on the strength of the reasoning in the case or its likely impact. It is not unusual for a commentator to be allowed to both place his or her version of a decision before the public, and *then* to comment on it. As a consequence, the focus can shift from the decision of the Court to a commentator's interpretation of the decision, leaving the decision and the perspective of the commentator interwoven. This is particularly problematic if a commentator does not clearly distinguish between fact and opinion. Over-reliance upon commentators occurs because many journalists view decisions of the High Court as if they were the pronouncements of the oracle at Delphi; authoritative, but so obscure and elusive as to require the aid of an interpreter. This holds great dangers for the High Court, which can find its decision misreported due to a commentator's error or misinterpretation, or perhaps even dissatisfaction with the decision itself.

The inaccessibility of a High Court decision can also allow manipulation of the facts for political ends. Where journalists cannot find "independent" commentators, they may turn to interested parties for clarification of a decision and, without understanding what the High Court has decided, uncritically accept such statements. This occurred after the handing down of the *Wik* case, where the decision was misrepresented, and remains largely misunderstood, in part because of the capture of journalists covering the case by interested parties. It continued to occur when journalists reported comments that, as a result of the decision, native title might put freehold title at risk.[32]

Reforming the High Court's Relationship with the Media

A central challenge now facing the High Court is to reconcile its very public work with the lack of community and media understanding of its

---

[32] In *Fejo v Northern Territory* (1998) 156 ALR 721, the High Court confirmed that this was not the case.

role and processes. Some judges of the High Court have been willing to communicate with the public through the media. Justice Michael Kirby is an obvious example,[33] as are former Chief Justices Mason and Brennan, who gave interviews to "Four Corners" and "The Law Report",[34] and "Lateline" respectively. The recent documentary by Daryl Dellora entitled "The Highest Court"[35] is also an excellent example of the Brennan Court opening up its processes and decision making to the public.

However, the Court should go much further and develop a media strategy based upon a partnership with the media that seeks to provide factual information about decisions of the Court to the public. Linda Greenhouse, Supreme Court correspondent for *The New York Times*, has argued that, despite the fact that the interests of the media and the Supreme Court "can never be entirely congruent"[36]—the media's interest in accessibility of information being at odds with the Court's need to protect the integrity of its decisional process—"I am naive enough...to think of these two institutions as, to some degree, partners in a mutual democratic enterprise to which both must acknowledge responsibility."[37]

A media strategy should be developed by the Court in consultation with members of the media and other interested parties. It should deal with the range of issues relevant to the provision of accurate information to the public by the media.[38] For example, the Court might consider lockups for journalists when one or more particularly important or lengthy cases is to be handed down on the same day.[39] This would allow journalists the time to read and understand a decision before filing a report. The Court should also consider the televising of its proceedings.[40] It was notable that, while the decisions of the Federal Court at first instance[41]

---

[33] See Kirby, M., *The Judges* (Boyer Lectures, 1983) at 78. However, Justice Kirby has also expressed deep concern about the standard of media reporting of court matters. See Kirby, M., "Judiciary, Media and Government" (1993) 3 *Journal of Judicial Administration* 63 at 70–71.

[34] This is reproduced in Lobez, S., "Interview with Chief Justice Sir Anthony Mason" (1994) 89 *Victorian Bar News* 44.

[35] Ronin Films, 1998.

[36] Greenhouse, L., "Telling the Court's Story: Justice and Journalism at the Supreme Court" (1996) 105 *Yale Law Journal* 1537 at 1539.

[37] *Ibid.* at 1561.

[38] See the list of suggested mechanisms to improve communication between the courts and the media in Nicholson, A., "The Courts, the Media and the Community" (1995) 5 *Journal of Judicial Administration* 5 at 15–16.

[39] See Sir Daryl Dawson, "Judges and the Media" (1987) 10 *University of New South Wales Law Journal* 17 at 25. Cf. Austin, R.P., "Occasional Address to Graduation Ceremony (Postgraduate Law)", 2 May 1998, University of Sydney, at 9.

[40] This has been supported by Sir Ninian Stephen, "Address on the Occasion of the President's Luncheon", Law Institute of Victoria, 19 August 1998, at 10, 12–14. Cf. Sir Daryl Dawson, "Judges and the Media" (1987) 10 *University of New South Wales Law Journal* 17 at 25–26.

[41] *Maritime Union of Australia v Patrick Stevedores No 1 Pty Ltd* (1998) 153 ALR 602.

[42] *Patrick Stevedores Operations No 2 Pty Ltd v Maritime Union of Australia* (1998) 153 ALR 626.

and on appeal[42] in the litigation arising out of the recent waterfront dispute were televised, the outcome in the High Court[43] was not. No great dangers lurk for the High Court in the use of television cameras in the courtroom, nor is it likely that High Court Cable would attract a large following.

Three changes should form the core of the Court's media strategy. First, the Court should appoint a public information officer,[44] responsible to the Chief Justice,[45] who would, according to Sir Anthony Mason, "serve a useful purpose by keeping the media informed of important cases, by giving the media a court perspective on issues as they arise and explaining the reasons for decisions".[46] A like appointment has been made by the Federal Court and several State Supreme Courts,[47] as well as by comparable courts in other nations, such as the United States Supreme Court.[48] The appointment of a public information officer is overdue at the High Court, which has suffered more in recent times than many other bodies from a misinformed press and public. The need for a such a position at the High Court is also reinforced by the fact that the Federal Attorney-General can no longer be expected to leap to the Court's defence against unwarranted criticism.[49] A public information officer would lessen the pressure upon the judges of the Court to engage in public debate about a decision, a course that could damage the standing and impartiality of the Court. On the other hand, as encouraged by the Federal Attorney-General,[50] judges of the Court should feel able to appear in the media to discuss general matters such as the role of the Court, judicial independence or the rule of law.[51]

---

[43] *Patrick Stevedores Operations No 2 Pty Ltd v Maritime Union of Australia* (1998) 153 ALR 643.

[44] This has been supported by Austin, R.P., "Occasional Address to Graduation Ceremony (Postgraduate Law)", 2 May 1998, University of Sydney, at 10; Sir Anthony Mason, "The Courts as Community Institutions" (1998) 9 *Public Law Review* 83 at 87–88.

[45] Robertson, "Media and judges in Qld: Time for Change?" (1997) 17 *Proctor* 7 at 8.

[46] Sir Anthony Mason, "The Courts as Community Institutions" (1998) 9 *Public Law Review* 83 at 87.

[47] Black, "Letting the Public Know—the Educative Role of the Courts" (1994) 1 *Canberra Law Review* 165 at 170; Nicholson, "The Courts, the Media and the Community" (1995) 5 *Journal of Judicial Administration* 5 at 9–10. See Evans, "Aiding and Abetting: Prue Innes Helps Judges and the Media" (1994) 68 *Law Institute Journal* 806 on the appointment of a Courts Information Officer in Victoria, and McColl, "Chief Justice Murray Gleeson AO—'Reasonably Calm'" *Bar News*, Autumn / Winter 1994, 11 at 11–12 on the appointment of a Public Information Officer in New South Wales.

[48] See Ginsburg, "Communicating and Commenting on the Court's Work" (1995) 83 *Georgetown Law Journal* 2119 at 2122.

[49] Williams, D., "Judicial Independence" (1998) 36(3) *Law Society Journal* 50. Cf. Sir Gerard Brennan, "The State of the Judicature" (1998) 72 *Australian Law Journal* 33 at 41–42.

[50] Williams, D., "Judicial Independence and the High Court" (1998) 27 *Western Australian Law Review* 140 at 150–151.

[51] Sir Anthony Mason, "The Australian Judiciary in the 1990s" *Bar News*, Autumn/Winter 1994, 7 at 9–10; Lord Taylor of Gosforth, "The Independence of the Judiciary in a Democracy" (1995) 4 *Asia Pacific Law Review* 1 at 10–11. Cf. Sir Daryl Dawson, "Judges and the Media" (1987) 10 *University of New South Wales Law Journal* 17.

This suggestion has obvious budgetary implications for the High Court. It would be difficult for the Court to cater for the position out of its existing resources, which are so stretched that the Court is currently unable to open on weekends for visitors. Accordingly, the extra costs incurred should be met by increased government funding. A strong case can be made out for this based upon the changed role of the Attorney-General and the need to improve civics education in this area. Such funding would reflect the money already spent on bodies such as the Parliamentary Education Office.

Secondly, the Court should reform how it communicates its findings. The Court currently writes only for a legal audience, and makes little effort to deliver its judgments in a form that is accessible to the wider community. In handing down its reasons, there is little justification for the repetition of the facts in several separate judgments. This is a frequent occurrence. For example, in *Nicholas v The Queen*,[52] a 1998 case involving the separation of judicial power and the criminal justice system, the seven members of the Court delivered seven separate judgments, each of which separately recited the facts of the case. The Court should also consider making a greater effort to produce joint judgments. In the *Wik* case, for example, which involved enormous political sensitivity and was handed down just before Christmas 1996, five judgments were delivered, amounting to 204 pages of the *Commonwealth Law Reports*. The Court did make a small effort to outline the effect of its decision. Buried deep in the decision at the end of his judgment, Toohey J, with the concurrence of the other members of the majority, sought to explain the effect of the majority's reasoning.[53]

Thirdly, the Court should produce plain English summaries of its judgments.[54] The Court took steps in this direction in producing summaries for its decisions in the *Tasmanian Dam* case[55] and the *Patrick Stevedores* case. A summary should be short at one to two pages — no longer than the length of the headnotes currently produced for the judgments of the Court. The summaries should be produced by the public

---

[52] (1998) 151 ALR 312.

[53] *Wik Peoples v Queensland* (1996) 187 CLR 1 at 132–133.

[54] This or a like idea has been supported by Austin, R.P., "Occasional Address to Graduation Ceremony (Postgraduate Law)", 2 May 1998, University of Sydney, at 10; Sir Ninian Stephen, "Address on the Occasion of the President's Luncheon", Law Institute of Victoria, 19 August 1998, at 10–12.

[55] *Commonwealth v Tasmania* (1983) 158 CLR 1 at 58–59. See Sir Daryl Dawson, "Judges and the Media" (1987) 10 *University of New South Wales Law Journal* 17 at 24.

[56] Cf. Sir Gerard Brennan, "The Third Branch and the Fourth Estate", second lecture in the series "Broadcasting, Society and the Law", Faculty of Law, Radio Telefís Éireann, University College Dublin, 22 April 1997, who argues that: "The media would abandon their responsibility if they were to publish uncritically summaries of cases or other media releases issued with the authority of the courts. The media must themselves probe and analyse the reasons for judgments of public importance ... If the courts were to furnish digests of information for the media to publish, they would abandon the independence which both must assert and defend in the public interest."

information officer with the assistance of the judge's associates, and then checked by a member of the Court. A summary should be available at the handing down of a judgment and should be in a form that could be reproduced in the daily press,[56] along with appropriate commentary and analysis. This would be a breakthrough for the Court in that it would enable a decision to be more accurately communicated to the public via the media. Concerns about whether such a summary would be seen as having legal force are unfounded. The Court already participates in the production of authorised headnotes to its decisions when they are reported in the *Commonwealth Law Reports*.

Conclusion

Great challenges face the High Court. It stands the risk that its decisions will continue to be misconstrued and misinterpreted by an Australian public that knows little about it. This has the potential to undermine public confidence in Australia's justice system and the integrity of the Court. To respond to the current environment, in which there is considerable interest in the Court and its role as a law maker and protector of fundamental rights, the High Court must re-examine its relationship with the media. It should appoint a public information officer and hand down its decisions in a form that reporters can understand and communicate to the public. Changed perceptions and understandings of the Court mean that the Court can no longer afford to communicate its work solely to the legal profession. It must speak to the wider community.

COURT RADIO COMETH

Susannah Lobez

"The Law Report", ABC Radio National *

In recent years, the debate about whether court cases should be televised has raged—at legal conferences, in academia and in the media itself. It was great fodder, juicy issues about "public interest", "open justice" and "the rights of the accused to a fair trial" all up for grabs. Protagonists and opponents armed themselves to the teeth with analysis, expert opinion and at a pinch, anecdotal evidence about the dangers of the media *inside* the courtroom.

Of course print journos have always been in there, scribbling away with their quills and ink, entrusted by the courts to go away and write up a fair account of the case (and the judge's sometimes poorly chosen phrases!). We'd also had the odd broadcaster (including this one) get into a court to film or tape material to be used in various docos or current affairs features.

In 1995, the Victorian Supreme Court's Justice Bernard Teague put a tentative (but brave) toe in the water of "Court TV". He allowed a camera to record the sentencing of a confessed child killer (Avent). It was hardly gavel-to-gavel coverage, but it created a storm of controversy, provoked some unkind aspersions about Justice Teague's motivations and polarized public and legal opinion about the merits and evils of allowing cameras into courts.

Among the concerns expressed by those opposed to cameras in courtrooms were:
* it will turn court cases into entertainment;
* it will invade the privacy of the accused and his family;
* it will make judges, counsel, witnesses and juries self conscious or tempt them to perform for the cameras;
* coverage will be sensationalist and superficial, squeezed into two minute time slots;
* it may prejudice the fair trial or hearing, which ultimately is the goal of the courts.

The finale of the O.J. Simpson criminal trial put the big boot on any court television prospects in Australia for a while at least. It wasn't actually what the camera in the courtroom recorded and presented which seemed

---

*"The Law Report" is produced and presented by actor-turned-barrister-turned-broadcaster, Susannah Lobez. Damien Carrick is co-producer and reporter. It can be heard on ABC Radio National at 8.30 a.m. and 8.30 p.m. every Tuesday. "Law Report" transcripts are available at www.abc.net.au/rn.

to offend most people. It was the circus, the media feeding frenzy—constant commentary, media operators interviewing each other, speculation on evidence or argument put by counsel—all the kind of things which would make most Aussie lawyers think of the "Big C"—contempt.

Amid all this (and working on the premise that you "love the one you're with" and I'm with radio), I decided to have a go at "Court Radio"! After all, radio is an *ideas* medium, often less frivolous and superficial than telly. It lends itself to "infotainment". Radio will keep the audience from being distracted by the defendant's mother snivelling in the second row or the judge's funny looking wig and gown or the tipstaff dozing off. Counsel and judges won't be tempted to ham it up as they won't even be conscious of an audience, microphones already being on the bar table. Radio allows more focus on the issues and the argument than the personalities and appearances.

The judiciary and the media often seem suspicious of each other. It was going to take some diplomacy so I decided I'd try to be the intermediary. I put out the word that I was looking for some sensitive new age judges (SNAJs) to be part of this experiment and that I wasn't out to get 'em.

The South Australian judges proved receptive. The Chief Justice could say "yes" till he was blue in the face but what if when we found a case to record, the presiding judge said "no" or the defendant himself pulled the plug? Chief Justice Doyle and I, together, drafted a letter explaining the project and seeking the consent of litigants and their lawyers. His Honour and the Chief Judge of the District Court of South Australia provided a written endorsement of the project and I worked on the guidelines to cover the recording of a case.

It was then a question of finding the right case to record and getting the consent of all involved. After some false starts—judge, prosecutor, defence counsel, witnesses and defendant all agreed to allow recording of a case of alleged "possession of cannabis for sale". It was heard (and recorded) before judge and jury in the Adelaide District Court late in November 1996.

The Crown case was that the accused, having in his possession some 4.2 kilograms of cut cannabis and a 2.5 metre, silver-headed cannabis plant in his garden, had more than he was allowed to have for personal use (100 grams). Unless he could prove otherwise, he was deemed to have cannabis for sale (which carries pretty hefty penalties.)

The accused's case was that he was a habitual user of cannabis and smoked it as a kind of medication. He had grown a small crop of cannabis every year for over 20 years for his own personal use. Along the way, he had become a bit of an amateur geneticist. Despite failing grade six several times, he had experimented with the pollination process and developed unusual protein combinations to feed his plants.

"...I figured why should I feed a plant a bowl of chook shit...I wouldn't eat a bowl of chook shit...It's better with amino acids and proteins..."
Q. "What do you add to your plants?"
A. "Beer, malt, brewers yeast, eggs, bananas...I make it into liquid fertiliser and pour it onto my plants...and my chemistry works, the root structure is f...ing astronomical!"

This very first experiment with "Court Radio" was heard on Radio National's "Law Report" on Tuesday, 4 February 1997. Listeners were able to consider their verdicts after hearing both sides of the case and the following week the jury foreman delivered the verdict in the case. Another example of *"courtus interruptus"*.

Since the Law Report's first foray into "Court Radio" which aired in 1997, a number of discussions have taken place to try to produce a court radio documentary in other jurisdictions. Several judges seem willing, in a range of courts, but for a variety of reasons we haven't yet secured a recording opportunity.

So "Court Radio" is now a happening thing, on Radio National at least. Listeners will be taken right into the court for the trial. They may feel sort of like the thirteenth juror and will hear an abridged version of the case.

The South Australian judges and court staff have facilitated another recording opportunity of a Commonwealth prosecution of a person who was charged with arranging a marriage to circumvent immigration law. It was a longer trial than previously thought and we hope it will be edited and broadcast some time in 1999.

WHAT THE COURTS AND THE MEDIA CAN DO TO IMPROVE THE STANDARD OF MEDIA REPORTING OF THE WORK OF THE COURTS

Patrick Keyzer

Senior Lecturer in Law, University of Technology, Sydney; Convenor of the Courts and the Media Forum at UTS Law School, 13 November 1998

Fear and Loathing

How much of the hysteria which followed the High Court's decision in the *Wik* case[1] was the consequence of sensational reporting? The headline of *The Sydney Morning Herald* the following day was "A Judgment For Chaos". The editorial of *The Australian Financial Review* was entitled "Wik decision disappointing" and commenced with the comment that "[F]armers and miners have every right to be alarmed at yesterday's long-awaited High Court decision in the Wik case."[2] The editorial went on to say that the native title system, "which was already bogged down in complexities" would be thrown "into complete confusion. The system is now as clear as mud". The decision was a "setback" and had created a "mess".[3] A columnist for the Melbourne *Herald Sun* described *Wik* as an "utter disaster" which would give rise to "complex litigation" and stall development.[4] *Wik* would "leave the mining and pastoral industries facing an endless road of litigation to determine in the case of each and every lease whether native title exists and how they might be required to co-exist with it."[5] Headlines shrieked of the "anger", "dismay" and "disappointment" which greeted the "confusing" decision, the "obstacle" it created for Aboriginal reconciliation and resource security, how the decision had put the government in a "tough spot", "turned up the heat" on them and drew them into a "legal and political nightmare".[6]

---

[1] (1996) 187 CLR 1.

[2] "Wik decision disappointing", *Financial Review*, 24 December 1996, p 12.

[3] Ibid.

[4] McCrann, T.,"Mabo II decision will add to the perils of Pauline", *Herald Sun*, 1st edn., 24 December 1996, pp. 35 and 37.

[5] Taylor, L., "Ruling puts Coalition in a tough spot", *Financial Review*, 24 December 1996, p. 4.

[6] Tingle, L., "Government faces nightmare over High Court's judgment: Comment", *The Age*, 24 December 1996, p. 5.

With a few exceptions, journalists were *not* responsible for generating the *heat* in the *Wik* debate. We need to distinguish between *reportage* of alarmist or extremist opinions by the media and *expression* of alarmist or extremist opinions by the media. Stakeholders reacted sharply to the decision and adopted strident and rigid positions: simply reporting the opinions of the stakeholders produced ample drama for a good story. And it might be expected that the stakeholders would express their messages in a way which would maximize their impact. However the press was deficient in shedding *light* during the *Wik* debate. While a few journalists reported the mixed reactions to the *Wik* decision, the large majority of the reporting emphasized the negative reactions to the decision. Overall, there was a lack of balance and depth in the reporting and in the commentary. In that environment, the High Court was a soft target. The strident criticism of the Court left many with the impression that the judgments were not supported by extensive and careful legal reasoning.[7] This helped create an environment in which misinformation could thrive. Facts were swallowed by opinions. Native title claims could and, it was intimated, would, be made over pastoral leases, mining leases, forestry licences, irrigation agreements, the ocean, and even *backyards.*

When the *Wik* decision was handed down, the policy of the Chief Justice, Sir Gerard Brennan, was to decline to respond to the criticism.[8] Brennan CJ outlined his perspective on the relationship between the courts and the media in a speech called "The Third Branch and the Fourth Estate".[9] Sir Gerard pointed out that the judicature has no power base but public confidence in its integrity and its competence in performing its functions. But to secure the rule of law, there must be an arbiter whose authority is accepted by the powerful and the weak, the rich and the poor, the government and the governed, the majority and the minority. Yet the public knows little of the functions and methodology of the courts. While it might be tempting to say that the courts and the media share a responsibility to create or maintain confidence in the work of the courts, that would cast the media in the role of apologist for the courts. Ideally, the media should report and analyze the work of the courts. According to Sir Gerard Brennan, the courts must ignore the media lest they be

---

[7] Austin, R.P. (the Hon. Justice), "Occasional Address to Graduation Ceremony (Postgraduate Law)", 2 May 1998, University of Sydney, also cited by Williams, G., *infra*, n. 39.

[8] Chief Justice Brennan had already taken the exceptional step of writing to Deputy Prime Minister Tim Fischer to scold him for his attacks on the Court. Fischer had criticised the High Court for, as he put it, delaying the delivery of the *Wik* judgments. Fischer later apologised to the Chief Justice, but was one of the principal critics of the judgment, and later remarked that the government would be replacing retiring judges with "Capital C" conservatives.

[9] Brennan, the Hon. F.G., "The Third Branch and the Fourth Estate", (1997) 16 *Australian Bar Review* 2.

influenced by its views. The courts and the media have interlocking but *disparate* functions which, if properly performed by both institutions, should produce public confidence in the maintenance of the rule of law by the courts.

Certainly, judges should not be expected to hold news conferences to explain their opinions. They do not have a *political* message to *sell*. The maintenance of both the reality and the public's perception of the impartiality and independence of the judicature is a constitutional fundamental.[10] As Sir Frank Kitto warned:

> Every judge worthy of the name recognizes that he must take each man's censure; he knows full well as a judge he is born to censure as the sparks fly upwards; but neither in preparing a judgment nor in retrospect may it weigh with him that the harvest he gleans is praise or blame, approval or scorn. He will reply to neither; he will defend himself not at all.[11]

A judge influenced in judgment by what was said in the media "would not be fit to be a judge".[12]

The Power of the Press

The mainstream media is the most prominent producer of news about the courts, and is therefore in a unique and powerful position in respect of its relationship with the courts. People rely on the media for their information about the courts. It is unrealistic to expect people to converge in the public galleries of Australian courts to improve their understanding of the court system.[13] The media has the power to create and to destroy the reputation of the courts. It can enhance or destroy understanding of judgments. It can control the degree of prominence given to public exposure of a court case or decision. It settles the agenda of legal reform and the parameters of discussion of the work of the courts.

But journalists inhabit a different professional and ethical universe to judges. Even experienced lawyers can come to grief attempting to understand some judgments. Pity journalists without legal training attempting to grasp the gist of a 150 page judgment handed down at 10.30 a.m. in time for a 4.00 p.m. deadline, and subject to all the other regrettable vicissitudes of news production.[14] And legal journalism is in a number of critical respects more difficult than other types of journalism. There are no sources, no leaks, no information derived from casual

---

[10] See for example, *Wilson v Minister for Aboriginal Affairs* (1996).

[11] Sir Frank Kitto, "Why Write Judgments", (1992) 66 *Australian Law Journal* 787 at 790, cited in McLelland, R., *infra*.

[12] *BLF Case* (1982) 41 ALR 171 at 90 per Gibbs CJ and at 123 per Mason J, both quoting Lord Salmon (see Anderson, D., fn 15).

[13] As Jenny Brockie pointed out in the panel discussion following the third session of the Forum, *infra*.

[14] Even the Attorney-General was prepared to make this concession. See also Campbell, R., *infra*.

contacts, no off the record briefings and no doorstops.[15] You cannot interview the newsmakers.[16]

Courts have to take account of the significance of the work of the media and the constraints on legal journalists and take steps to facilitate the dissemination of information about their work.[17] As Chris Merritt, legal correspondent for *The Australian Financial Review*, notes:

> ...on most big issues that have a direct impact on the judiciary, the point of view of the judiciary is either missing, late or it appears obliquely, through the voices of others whose interests are not always exactly in alignment with those of the judges. If this continues, the judiciary will effectively be vacating the field and leaving it to others to set the parameters of debate on these matters.[18]

How can the courts help the journalists in ways which do not compromise the public's perception, and the reality, of their independence and impartiality?

Court Media Officers or Court Public Education Officers?

The appointment of court media officers is a welcome development.[19] But their role is extremely delicate. There are real dangers. There is perhaps an *inherent* danger in having court media officers explain decisions. How can the danger of giving differing emphasis to different parts of a decision be avoided?[20] Would court media officers or public education officers correct misinformation? Poor court reporting by the media? *Substandard* court reporting by the media?

Caution must be exercised to ensure that a more cosy relationship between the courts and the media does not increase the power of the media to influence judges and judgments[21] or provide the media with information which would not otherwise be shared with the public. Emphasis should be placed on the "public education" function of the court media officer. Certainly, much could be done to enhance appreciation by the general public and journalists of the role of the judiciary in our system of government, the separation of powers, and judicial review.[22]

---

[15] See for example Greenhouse, L., "Telling The Court's Story", (1996) 105 *Yale Law Journal* 1537, 1539–1540.

[16] Greenhouse, L., 1543.

[17] *Infra*.

[18] Merritt, C., *infra*.

[19] Sir Anthony Mason AC KBE, "The Courts as Community Institutions", (1998) 9 *Public Law Review* 83 at 87, cited in Williams, G., *infra*, n. 44.

[20] A difficulty noted by Jenny Brockie during the panel discussion following the third session of the Forum.

[21] It has been said that *some* judges are "very astute at using the media", for lofty *and* grubby objectives: Campbell, R., *infra*.

[22] See Merritt, C., *infra*. There is an unfortunate tendency for newspaper articles describing cases involving judicial review of legislative or executive action to be headed "Judges Hitting Out" or "Judges Slamming Ministers": see the comments of Lord Lowry, United Kingdom House of Lords Debates, 5 June 1996, "The Judiciary: Public Controversy", p. 1297.

Court-Produced Headnotes and Judgment Summaries

One task for the court public education officer might be the dissemination to the public of a brief account of the facts and reasons for decision in every case.[23] Recently, several courts have adopted the practice of distributing judgment summaries at the time of judgment delivery.[24] A notable example was the High Court's summary of the orders and effect of those orders in *Patricks Stevedores Operations No. 2 Pty Ltd v Maritime Union of Australia*.[25] Media reports immediately following the decision were mixed, with some reporting the decision as a "win" to the Union, others as a "win" to Patricks. But by the time of the evening television news bulletins, most outlets reported the decision, accurately, as a "win" for neither party,[26] but simply as a faithful application of the policy of the Federal Government, reflected in its industrial laws.

Distribution of a judgment summary at the time of judgment delivery is unusual. Yet, some weeks, months or sometimes years later, when the news value of a judgment has evaporated, a selection of the judgments of superior courts are reported by private publishers headed by a judgment summary which is a brief and effective source of information about the content of that judgment: the *headnote*. Between the time of judgment delivery and this publication, an editor, typically holding legal qualifications, prepares a brief summary of the facts, the question of law to be decided and the judgment or judgments of the court.

At present, the "headnotes" for some of these publications are returned to the court for authorization. The judges who heard the case then have an opportunity to check the headnote for accuracy. In practice, the judge's associate reviews the headnote before the judge has a final look over it. This can sometimes require a complete re-drafting of the headnote. Then it is returned to the publisher, and the judgment is published as an "authorized" report. The court will then customarily require litigants to use the authorized report of a case where it is available.

What is the purpose of this explanation, other than to demonstrate that this is a complicated, time-consuming rigamarole? It is to ask this: why don't the courts prepare the headnotes for delivery with the judgments? The headnote could then be used by the media to pass on to the public in its reports.

---

[23] If prepared by the Court itself, this would also remove the spectre of "spin-doctoring". See Campbell, R., *infra*.

[24] A practice noted by Chief Justice Black, *infra*, Austin, R.P. (the Hon. Justice) "Occasional Address to Graduation Ceremony", 2 May 1998, University of Sydney, p. 10; Dawson, the Hon. Sir Daryl, "Judges and the Media" (1987) 10 *University of New South Wales Law Journal* 7 at 24; Sir Ninian Stephen, "Address On the Occasion of the President's Luncheon", Law Institute of Victoria, 19 August 1998, pp. 10–12.

[25] (1998) 153 ALR 643.

[26] But cf. Williams, G., *infra* and Campbell, R., *infra*.

This proposal will not bankrupt the private publishers of law reports. They will still be able to add value to the reporting of judgments by indexing and digesting case reports. The courts have given no credence to fears expressed by the councils on law reporting that electronic dissemination of reports by the courts will threaten the economic viability of the authorized reports. And, after all, we have already paid *once* for the information produced by the courts.

Publicizing Pleadings and Submissions

Reporting of the work of the courts would also be enhanced if, where appropriate, journalists had access to the pleadings and submissions which precede the hearings and the judgments.[27] Once a public announcement is made that a judgment shall be delivered (generally this announcement is passed to the parties in advance of the public release of a judgment to enable them to appear in court to receive it), journalists could prepare their articles in advance, and they would be better informed on judgment day. Better still, make these documents publicly available on the internet so the public can read them and form its own views.

Ultimately, courts *are* public places, and they should be subject to media scutiny just as the executive and the legislature are. If publicity is the hallmark of the exercise of judicial power, it might even be a constitutional requirement of our system of government that judgments, and perhaps even the materials which inform our judges, be freely available to the public. Public exposure of court documents might enhance the quality of the submissions, and would certainly increase public awareness not only of the functions of the courts but the people, organizations and polities who participate in the dynamic of the exercise of judicial power.

Judicial Leadership and Media Relations Policy

There are special problems in developing policy to govern court–media relations. First, no court can speak for any other court. Second, no Chief Justice can speak for any individual judge. Judges take an individual oath to the law. And judges have differing views and attitudes in respect of media reporting of their work. Judges are by their nature independent thinkers, many of them are fiercely independent thinkers, and it is unlikely that one single perspective would be shared by judges collectively, let alone a majority of them. Reforms will take place on a court by court and judge by judge basis.

The Commonwealth Attorney-General has proposed that the Judicial Conference of Australia, a judge's "peak body", speak on behalf of the judges. But it cannot.[28] First, the organization of judges which has the

---

[27] See the comments of Wendy Bacon in the discussion following the second session of the Forum.

[28] As Chris Merritt points out, *infra*.

actual power to develop policy which can bind the administration of the courts (if not the behaviour of its judges) is the Council of Chief Justices of Australia and New Zealand. The Judicial Conference simply does not have the authority to speak on behalf of the Australian judiciary. Second, even if it did, any suggestion that it respond to criticism of a court or justice of a court places its membership—other judges—in the invidious position of commenting on the work of another judge or court. This is clearly out of the question. Recognizing the problems outlined above, the Council of Chief Justices is the only organization which can develop a media relations policy for the courts. This could be time-consuming.[29]

What is "Judicial Accountability"?

Each of these proposals requires increased funding for the courts. Governments cannot expect courts to spend shrinking amounts of money on civics education when there are pressing demands on court resources, especially pressing demands caused by cuts to court budgets and to programmes which directly impact on the efficient management of court business.

The notion of "judicial accountability" has to be treated with some caution.[30] As Chief Justice Brennan said in "The Third Branch and the Fourth Estate":

> Court critics sometimes complain that judges are unaccountable. To whom should they be accountable and for what? In charging a jury, judges expose their conception of the law to be applied. In reasons for judgment, they give a full and public account of the facts they find and the law as they hold it to be. How otherwise are they to give an account of the exercise of their powers? Should the judge be accountable to the government of the day? Certainly not. Should the judge be accountable in some way to an interest group or to the public? The rule of law would be hostage to public relations campaigns or majoritarian interests. Should a judgment be fashioned to satisfy popular sentiment? That would be the antithesis of the rule of law.

Of course the community demands accountability of those in public office, including judges.[31] The administrators of courts should be and are exposed to the same measure of scrunity of their budgets as the various departments of government. But it is understating the true position to say that the judiciary "are not dependent on any group or body in society, least of all the Executive which appoints them".[32] They *are* dependent on the government for adequate funds to run the courts. These are funds

---

[29] As Jenny Brockie, Liz Jackson and Susannah Lobez pointed out in the Forum discussions, *infra*.

[30] Gleeson, the Hon A.M., "Performing the Role of the Judge", (1998) 10(8) *Judicial Officers' Bulletin* at 59, cited in Williams, D., *infra*, n. 4.

[31] As the Attorney-General noted in his paper. Of course, this comment applies with equal force to the members of the executive and the legislature.

[32] See Williams, D., *infra*.

that might be used to create court public education offices, among other things.

Courts and judges are only truly accountable to the constitutional requirements of their respective jurisdictions, not the policies of governments. Reduction of court budgets does not improve the prospect of improved education of the public by the courts. Continued decreases in court funding might threaten the constitutional separation of powers.

What Journalists Can Do

The courts do not have sole responsibility for improving the standard of media reportage of the work of the courts. Journalists should strive for accuracy and completeness in the reporting of the work of the courts.[33] Their *Code of Ethics* requires it. They should explain the reasons for the decision and resist sensationalizing their reports.[34] They should have the patience to deal with the important issues and mute the drama, the trivial and the salacious.[35] Journalists should fight to retain the integrity of their reporting right through the process of a story.[36]

These are ideals. But journalists have much to gain from improving the standard of coverage. Journalists should not assume that judges are not aware of their critics.[37] They are. All judges are conscious of criticism of their work in the media. They too are informed citizens. They read newspapers. They get upset when journalists get it wrong, just like anybody else. Judges read by-lines and the reputation of a legal correspondent can be destroyed in the eye of the judge by inaccuracy.[38] Journalists will command the respect of judges if they are accurate and strive to be complete in their coverage of the work of the courts. This might improve opportunities for access to the courts.

If the hallmarks of high quality legal reporting are accuracy and impartiality then greater exposure should be given to the commentary of observers who have the capacity to provide informed and impartial views on the work of the courts. Asking a lawyer who has appeared for one of the parties to explain a decision will produce a predictably biased response. Politicians will rarely have the capacity to greet a decision with an impartial response, particularly in constitutional cases. A barrister who appears for a party in constitutional litigation who is *also* a member of a political party cannot be expected to provide an impartial account of a given decision.

---

[33] Dawson, D., "Judges and the Media", (1987) 10 *University of New South Wales Law Journal* 17 at 23.

[34] See Williams, D., *infra*.

[35] See Campbell, R., *infra*.

[36] See Kimberley Ashbee's comments in the discussion following the third session of the Forum.

[37] See Anderson, D., *infra*, particularly at nn. 14 to 16.

[38] See Kimberley Ashbee's comments in the discussion following the third session of the Forum.

Conclusion

It is going too far to say that courts are "a public relations disaster". Many judges recognize that they need to make greater efforts to communicate with "the punters" about the issues.[39] Judges have made great strides in improving public education about their work.[40] Australian courts have, within their limited means, embraced the electronic media, with most courts having web sites and publishing judgments on the internet. The appellate courts have taken steps to develop an Electronic Appeals Project which would greatly enhance the efficiency of handling court information. That project might even be developed in such a way as to improve public access to pre-judgment information.

A number of senior judicial officers have expressed "cautious optimism" about the prospects for the relationship between the courts and the media.[41] Hopefully suggestions like these and the work and ideas of the many people involved in the Courts and the Media Forum will help to improve the flow of information and any fear and loathing in the relationship between the "third branch" and the "Fourth Estate".

---

[39] As Liz Jackson pointed out in the panel discussion following the third session of the Forum.

[40] The Hon. Michael Black AC, "Letting the Public Know—the Educative Role of the Courts", (1994) 1 *Canberra Law Review* 165. See also the comments of Chief Justice Black and Chief Justice Doyle, *infra*.

[41] See for example Black, M., *infra*, and Lord Cooke of Thorndon, United Kingdom *House of Lords Debates*, 5 June 1996, "The Judiciary: Public Controversy", p. 1291.

PANEL DISCUSSION

Associate Professor Chris Nash[1], Kimberley Ashbee[2], Jenny Brockie[3], Liz Jackson[4], Associate Professor Rod Tiffen[5]

CHRIS NASH:

There has been a bit of discussion here about the need for responsible media access policies to the courts. David Anderson pointed out that in the United States the horse has already bolted and, for structural reasons of cross-media competition there, there is no such thing as responsibility any longer. There is, in fact, rampant freedom of speech.

I just might point out that there is a very distinguished tradition in North American liberal democratic theories, especially to do with communications, that suggests, in fact, freedom of the press is a very bad thing in terms of its impact on freedom of speech. What the freedom of the press does is give power to the media monopolies, or large media organizations, which then act not only through the professional ethics of their employees, which they control, but also through their own institutional corporate interests to stifle sometimes what might be seen as the voice of the people.

We have seen allegations of that in Australia recently with the Pauline Hanson phenomenon, where the media were locked in with the elites, who the people are criticizing. So Harold Innes, in particular, who many consider to be the most distinguished communication theorist in North America this century, suggests that freedom of the press was, in fact, an abrogation of a democratic right to the freedom of speech. With the internet what we are seeing is a rampant outbreak of freedom of speech. To me, that underlies the larger issue: that, really, the media and the courts, or the media and the justice system, can, to a large extent, work hand in hand in an informative or educational role vis-a-vis the public. I think that fails to recognize that there is a profound political tension between the media and the courts.

The courts—the third branch of government—are an arm of government and in democratic political theory, at least, the role of the press is,

---

[1] Associate Professor of Media, University of Technology, Sydney and Director, Australian Centre for Independent Journalism; Session 3 Panel Chair.

[2] Acting Public Information Officer, Supreme Court of New South Wales.

[3] ABC Television.

[4] "Four Corners" programme, ABC Television.

[5] Associate Professor, Department of Government and Public Administration, University of Sydney.

on behalf of the people, to challenge the excesses of government or, perhaps, to limit the excesses of government.

So the courts, just as the executive and the legislature, are, therefore, fair game for the media. In fact, it is the media's constitutional role. It is what their very right to freedom of the press depends upon—taking a distant and critical relationship to the courts.

Now the Westminster traditions in some ways disguise this because one is born a subject of the Crown. The various arms of government emanate from the Crown, at least in theory, which is quite different from government being of the people, by the people and for the people. So there is, I think, a difficulty under the Westminster system of actually grappling with what precisely the rights of people are, vis-a-vis the institutions which are constituted under the Westminster system. But there is no doubt that the political reality is there, and the One Nation phenomenon, where they attacked the media, the courts and the government, is all part of an elite and very real manifestation of that.

Tim Fischer, the Deputy Prime Minister's, call for installation of a "capital C conservative" onto the High Court was another instance of that political pressure being felt by politicians which they are then turning onto the other branch of government. So it seems to me it is absolutely important that there not be a woolly notion that the media and the courts can work easily together.

Our system of government, if you like, depends upon there being quite a profound political tension between the two.

KIMBERLEY ASHBEE:

I was interested in Justice Teague's gradings for proceedings and televising of proceedings. My observations in terms of the Supreme Court in New South Wales are only three months old but, prior to that, having spent time with the Bar Association, the Law Society and a top tier law firm, I have an overall picture of all the players in the game and what roles they can play and improve on. Generally, I think the community's understanding of the whole court system show that courts seem to get sometimes unfairly criticized for some of the things that happened further down the food chain, if you like.

The gradings, I thought, were fair, but I don't think there is anything too hard that can't be done with planning, with consultation and having very strong professional working relationships with the media. I believe that the sentences that I have observed myself were actually right for broadcast because you have got a neat summary, if you like, of what has happened in the trial. Probably the sentences in jury trials are more interesting, and challenging—for the judiciary to explain how they have arrived at that particular sentence. However, on the other side, I think that journalists need to take particular care in really owning their story right through the whole process of writing, the subbing, what picture goes with it, and fighting strongly internally for that. I think that is very important.

You educate at the same time as doing that because it is your by-line that the judicial officers read and see and, whilst I will believe you about a subbing or a photograph you didn't know was going to accompany your story, and I will always pass that on, that is your reputation, if you like, and how you are seen in the eyes of the judicial officers.

Recently we had a judgment where a cautioning note was issued at the end—it should have been at the front, in my view—which said what a judgment *wasn't*. That was superb because it is exactly what the media thought it would be, and it turned out not to be that, so it was there in black and white. Of course, when I turn up for a judgment to be handed down they know something is on any way, so that worked very well.

CHRIS NASH:

Jenny, do you want to add anything?

JENNY BROCKIE:

Only that I find it rather depressing that I was asked to be here actually. The only real qualification I have for being here is that I am one of the few people who have managed to get cameras inside a courtroom. It was four years ago. For those of you who don't know, it was a feature-length documentary about Campbelltown Local Court, called "So Help Me God".

I think the point that Chris makes about the separation in this talk of co-operation between the media and the courts is a very good one. At one level, that is true. But at another level, it is essential that the respective roles are kept separate and there is a mutual respect for those roles.

When I set out to make a film in a Local Court, in a magistrate's court, the main reason was that it is or was where 90 per cent of court business was carried out and the "LA Law" image of court was very much people's television diet. It seemed to me that what really went on in Local Courts, in particular, was quite likely to be of considerable interest and also might surprise our audience.

I went to Ian Pike, who was then the Chief Magistrate in New South Wales, and explained to him that I wanted to make a feature-length film about the life of a courtroom, that I wanted to contextualize things like magistrates' decisions, and contextualize the whole court procedure by looking at not only what went on inside the courtroom itself but what went on in the Legal Aid Office and solicitor's office around the court and so on. He agreed it was a wonderful idea and said: "I think it is very unlikely you will find a magistrate to do it but, you know, go ahead and try". As it was, we approached dozens of magistrates. Only two were interested. Nearly all the others said they thought it was a fabulous idea for someone else to do and, in the end, I had several meetings with Kevin

Flack, who was then the senior magistrate at Campbelltown Court, and he agreed very much along the lines that I think were appropriate for that film. Now, in a sense, that relationship was very dependent on our mutual regard for not stepping on one another's toes, if you like.

My biggest fear in making the film was, frankly, that I would find a magistrate who would say yes, but who would want to pick and choose the cases that we filmed. That seemed to me to be overstepping what I wanted my film to be, which was very much an overview of the life of a court over a period of six weeks.

As it turned out, Kevin Flack didn't do that but did lay down a condition that we would require consent from all the participating parties. His concern was that in opening the courtroom he did not want to invade people's privacy. I mean, this idea that a court is an open place is nonsense when the majority of people get their information from electronic media. You know, people do not go into courtrooms *en masse* and sit in the public gallery and that is part of the reason they don't understand how the legal system works. They rely on electronic media, and they rely on print media for coverage of court cases. So, it was interesting, in a sense, that this issue of privacy co-existed with the idea of an open court, but, indeed, it does. I was more than happy to agree to that because we felt, as filmmakers, that it would be inappropriate, I suppose, to go blasting in on a one-off basis and expose people to national television when there is not a prevailing culture that actually has courtrooms open to a television audience.

What ended up happening was that an extraordinary number of people agreed to be filmed. Written consents were obtained from everybody involved. Double consent forms were signed both for Legal Aid Office purposes and for the ABC's purposes. As a result, the film went to air and the sky didn't fall in. I mean it was not the end of the world that court proceedings made it onto television. I do find it depressing that while, as Justice Teague says, the question seems now to be not whether but how courts will be televised, it is still not happening. For all the talk, for all the conferences, for all the number of times this discussion has been had, by and large, I have yet to see a major trial covered by a television camera and put to air as a documentary, or whatever, after the event.

Now, it seems to me there are big transitional issues to think about. I think the whole issue of privacy is something that is quite complex and interesting in relation to this issue because I think we have a culture where court proceedings don't appear on television. When they do, those people do get singled out.

I just returned from the United States a couple of weeks ago and I have to say, while the horse has bolted, I had a fascinating conversation about the O.J. Simpson trial with somebody over there who said that the most intriguing thing about it was discovering just how truly boring the legal system can be. This was because people were turning on their television day after day wanting something salacious and wonderful or exciting to happen and were finding that day after day, it was bogged down in legal argument.

There is an argument to say that a court TV network, while we might gasp and say "shock, horror" and "how outrageous" and "how exploitative that is", in a sense, if you are looking for contextualizing your court proceedings where you have ongoing coverage of court proceedings in all their boring glory, you are, in a sense, educating people much more to the system than you are if you are taking snippets out. So you can argue either way.

I guess it just seems to me that it is a discussion that has been had endlessly, that people are slowly coming to the view that perhaps it might be worth opening that door slightly. I would just sound a note of caution about respect. I don't think journalists want to tell judges how to do their job. I would be worried if judges started trying to dictate to journalists what particular aspects of the case they could cover for television. For example, if they, in fact, were prepared to agree in principle to the idea of coverage. Then you get into all that real messy territory of what do you single out, how do you safeguard against people being exploited, or whatever, but we have got to move on it. The most staggering thing to me at Campbelltown was the extent of ignorance these people had about the system they were about to walk through the doors into. They had no idea, half of them. The people who had never appeared in court before had no idea what was going to happen when they walked through those doors and I think that is a real worry.

LIZ JACKSON:

We actually did think at one point about trying to do a "Four Corners" programme where we gained access to the court, but failed utterly when absolutely everybody refused to allow us in.

It seems to me that there are the easy things and there are the hard things. I mean, the easy things that we could all agree on would be a public information officer for the High Court of Australia. About five weeks ago, I rang up the High Court of Australia wanting a number for Sir Anthony Mason and no one there was able to tell me. The conversation went something like: "Sir Anthony Mason? You want to know where Sir Anthony Mason is?", "Yes, he was the Chief Justice. You know, the one before last". There was no one actually—you might think that is a very minor point—who answered the phone who was able to actually give me that number. Far more important was, I think, in terms of getting that position and the difference it makes is an acknowledgment by the Court that there is a problem.

It is fantastically important that people who are judges go on a populist medium (even if it is an elitist programme) and actually talk to the punters about the issues.

That, for instance, in the case of persuading Sir Anthony Mason, was something that was fantastically difficult but for which I think he ought to be acknowledged. He was actually prepared to go on television and answer questions, albeit as he was walking in, and saying: "I don't know if I can talk about *Mabo*." I said: "Hang on, you've got to. Everybody wants to know about it."

Excuse me for relating that. But when push came to shove, he was prepared to articulate of his own volition. If you look back at the interview, he was prepared to say why a judgment like that was important and was prepared to answer a question like: "When it comes down to implied rights, I have picked up the Constitution and I can't find any here. Did you make it up?". He was prepared to answer a fairly direct television question and I thought he acquitted himself admirably, and, as Jenny said, the sky didn't fall in.

At the end of the program, the High Court—and correct me if I am wrong—was happy with it and felt that it was a fine thing to have done and ought to have been done. As I say, my job is often persuading people that it actually is really quite important to break down the sense that there is an elite, which I accept does not just constitute the High Court, and journalists like myself find ourselves uncomfortably classed in that elite.

I also wanted to quickly touch on the fact that there is not always going to be, as I think Chris and Jenny have alluded to, a congruence of interests. I think certainly there is something that remains to be discussed about what is proper to be talked about in the media. I don't think there is agreement between the courts and the media about what it is proper to be talked about, and I think that comes down to a different view about how we go about, for instance, maintaining confidence in the judiciary. I am slap bang against this in terms of the recent programme that "Four Corners" did in which we finally ended up, after a certain debate about what the programme should actually be about, looking at the long, close attention to the case of Justice Ian Callinan. In terms of an agreement among the courts and among lawyers generally about what was proper to go on television and be prepared to say, we encountered the full range from people who weren't, for instance, judicial officers, who would not allow us to film in foyers of courts, where some stage of the proceeding might have happened in that foyer in that court.

We were not allowed to film barristers' admissions (for the sake of discretion they will remain unnamed); just where the barristers walk in and say: "I hereby swear a public duty to the court." This is obviously absolutely critical to a discussion of that case to understand that that is what baby barristers do, they swear a duty to the court. That wasn't on.

I think right through the legal profession and right up to the very top in the political area of this, there was a general disappointment that we should even look at this case, that it was simply inappropriate and would undermine the standing of the judiciary. This was expressed to me at the highest levels, that this was simply something that they were extremely disappointed that we were even looking at.

But let me say also, some people were, despite the imposition, prepared to at least elucidate what were the general principles and I would like to express my gratitude to those people. I do feel that the sky didn't fall in as a result and, without trying to be too pompous, that it was fair.

So all I am saying is that we can agree that certain things are easy but certain things are hard and the hard things, it seems to me, are what is proper for the media to talk about and what is proper for judges to engage in. There is not an agreement about what it is proper to talk about in terms of maintaining public confidence in the judiciary. I think you may have to be a bit bolder in the current climate where, as I say, we are dealing with a perception of elitism and self serving mysticism.

ROD TIFFEN:

When lawyers and journalists talk about increased media access to the courts, the emphasis is overwhelmingly on the external interface—how they can communicate better outwards.

What tends to be neglected somewhat are the internal workings of the courts and how these may contribute to the problem. A related point I would like to make here is that when people talk of law reform, overwhelmingly they are talking about a matter of reforming the content of the law. It seems to me that a lot of the procedures are not to do with the content of the law but its procedures. Here I think the most crucial thing of all is simply the matter of delay. Let me give you a couple of examples.

In April 1997, I strongly believed in Senator Colston's right to a presumption of innocence. I thought it would have been a very dangerous precedent to expel him from the Senate without having gone through a criminal trial. Eighteen months later I find it just ridiculous that that trial has not happened, that we are still talking about a presumption of innocence and that a senator elected in 1993 for Labor may be crucial to fulfilling the Government's mandate.

I also would like to make the point, for example, about one of the best pieces of reporting in Australian current affairs history, namely the "Four Corners" programme, "The Moonlight State". It went to air in May 1987. Subsequent legal action by one of the Bellino brothers, the gangsters exposed or some of the gangsters exposed in that programme, finally finished in June this year, eleven years and one month after the program went to air. Five Queensland Premiers came and went during the time that that court case dragged on, and a sixth one departed about three weeks later. The ABC won every step of those legal proceedings except for one rather bizarre High Court judgment, where several justices seemed to me to consider that they were better editors than the people at the ABC.

I would like to know the cost, including the hidden costs of staff time, on cases here for the ABC which they have won. Let's be clear about this. These are cases the ABC has won that have cost them so much. Their legal fees now must be well over half a million dollars. I hope that Mr Bellino doesn't go bankrupt before he can pay.

Now, one of the problems, I think, with cases like this, is that the stop-start nature of political cases means that the reports to the public and the public's capacity to form a coherent view of what is occurring are almost nil unless they are dedicated researchers. Reports go on, with daily reports while the court is sitting each day, with different witnesses, giving different pictures, and then the case may disappear for several months. It is very hard to get reports that integrate the proceedings and I don't think this sort of haphazard, erratic, unpunctual procedure helps the public's right to know at all.

It is very difficult at times, I think, to distinguish legitimate claims of the media as a vehicle of public information from their self interested grandstanding. The example which came to my mind today was, some years ago I was in Perth doing some work on WA Inc., and that Royal Commission, which was exemplary in its relations with journalists, held one meeting, a press conference between the three judges, an all-in press conference. Unfortunately for Howard Sadler, this was at 10 a.m. in the morning, which clashed with his programme. He then wanted the judges to meet him individually, separately and, in a discussion with another member (the breakfast announcer on his station), their refusal to meet him individually was referred to as a Goebbels-like tactic. So this sort of grandstanding, I think, is an enormous inhibition in trying to get rational discussion of these issues.

The last two issues I mentioned are about what I think are weaknesses of media reporting. The first is to do with the lack of editorial imagination, especially the lack of an effort to produce—and maybe this runs into contempt of court problems, I'm not sure—integrated reports that try to interrelate the testimony of different witnesses, sometimes heard weeks and months apart, that no casual readers of a newspaper could ever hold in their minds properly.

The second and the last point I would like to make is the moral simplicity of much of our media. In commercial broadcasting, current affairs in particular, in tabloid newspapers to some extent, marketing people have discovered that uncertainty is uncomfortable. If you can offer your audience certainty, if you can offer them a picture that the truth is simple, that virtue is on one side and vice is on the other, then they go away feeling much better. Unfortunately, of course, truth is the primary casualty in that sort of reporting. And I might just leave it at that.

Questions and Comments from the Floor

KIRSTEN EDWARDS (ASSOCIATE LECTURER, UNIVERSITY OF
TECHNOLOGY, SYDNEY):

I think, at the end of the day, when you get past some practical
things, there is a fundamental conflict between the role of the courts
and what we try to achieve in trying to make it more accessible to the
public.

We have heard a lot about practical things, and certainly a lot of these
are great: the web page is great, the media officer is great, maybe a bit of
court TV, maybe a few more joint judgments, more people who know
what they are talking about but can also communicate it in an accessible
way to the public. But there are also certain things that the courts just
cannot do.

One commentator pointed out that courts sometimes release six
judgments in one day. But you can't expect the High Court to stagger the
release of judgments and have people withholding on their legal and civil
rights in order that the media can digest them more comfortably. You
also can't expect them to be contactable, like when you try to contact
Anthony Mason. I know that if I called the ABC and asked for Geoffrey
Robertson—because, you know, he used to be there a while ago—they
would probably be equally oblique as to how I could get hold of him.
And there are certain other practical difficulties, things like the delay
that was criticized in the *Wik* decision. There are so many appeal books
to digest.

The High Court is not accessible to the public ever, no matter how
much we try to make it simple, because it is the most legally sophisticated
institution that you will ever come across and you can give people plain
English summaries, you can explain to them the role of the people, you
can explain to them what the case is about, you can have a law degree,
and you will still have a lot of trouble following what is going on.

I sat in the High Court for the year, having read every single thing that
came before me and I didn't know what was going on, so I think, perhaps,
we should give up certain expectations that anybody is ever going to be
able to walk into the High Court and understand what is going on because
it is so complicated. It is so difficult and the judges don't want to make it
easier. They don't want to make their judgments shorter, and they don't
want to make their judgments more accessible to the people because
they consider themselves legal experts. They don't consider that that is
their role and they won't.

I agree with Liz Jackson that when we do these little things the sky
doesn't fall in, but there is a huge legal backlash whenever a judge tries
to be more populist. There is a huge legal backlash whenever a judge
tries to be accessible to the public and they have to bear that on their
own. They do believe that the sky will fall in if they start having to think,

"Maybe I should only write a 20-page judgment and release it before 4 p.m. so the journalists will get hold of it." So it seems to me that maybe we should be giving up in a way on the High Court apart from those commendable practical initiatives that are under way and start doing what Jenny did, and just get to the magistrates courts, the District Court, where real justice is done about real people. There will always be a perception of elite when we talk about things that are just so intellectually sophisticated that lawyers can't understand themselves, and that is just inevitable.

Maybe we should give up on that because I don't think it is ever going to be fixed and I don't think lawyers will ever be able to write judgments on the most sophisticated legal issues that are immediately accessible. Maybe we should forget about the High Court and just go back to these District Courts and show how real justice operates on real people, as it is more comforting.

GEORGE WILLIAMS:

I think that is a failure to acknowledge that the High Court has itself made great steps. I mean, you might as well say they have done nothing in recent years and they have. To say there is nothing that can be done about the High Court is to say what the High Court has done in recent years in terms of an effort to make itself more accessible and an effort to get out there and get more comprehension has not been worth the trouble. It has done things.

ROD CAMPBELL:

I cover the High Court all the time. I don't think you need to give up because at least one judge of the High Court has proved that it can be done—Justice Michael Kirby. He has not written shorter judgments but he has certainly written judgments that are a delight to read as a journalist. He actually has headings. He actually says: "these are the facts, this is the legislation, these are the legal principles, this is how I apply them and this is my conclusion". He is a delight to read. He gets reported by journalists all the time because of that. So it can be done.

So far as expecting the High Court to stagger its judgments, I think leadership from the Chief Justice might have something to do with it. One of the horror days of all horror days was—I can't remember the year now—but the High Court handed down four, five interrelated judgments all on the acquisition of property other than on just terms and my recollection is that there were four judgments; three went one way and one went the other. The three that the plaintiffs lost were 16 individual judgments. The other one, which was *Georgiadis* I think, had seven or five.

There were something like 21 separate judgments to be digested. What it was, in fact, was one news story at the end of it. A couple of journalists woke up to the fact that they were all about the same section of the

Constitution. I really would like to see some more guidance from the Chief Justice. If you do an analysis of minority judgments and separate judgments, you see an extraordinary correlation between judges who can't ever manage to get a majority and those who are capable of writing joint judgments, but some Chief Justices are more successful in encouraging it than others.

JENNY BROCKIE:

Could I just say that I agree with what Liz was saying about you should not give up, but I do sympathize with what you are saying. I spent six weeks at Campbelltown. I heard Kevin Flack referred to as "Your Honour". I saw people jump up and say "objection!" because all they had seen was "LA Law". I heard him called "your Holiness" by a litigant.

You have a fundamental problem in a society where people are appearing in a court and have not a clue about court procedure, how it works or what they are supposed to do, or where they are supposed to sit or stand, or who takes their turn. So I agree with Liz but I think what we have got to do is attack the lot, have a go at the lot, and start recognizing that courts are not the private domain of judges and magistrates. They are supposed to be public places, and that seems to me one of the fundamental problems, that there is a kind of legal culture that has almost created this privacy about the whole procedure which is presided over by the person up behind the big bench who really has the say about this thing called the electronic media, which is so much more evil in its intentions and its potential than a tabloid newspaper. Come on! We are about to head into the next millennium!

CHRIS NASH:

I would just like to comment, too, that the judgment of the High Court that landed it in the most trouble was, as George described, absolute black letter law—*Wik*. It was absolutely imperative for them to respond politically to the sorts of attacks that Robert McClelland talked about. You know, it just was not an option for them to sit there. Something had to be done. It was a profound constitutional battle.

SPEAKER:

I was interested in some of the remarks that Justice Teague made in regards to the electronic media in the courts, the television in the courts. What would he think about the televising of royal commissions? I was actually in a royal commission for two years. As a consequence of the barrister addressing the commissioner on the evidence, that barrister was actually taken before the disciplinary tribunal of the Bar Association on his remarks about one of the witnesses.

He said things like: "He is redolent of the John Cleese character". He shrugged his shoulders and said: "well, a few people died. So what!".

And they took offence at that. There was a three day hearing at the disciplinary tribunal. Because there was no actual video of the witness's attitude, they had difficulty seeing what the barrister was getting at. He was talking about the witness's attitude and I feel that if things go to appeal, or in this case it went to the Bar Association, that it is important that there is some kind of a record on video tape of what the witness's attitude and demeanour was.

JUSTICE TEAGUE:

Perhaps two things. One concerns royal commissions. Essentially, it will be a matter for the royal commission to determine the appropriate practice to be adopted in front of the commission. It is very much an individual thing. Whatever it decides to do is not going to affect other people so it may be relatively easier to be more permissive in relation to that sort of situation, but it will depend upon, I would have thought, the making of the right sort of approach at the right time.

The second matter concerns video recording of the proceedings. In fact, substantial research in Victoria has suggested if cameras are placed in the right way with split screens and so on, it is the most cost-effective way of providing a record of proceedings for the use of transcript and so on.

Chief Justice Black probably can say what is going to happen, at least in the new Federal Court in Melbourne, but I think that is the way to go, based on the Victorian research. In fact, in a significant number of courtrooms in Victoria now, the transcript is effectively provided, even in remote locations—Geelong, Mildura and so on—by the four cameras that are set up in the courtroom where the image is relayed back to Melbourne, the transcript is provided in Melbourne and sent back if necessary through other channels. But it may be that that will give rise to possibilities in the near future as to the way in which that sort of record can be made available. In fact, that particular record was used in contempt proceedings recently in relation to an accused who performed badly immediately prior to the judge coming into court.

ANDREW KENYON:

Just a brief comment on the reporting of the High Court–District Court–magistrate's court issue. I can understand how reporting the legal changes made by a High Court judgment can be difficult. It is difficult to get a concise summary and to get that out into the media in a good way. But there is an aim that is the same for reporting the High Court or the District Court, televising, doing documentaries, whatever, which is about the public understanding of the legal process.

The High Court has a particular constitutional role. It may well be that particular efforts that the High Court has made, and will continue to make, will be very important in clarifying that role among the general population, just as documentaries at the District Court or magistrate's court level can be very important in helping people realise our courts don't look quite like "LA Law".

SYLVIA CRIVEN (PUBLIC RELATIONS MANAGER, COURTS ADMINISTRATION AUTHORITY IN SOUTH AUSTRALIA):

I would like to say that there is very much a popular interest and demand for knowledge about the courts in South Australia. You may not know about this but "Today Tonight" filmed a documentary in the magistrate's court. It went for an hour and when it was screened on a Friday, just before the footie, it had 210,000 viewers, according to their ratings, and we had such a lot of tremendous feedback from the community. As you say, Jenny, they had no idea what they were going to come to terms with and that followed a sentencing, it followed some of the preliminary work in the solicitor's office, so the audience was able to see the legal process at various stages in a sort of a piecemeal fashion and, as you know, we haven't done a complete court case. But there certainly was a demand.

CHRIS NASH:

Other questions?

SUSANNAH LOBEZ:

I would like to make a brief comment about the relative merits of gavel-to-gavel coverage, which is literally from start to finish in a court case, à la court TV in the United States, and edited documentaries like, "six weeks in the life of the magistrates court" or what we have done with the "Law Report", a day in the life of the magistrate. Lots of those have been done, as Sylvia has said. I think that is going to be a really big issue. I could not help wondering in the previous session whether if we had gavel-to-gavel coverage, we just went out on a dedicated network— perhaps when digitalisation comes we will have that—where everyone would be, literally, like in the old days, sitting in the back of the court knitting, watching the daily grind through the courts. Maybe that would alleviate some of the difficulties about commentators getting it wrong or the wrong slant or, you know, the mistakes in the reporting, et cetera.

The other thing I have to say is that it takes an awful lot of smooching. It was in 1993 when I first started at the "Law Report" that I met Chief Justice Anthony Mason down in Tasmania, at a conference, and he had just come back from England a little bit concerned about illegitimate recording in England, and it was in that context that I said to him: "hey, how about an interview?" and it took, until May 1994 to actually achieve that with all the negotiating about how it might happen.

Now, that was because it was a one-off and we had to set the terms. Chief Justice Doyle will agree that from the first time when we spoke about court radio, and I think I spoke to Justice Olsson first, it was nearly

18 months by the time Chief Justice Doyle and I had both organized the guidelines and found the case and worked out how all the practicalities would be resolved.

I know that Justice Teague said collectivism is the way to go but I am damned if I am going to put 18 months of my own time and make that available to every other judge who requires these kind of precautions. I just urge those members of the judiciary who are here to go to their Chief Justices committees or their AIJA meetings and say: "listen, we need to do some work, too. We need to work out what is a fair deal here". I think things will progress much more happily and, next time we all meet, Jenny won't be so depressed.

GEORGE WILLIAMS:

Sir Ninian Stephen has supported the idea of television in the High Court and, indeed, all the time. He seems supportive of some idea like High Court cable. I'm not sure it would be a big ratings winner but a former High Court judge has certainly seen that as a good idea.

The High Court itself has television cameras already for internal consumption. The problem is they are in black and white and you might have a problem of people thinking they are watching re-runs of "Lost in Space" or something like that, I suppose. All I am trying to say is, yes, there has been support from a former High Court judge and, yes, it could be done, but I can't see any great dangers for the High Court in this. The main thing is, well, would anybody watch it?

SPEAKER:

But that is not the point, I don't think. I mean, I think whether it rates or not, frankly, is not the problem that everyone here is facing.

PATRICK KEYZER:

It depends who pays for it: the funding. The governments of the day don't want to give extra funding to the courts to assist them in developing public education media strategies. The courts, of course, are doing more with less. They have more litigants, and it is a time that has been very difficult for them over the last few years. They are feeling a little embattled.

JENNY BROCKIE:

At the same time, Liz is right. I mean, she has tried to film a case from go to whoa for "Four Corners". I have been interested in filming a case from go to whoa. We are not getting anywhere.

SPEAKER:

I think there is probably a problem of goodwill in some jurisdictions toward this sort of thing but I think there is an issue of resources for public education media. The idea of one-off interviews, documentaries and engagements with different courts and different jurisdictions has progressed a lot in the last few years. We have a High Court documentary. Liz has interviewed Sir Anthony Mason. Maxine McHugh interviewed Sir Gerard Brennan and Chief Justice Doyle has been on talkback radio. So we have these developments over the last few years and people are starting to sit up and take notice of various jurisdictions. But, if we are looking at longer term public education media strategies, I think a lot of the courts are, quite rightly, saying to the executive government, "If you want us to extend ourselves, you are going to have to pay us so that we can do this."

FACULTY OF LAW, UNIVERSITY OF TECHNOLOGY, SYDNEY

Professor and Dean of Law

D. Barker, LLB (Lond), MPhil (Kent), LLM (Hons) (Cantab), DipLG (Kent), GradDipLegPrac (UTS), FCIS, ACIArb, FAIM, FIMgt, MACE, Solicitor of the Supreme Court of NSW and the High Court of Australia

Associate Dean

A.S. Mowbray, BSc, LLB (UNSW), Solicitor of the Supreme Courts of NSW and ACT

Professors

S.K.N. Blay, LLB (Hons) (Ghana), LLM (ANU), PhD (Tas)
D.E. Flint, AM, LLM (Syd), BSc (Ecs) (Lond), DSU (Paris), Solicitor of the Supreme Court of NSW and the High Court of England

Associate Professors

M.A. Adams, BA (Hons), LLM (Lond), FCIS, AIMM, MACE
K. Cutbush-Sabine, Dr Jur (Zur), LLM (Hons) (Lond), MInstAM (UK)
P.B.C. Griffith, LLB, BJur (Monash), LLM (Lond)
R.J. Watt, BCom, DipLib (UNSW), LLB (Syd), LLM (Hons) (UTS), Solicitor of the Supreme Court of NSW (Law Collection Consultant)

Senior Lecturers

K. Bubna-Litic, BJuris, LLB (UWA), LLM (Syd), Barrister and Solicitor of the Supreme Court of Western Australia
S. Carr-Gregg, BCom, LLB (UNSW), LLM (UTS), Solicitor of the Supreme Court of NSW
T. Chiu, BSocSci (Hons) (Chinese HK), LLB (UNSW), GradDipLegPrac, PhD (UTS), Solicitor of the Supreme Court of NSW and the High Court of Australia, Solicitor and Barrister of the Supreme Court of ACT, Mediator CCPIT, Henan, China
P. Egri, BA, LLB (Syd), MCogSc (UNSW)
I.D. Ellis-Jones, BA, LLB (Syd), LLM (UTS), Solicitor of the Supreme Court of NSW and High Court of Australia
M.B. Evans, BA (Hons), LLB, LLM (Syd), LLM (Hons) (Cantab), Barrister of the Supreme Court of NSW
P. Keyzer, BA (Hons), LLB (Hons), LLM (Syd), GradDipLegPrac (UTS), Barrister and Solicitor of the High Court of Australia, and the Supreme Court of NSW
D. Meltz, LLM (Syd), SJD (UTS), Solicitor of the Supreme Court of NSW

G. Monahan, BA (Macq), LLB (Syd), LLM (UNSW), Grad Certificate in Higher Education (UTS), Solicitor of the Supreme Court of NSW and the High Court of Australia, Notary Public

G.A. Moore, BA, LLM (Syd), Barrister of the Supreme Courts of NSW, ACT and the High Court of Australia

V. Nagarajan, BEc, LLB (Macq), LLM (Monash), Solicitor of the Supreme Court of NSW

S.F. Smith, BA, MHA (UNSW), LLM, SJD (Syd), Solicitor of the Supreme Court of NSW

W.J. Taggart, RFD, BA, LLB, LLM (Syd), Solicitor of the Supreme Court of NSW and the High Court of Australia, Registered Migration Agent

P. Underwood, BA, LLM (Syd), Solicitor of the Supreme Court of NSW

C.Ying, BA (Manit), LLM (Lond), Barrister at Law of Lincoln's Inn and the Supreme Court of NSW

J. Zetler, RGN, RPN, BA (Syd), LLM (UTS) RCNA, Solicitor of the Supreme Court of NSW

Lecturers

J.A. Cooper, BEc, DipEd (Syd), LLB (UNSW), LLM (Syd), MHEd (UNSW), Solicitor of the Supreme Court of NSW and Attorney of the New York Bar

P. Crofts, BEc, LLB (Hons), LLM (Syd)

R.A. Davis, Bec, LLB (Hons), LLM (Syd), Solicitor of the Supreme Court of NSW (Director, Undergraduate Programs)

P. Edmundson, BJuris, LLB (UNSW)

K.C. Gould, BA, DipEd (Macq), LLB (Hons) (UTS)

P.L. Hutchison, BCom (UNSW), BCom (Hons 1) (Witw), MA Law (Oxon)

J.A.H. Lancaster, BA, LLB (Hons) (Macq), RGN, Solicitor of the Supreme Court of NSW

M. Langford, BA, LLB (Macq), LLM (Syd), Graduate Certificate in Higher Education (UTS), Solicitor of the Supreme Court of NSW

T. Libesman, BA, LLB (Macq)

B.M. Olliffe, BA (Hons), LLB (Syd), Solicitor of the Supreme Court of NSW (Director, Professional Programs)

R. Pettit, BA, LLB (Macq), LLM (Syd), Graduate Certificate in Higher Education (UTS), Solicitor of the Supreme Court of NSW and the High Court of Australia

M.A.K. Scott, BA, DipEd, LLB (UNSW), GradDipLegPrac, LLM (UTS), Solicitor and Barrister of the Supreme Court of NSW

P. Stewart, LLB, LLM (Syd), admitted as a Solicitor of the Supreme Court of NSW and the High Court of Australia

A. Stuhmcke, BA, LLB (Hons) (Macq), LLM (Hons) (Syd), Solicitor of the Supreme Court of NSW

R. Tong, LLB (Syd), LLM (Lond), Solicitor of the Supreme Court of NSW and the High Court of Australia

P.M. Whitehead, BA, LLB (UNSW), LLM (Lond), Solicitor of the Supreme Court of NSW and the High Court of Australia

Associate Lecturer

K. Edwards, BA, LLB (Hons) (ANU)

Visiting Professors

M. Pryles, LLB (Melb), LLM (SMU Texas), SJD (Melb), Barrister and Solicitor of the Supreme Courts of Victoria and ACT, Solicitor of the Supreme Court of NSW
The Hon. A. Rogers, QC, LLB (Hons) (Syd)
R. Vermeesch, LLM (Syd)

Adjunct Professors

D. Bennett, QC, LLB (Tas)

Australasian Legal Information Institute ·

Co-Director — A.S. Mowbray, BSc, LLB (UNSW), Solicitor of the Supreme Courts of NSW and ACT
Manager — P.T.H. Chung, BEc (Hons), LLB (Syd)
Project Officer (Primary Materials and Software Support) — D. Austin, BSc, LLB (ANU)
Project Officer (Primary Materials) — J. Kwok
Project Officers (Secondary Materials) — D. Irvine, BA (Hons), LLB (UNSW), S. McCann, BA, LLB (Tas)
Administrator (part-time) — T. Gill, BSc (Hons) (Uni College of Swansea, UK)
Editorial Support (part-time) — C. Thomson

Community Law and Research Centre

Director — I.D. Ellis-Jones, BA, LLB (Syd), LLM (UTS), Solicitor of the Supreme Court of NSW and High Court of Australia
Manager — P. O'Brien, BBus, LLB, GradDipLegPrac (UTS), Solicitor of the Supreme Court of NSW
Solicitor — K. McFarlane, LLB

UTS Law Review Student Editorial Board

Kon Asimacopolous
Rhys Bollen
Julia Colagiuri
David Dimouski
Julian Hammond
Lyndall Foldvary
Michelle Shek